Contributions to Economics

For further volumes:
http://www.springer.com/series/1262

Anastasios Karasavvoglou
Persefoni Polychronidou
Editors

Balkan and Eastern European Countries in the Midst of the Global Economic Crisis

Physica-Verlag
A Springer Company

Editors
Prof. Anastasios Karasavvoglou
Dr. Persefoni Polychronidou
Kavala Institute of Technology
School of Business and Economy
Accountancy Department
Agios Loukas
Kavala
Greece

ISSN 1431-1933
ISBN 978-3-7908-2872-6 ISBN 978-3-7908-2873-3 (eBook)
DOI 10.1007/978-3-7908-2873-3
Springer Heidelberg New York Dordrecht London

Library of Congress Control Number: 2012943347

Printed on acid-free paper

Physica-Verlag is a brand of Springer
Springer is part of Springer-Science+Business Media (www.springer.com)

Preface

The developments in Europe and in the world are rapid. The global financial crisis has led the economies into deep recession, exaggerated the problems of employment in the job market, limited the investments and pointed out the dangers that uncontrolled expansion of the credit system over real economy bears. The collapse of banks and financial organizations, the widening of economic and social inequalities and generally the weakening of the growth rates of the economies are some of the consequences of the global financial recession.

In Europe, the results of the crisis have led to serious problems in the European Union (EU) and especially in the peripheral countries. The developments therein have shown the main issue to be the debt problem in countries such as Greece, Ireland, Portugal and Spain and the difficulties of refinancing. This issue has led to a lively debate in the EU over the formation of institutions and policies that make the economic policies of member states more flexible and effective and, at the same time, offer the opportunity for the EU to coordinate the national policies at the EU level.

The developments at the European and global levels are sure to have an effect on the economies of the Balkan and Black Sea countries. The global financial crisis has caused a recession in economic activities, has limited the flow of foreign funds in the wider region, has created serious problems in each country's job market and has decreased the incomes and the living standards of the citizens. Furthermore, the financial character of the crisis has created conditions of economic instability, has caused problems in national budgets and made the countries with limited exporting orientation vulnerable. Finally, the foreign businesses that are working in this area have postponed investment plans and, in addition to limited funding for the banking sector, have slowed down the growth rates of the economies.

At the same time, however, the countries of the region constitute undoubtedly a very promising financial area with many possibilities for development. Specifically, the Black Sea and South-eastern European regions are an important reference point for investors and exporters, especially European ones, as the population in these regions increases rapidly and their oil and natural gas reserves make them enormously appealing. The needs for development and expansion of infrastructure, investments in new technologies, energy, environment, waste and water management as well as investments in the health sector are common for all countries. It is interesting that according to some views, the economic area covering the Balkans and the Black Sea can become as significant as that of China and India, while much is said about "Europe's tigers".

The third International Scientific Conference, "The Economies of Balkan and Eastern Europe Countries in the changed world" (EBEEC 2011), which was co-organized by the Department of Accountancy of the Kavala Institute of Technology, Greece, and the Faculty of Economic Sciences of the University of Pitesti, Romania, took place in May 2011 in Pitesti, Romania, and introduced the issue of economic developments in Eastern Europe, Balkan and Black Sea countries. There was a discussion of the past, present and future economic issues regarding the region as well as an in-depth analysis of the aspects and domains of the countries' economies; policy suggestions were also made concerning the achievement of 80 remarkable growth and improvement in the residents' standard of living.

The papers in this volume are contributions of the suggestions made by some scientists who participated in the conference mentioned above.

In Part I, Joel I. Deichmann analyses the origins of FDI in the Republic of Croatia and records the important factors that have facilitated FDI during Croatia's transition period. The factors that affect the attraction of foreign investments are revealed, and an expanded gravity model is used in order to conclude to important policy implications. The results show that Croatia fits into the typical transition economy scenario, favouring follow-the-leader firms from nearby (especially EU) origins.

The chapter of Eftychia Tsanana, Constantinos Katrakilidis and Panagiotis Pantelidis focuses on the convergence of the Balkan economies with the EU-15 average over the period 1989–2009. With the use of an econometric model, the existence of dissimilarities among the examined Balkan economies in the process to catch up with the EU-15 is pointed out. The results support income convergence with the EU-15 only for Greece and Slovenia.

George D. Borovas refers to the economic relations between two countries of the Center and Western Balkans, especially those of FYROM and Bosnia-Herzegovina, and he also analyses interesting social and economical aspects of these relations. Emphasis is laid on the phenomenon of "Yugonostalgia", in order to interpret the relations of the past, the present and the future.

Özcan Karahan and Olcay Çolak analyse the effect of inflation target policy on inflation uncertainty in Turkey. For this purpose, they use a GARCH model. The results show that inflation target policy is a strategy to illuminate the inflation uncertainty.

Georgios Makris and Konstantinos Filippidis study the role of fiscal policy under the framework of the Stability and Growth Pact (SGP) in Economic and Monetary Union (EMU), taking into consideration the financial crisis in Europe and especially the high deficits. Under this framework, they argue on the point that the macroeconomic and financial imbalances can be dealt with a flexible labour market.

In Part II, Felix-Constantin Burcea, Victor Balau, Cristina Baldan, Tiberiu-Cristian Avramescu and Emilia Ungureanu refer to the role of the central banks; especially to the role in correcting imbalances in the economy and in creating grounds for vi Introductory Note durable economic performance. Using the case of the Romanian central bank, the authors deduce that the Romanian National Bank's momentary policy, inflation policy and change rate policy play a very important role in macroeconomic and monetary stabilization.

In the paper of Eftychia Nikolaidou and Sofoklis D. Vogiazas, the determinants of credit risk in the Romanian banking system over the period 2001–2010 are investigated by applying the autoregressive distributed lag (ARDL) approach to cointegration. The empirical results indicate that bank-specific factors as well as macroeconomic activity factors have a significant impact on Romania's credit risk, both in the short and in the long run. Furthermore, the findings strongly support the hypothesis that the Greek crisis has a significant impact on Romanian non-performing loans.

In Part III, Alexiadis Stilianos, Ladias Christos and Milionis Sotirios investigate the extent of cohesion amongst European regions in the light of the current policy dilemma of "cohesion-competitiveness". They take into account the notion of knowledge-based economy in a model of regional growth. The model suggests possible ways to overcome the "development gap", identifying certain areas of policy intervention.

Fotios Chatzitheodoridis, Anastasios Michailidis, Georgios Theodosiou and Efstratios Loizou investigate the role and importance of local cooperation for endogenous rural development. By using a two-step clustering analysis, the authors investigate the relation between social characteristics and willingness to adopt endogenous development.

Lambros Tsourgiannis, Anastasios Karasavvoglou and Michael Nikolaidis explore consumer buying behaviour towards organic food in the region of East Macedonia and Thrace in Greece. With the use of proper tools (principal component analysis, cluster techniques, discriminate analysis), they find interesting correlations between the factors that affect consumer buying behaviour, such as personal consumer characteristics and preference for consumption of organic wine.

Kateryna Kononova indicates the composite Information and Communication Technology's Development Index (IDI) and analyses the growth in relation with the progress of Information and Communication Technology's (ICT's) use in developed countries. It is indicated that national strategies can facilitate the introduction of ICT in Ukraine, Belarus and Moldova and contribute to the intensification of their transition to information society.

We would like to thank all the participants of the conference EBEEC 2011 held in Pitesti, Romania, and especially the authors of this volume. We are indebted to the Kavala Institute of Technology and especially to the Department of Accountancy for offering valuable support for the realization of this conference. Also, we would like to thank Dr. Theodosios Theodosiou, Dr. Ioannis Kazanidis and Ph.D. candidate Dimitios Chatzoudes. Finally, we express our sincere gratitude to Fotini Perdiki for editing the volume.

Kavala
February 2012

Professor Anastasios
G. Karasavvoglou
Dr. Persefoni Polychronidou

Contents

Part I
European Union, Economic Relations and Macroeconomics

Origins of Foreign Direct Investment in Croatia: Application of an Expanded Gravity Model

Joel I. Deichmann

1 Introduction

Situated in the Western Balkan region of Europe, the Republic of Croatia is among the most interesting contexts for examining flows of foreign direct investment (FDI). Croatia's geographic location straddles western and eastern Europe, as well as many of the continent's historically-competitive political and cultural forces. Most recently, Croatia's emergence from the violent dissolution of Yugoslavia as a new nation-state in 1991 continues to shift towards greater integration with the European Union. As a form of spatial interaction, foreign direct investment has been shown to flourish between locations with cultural (Bandelj 2002) and spatial proximity (Brenton et al. 1998), while avoiding areas that are isolated or otherwise impacted by political instability and war (Brada et al. 2006). Following the gravity model's simple tenet that spatial interaction increases with two objects' masses and decreases in response to the distance between them, this paper takes gravity variables into account in order to help understand the factors that enable and those that deter FDI.

In the voluminous FDI literature, very little has been published about the gravity model, and even less about the Republic of Croatia. Croatia provides an interesting context in which to study FDI, also because its present existence is a consequence of the dissolution of Yugoslavia, yet its future almost certainly holds in store membership in the European Union. Simultaneously, therefore, it represents both a case of devolution and of supra-nationalism. Croatia's FDI stock continues to grow rapidly, at the end of 2009 having reached 7,358 projects of various sizes, and representing a cumulative total of 27 € billion, or 6,136 € per person (Croatian National Bank 2010).

J.I. Deichmann (✉)
Global Studies Department, Bentley University, 175 Forest Street, Waltham, MA 02452, USA
e-mail: jdeichmann@bentley.edu

A. Karasavvoglou and P. Polychronidou (eds.), *Balkan and Eastern European Countries in the Midst of the Global Economic Crisis*, Contributions to Economics,
DOI 10.1007/978-3-7908-2873-3_1,

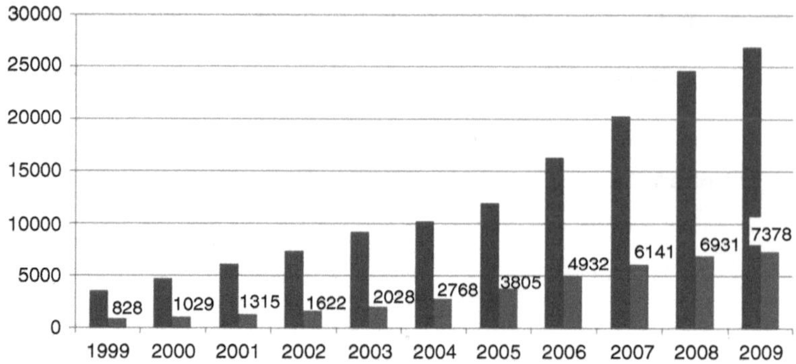

Fig. 1 Cumulative FDI to Croatia, 1999–2009 (in million €, number of transactions) (Data source: Croatian National Bank (2010))

1.1 Foreign Direct Investment in the Republic of Croatia

As illustrated in Fig. 1, FDI in Croatia has increased more than fivefold over the past decade. According to the Croatian National Bank (2010), more than 88% of the total number of FDI transactions took place between 2000 and 2009, the period under investigation here. As was the case in many of its former Yugoslav-Republic neighbours, inflows to the country languished during the war-torn years of the early 1990s (Brada et al. 2006). However, at the start of the new millennium when it became clear that stability had returned to the region and plans for EU accession began to take shape, the inflows quickly began to accelerate. In Central and Eastern Europe, only the Czech Republic, Estonia, Hungary, and Slovakia have attracted more FDI per capita (EBRD 2010). The vast majority of Croatia's FDI stock is in financial intermediation (9,396 € million), manufacturing (5,482 € million), wholesale/retail trade (3,961 € million), or transport/communication (2,170 € million), together representing more than 82% of the total. Investment in Croatia's manufacturing sector is dominated by chemicals, fuel production, mineral products, and food products (Croatian National Bank 2010; Hunya 2010).

The leading origins of Croatia's incoming FDI are listed in Table 1. Because most of the countries are European, it is both feasible and worthwhile to present them spatially on the map in Fig. 2, as done in a recent contribution by Zademach and Rodríguez-Pose (2009) on European mergers and acquisitions.

Even the most cursory examination of Fig. 2 leads to the expectation that cultural and geographic proximity to Croatia may be at work as facilitators of inward FDI. Austria, Hungary, and Slovenia all share a common history with Croatia, and all three are among the leading origins as counted by the number of transactions and value of FDI. As the world's largest economy, the United States is the lone non-European entity among the top FDI origins, but it is important to note that most of the 1.12 € billion in FDI from the USA was later "withdrawn" from the data tables in 2008 as Teva Pharmaceuticals (Israel) acquired Barr, the lone major US investor

Table 1 Cumulative FDI in Croatia as of December 2009 (transactions) value in thousand €

1	Austria (1219)	6706465	17	Denmark (116)	179817.1
2	Netherlands (426)	4155866	18	RUSSIA (363)	128530.6
3	Germany (707)	3065234	19	Cyprus (89)	128368.7
4	Hungary (213)	2319712	20	Malta (43)	93841.33
5	United States (253)	1471043	21	Norway (83)	86336.83
6	France (118)	1361125	22	Czech Republic (75)	82912.02
7	Luxembourg (133)	1280377	22	Bosnia and Herz (123)	78921.89
8	Italy (949)	1153523	23	Poland (72)	67131.81
9	Slovenia (767)	1069254	24	Ireland (115)	67057.51
10	Neth Antilles[a] (8)	869930.2	25	Brit Virgin Isl (47)	60766.37
11	Switzerland (251)	565268.9	26	Spain (37)	45415.46
12	United Kingdom (429)	446003.7	27	San Marino (6)	37686.97
13	Belgium (83)	417962.4	28	Slovakia (59)	26719.51
14	IFIs (1)	329882.1	29	Israel (31)	23578.91
15	Sweden (86)	271557.5	30	Iran (1)	20861.17
16	Liechtenstein (96)	183389.1		Total	26904045

Source: Croatian National Bank (does not include divestment)
[a]Netherlands Antilles ceased to exist on 10 October 2010

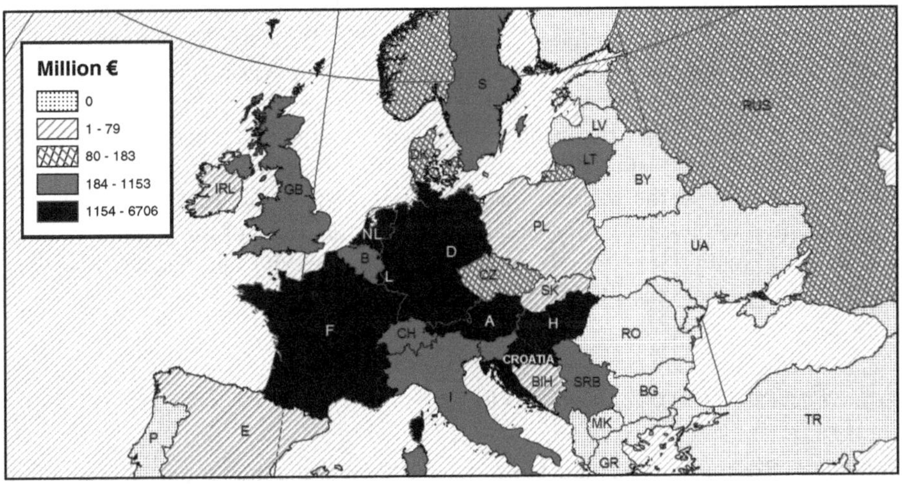

Fig. 2 Origins of FDI in Croatia (cumulative value through 2009) (Data source: Croatian National Bank (2010) Cartography: Joel I Deichmann)

that had earlier purchased the Croatian firm Pleva. Also, the Netherlands is over-represented in the rankings; because of its favorably low corporate income tax rate, many foreign firms including those from the USA establish holding companies there as bases for investment in third countries such as Croatia, thereby distorting the positions of some countries in Table 1 (Hargitai 2010).

2 Literature

Until recently, very little scholarly work had been published on any aspect of FDI in Croatia. One exception is an analysis of destination-specific location determinants by Botrić and Škuflić (2006). Using data from 1997 to 2002, these authors highlight the importance of agglomeration and infrastructure, but their speculation about privatization as a factor remains inconclusive. In a subsequent study at the Croatian county level (Škuflić and Botrić 2009), the same authors find that workforce education level, export orientation, and domestic local investment are statistically significant and intuitively meaningful explanatory variables. In their macro-level analysis, Redžepagić and Richet (2009) discover the importance of EU accession as well as some evidence of former industrial specialization, proximity, and growth in local demand.

Hunya and Škudar (2006) examine the impact of FDI in the country, associate it with export output, and argue that more should be done by the government to promote inward FDI. Examining FDI flows throughout the European Union and its candidate countries including Croatia, Dabić and Pejić-Bach (2008) examine both the drivers of FDI and the extent to which it drives growth in GDP, technology, and employment. Brada et al. (2006) compare FDI into Croatia and its Central European neighbors, identifying the economic costs of instability in the region that have been slowly overcome as peace returned in the late 1990s. Bandelj (2002) finds cause to expect that the temporary negative impact of the Balkan War was in part overcome in the case of some major origins (namely the USA and Australia) by remittances sent back to Croatia after that conflict subsided. In large part, because so little has been published on Croatia, before embarking on this exercise it is worthwhile to take a quick look at the scholarly work on origin effects of FDI. Because many mainstream variables are gravity-related (various measures of mass and distance), and existing studies tend to rely upon augmented gravity approaches, it is also instructive to consult the literature on gravity models.

2.1 Foreign Direct Investment

Following Rodríguez-Pose and Crescenzi (2008), like other forms of economic activity, FDI's location is sensitive to place-specific characteristics such as agglomeration and proximity. A pioneer of geographic explanations for international business, John Dunning (1980) famously set forth the "OLI" eclectic paradigm of FDI. Rather than a theory per se, the OLI approach takes into account the "O" (Origin), "L" (Location), and "I" (Internalization, or entry mode) behind each investment. Especially following its (1998) reintroduction, the approach is recognized as being inherently spatial, as it examines the ways in which place related advantages (such as research and development expenditures or economies of scale) can give rise to higher revenues or lower costs (such as an ability to overcome the friction of geographical or cultural distance). Dunning (2008, p. 185) later observes that "technological advances and sweeping changes in the global economic scenario" (continue to alter)"country-specific opportunities and challenges, and none so much as those within the transition economies of Central and Eastern Europe". Many authors such as Deichmann et al. (2003) and Brada et al. (2006), as well as Dunning himself (2008) have heeded the call to examine and compare Central and Eastern European countries as destinations for FDI as the floodgates opened following the demise of the Iron Curtain. To further approach this timely issue and in keeping with Dunning's framework, the chapter focuses upon the *origins of FDI only*, holding the location fixed as the Republic of Croatia, and aggregating all levels of internalization in order to manage the scope of the analysis.

Following Dunning's taxonomy of origin-effects, considerable research has focused specifically on the enabling factors at home that facilitate investment abroad. These studies include Ó hUallacháin and Reid (1992) and Grosse and Trevino (1996) in the United States, both of which identify as important both geographic and cultural distance, among other factors. The role of distance is amplified by the work of Brenton et al. (1998), who explicitly invoke gravity rules in their paper, using population as a measure for origin-country mass and trade as an additional enabler for FDI. These results are corroborated by Hunya, who argues that "the size of the home and host country and the distance between them matter" (2000, p. 90). Head et al. (1999) find that firms from the same origin - and especially those in the same industry- tend to agglomerate in the host country, adding that host offices located abroad can be successful in attracting investment, a finding that is recently explored and confirmed by Deichmann (2010) in the case of the Czech government agency Czechinvest. Bandelj (2002) finds that both cultural distance and trade facilitate FDI, while Bevin and Estrin (2004) cite labour costs, market size, and geographic proximity. Building upon existing work, Brada et al. (2006) find that instability in the Balkans resulted in lost FDI to the region, including Croatia. Bitzenis (2004) highlights the importance of historical links between countries, a factor that will be examined here given Croatia's historical ties to other successor states of the Austro-Hungarian Empire and Yugoslavia.

The oligopolistic reaction theory suggests that firms attempt to reduce uncertainty by following-the-leader into uncertain markets (Knickerbocker 1973). Head et al. (1999) and Deichmann (2010) find evidence that this tendency also holds in Central and Eastern Europe. In Table 2, one can observe that some of the leading early origins, including the United States, which was the top origin at the time, have fallen away during the past decade. Although the Dayton Accords in 1995 officially brought Yugoslavia's war of dissolution to a close, 1999 is an important year because it marked the return of relative stability and the beginning of significant FDI (Fig. 1).

Brada et al. (2006) provide the most comprehensive analysis thus far of the impact of the Balkan conflict on FDI. The authors compare FDI flows between two regions of European transition states: those in Central Europe and those in the Balkans. They highlight Croatia and Slovenia as exceptions to the pessimistic appraisal of the war-torn region, observing that as of 2001, Croatia alone had attracted inflows relative to GDP and population comparable to the well-known Central European success stories. Because FDI is a "forward looking activity", the

Table 2 FDI in Croatia as of December 1999 (in million €)

1	USA	907.1	14	Hungary	13.9
2	Austria	666.3	15	Bosnia and Herzegovina	12.2
3	Germany	940.6	16	Russian Federation	6.4
4	Netherlands	218.0	17	Belgium	6.1
5	UK	89.8	18	Malta	3.3
6	Slovenia	84.6	19	Luxembourg	3.1
7	Sweden	68.2	20	Cyprus	1.5
8	France	59.3	21	Virgin Islands	1.3
9	Italy	58.9	22	Ireland	0.7
10	Switzerland	52.6	23	Israel	0.7
11	Liechtenstein	51.7	24	Spain	0.3
12	IFIs	46.3	25	Slovakia	0.3
13	Denmark	23.9	26	Poland	0.2

Data source: Croatian National Bank (2010). It does not include divestment

authors cite political instability as the main deterrent to investor confidence in the region, as conflict can interfere with the profitability of sales or production, as well as reducing the value of assets through a reduction in the value of the host country's currency. The authors attribute Croatia's comparative success in attracting greater-than-predicted FDI to the restoration of peace to the region by the 1995 Dayton Peace Accords.

2.2 *Gravity Models*

Gravity models have been used in analyzing many forms of spatial interaction. Newton's Law posits that any two bodies attract one another with a force that is proportional to the product of their masses and inversely proportional to the square of the distance between them. In other words, the larger two objects are the more likely they are to interact, and the farther away they are from one another the less likely they are to interact. In econometrics, masses or objects can be countries, measured by variables such as population size or GDP. Interaction may take the form of flows such as trade, migration, or foreign direct investment. For example, other things being equal, we would expect more interaction between Croatia and its immediate neighbor Hungary than with Estonia, a smaller country located farther away. Apart from Estonia having a smaller mass than Hungary, this example is also an illustration of distance decay or a decreasing likelihood of interaction as distance increases. The simple gravity model is presented as follows:

$$\mathrm{FDI}_{ij} = e\left(\mathrm{M}_i\mathrm{M}_j/\mathrm{D}_{ij}\right)$$

where, FDI = value of foreign direct investment
e = constant
M = mass (GDP or population)
D = resistance (geographical or cultural distance)

Jan Tinbergen (1962) is credited with the first application of the gravity model to explain international trade patterns in *Shaping the World Economy: Suggestions for an International Economic Policy*. Ok (2010) assesses current intra-EU trade flows using an augmented gravity model. Introducing measures of trade competitiveness, income, remoteness, and culture (adjacency and language), he tests and validates his model using EU manufacturing data over 9 years, confirming the significance of the extensions.

The model has since been extended to other trans-border flows including immigration and FDI. Lewer and Van den Berg (2008) apply the gravity model to international migration, where the population of the origin country is a push factor (crowding) and the population of the destination country is a pull factor (employment opportunities), with the difference between labor incomes serving as an attractive force for overcoming the friction of geographic distance. The authors demonstrate the approach's utility in studying migration, adding that the marginal influence of additional variables can be added to the model.

Like trade, migration, and other flows, FDI is driven by the attractive force a destination country has upon decision-makers in the FDI origin country. Brenton et al. (1998), Buch et al. (2003), Bevin and Estrin (2004), Borrmann et al. (2005), and Zademach and Rodríguez-Pose (2009) are among the few scholars that have employed gravity models in their work on foreign direct investment. In the context of Europe and its transition economies, Brenton et al. (1998) find that trade and FDI as dependent variables are driven by the same factors, underscoring the complementarity of these flows as alternate levels of internalization. Buch et al. (2003) use a similar technique to find evidence that refutes suspicions that the opening up of transition economies has diverted FDI from Spain and Portugal. Bevin and Estrin (2004) attribute FDI to both origin and host country GDP, and confirm their expectations that distance has an adverse effect on it. Borrmann et al. (2005) question whether distance can sometimes be an advantage rather than an impediment, then confirm the notion that it serves as a deterrent to FDI, noting that in economically integrated regions such as Europe, cross-border leakage can deem market size problematic as a measure of gravity mass. These findings are based only on the current (2010) Central European members of the EU; therefore no direct reference is made to Croatia. Finally, examining both the numbers and the values of mergers and acquisitions in Europe, Zademach and Rodríguez-Pose (2009) confirm that geographic proximity matters for FDI, and reinstate the importance of GDP, while conceding that the European corporate landscape is changing in unclear ways due to dissolving borders, calling for further research on the "imperfect integration" (2009, p. 784). In altering the gravity model to accommodate additional considerations such as trade links that have been shown elsewhere to facilitate FDI, the approach here is similar to the aforementioned studies. Following Zademach and Rodríguez-Pose (2009), it examines both the value of FDI and the number of transactions. What distinguishes the present work from most other gravity studies, however, is the examination of the origins (rather than the destinations) of FDI, and the data that are much more current.

3 Data and Methodology

This inquire applies ordinary least squares (OLS) regression to better understand origin effects based upon a cross-sectional data set of 190 countries (see appendix), from 2000 to 2009, examining both the value and the number of FDI transactions. This period marks the return of substantial stability to former Yugoslavia (EBRD), through the most recent publication of data, and a time in which more than 88% of all transactions in Croatia took place, as illustrated in Table 1. The OLS approach is inspired by similar research on origin effects in the USA by Grosse and Trevino (1996), in China by Zhao and Zhu (2000), and in Poland by Deichmann (2004). The software used is SPSS 18.0, and the first two models are specified by the author and are intended as illustrations of the basic gravity model, and an augmented one with all hypothesized determinants. The rest of the models are generated by SPSS using a forward selection algorithm, adding the variables to the models in order of their importance.

Most of the independent variables used in this project are from the World Bank's World Development Indicators, and the dependent variables are provided by the Croatian National Bank. The coverage of our variables begins in 2000 because this is the year that marks the return of substantial stability, and as shown in Table 1, the beginning of FDI acceleration. Moreover, as we are focused mainly on gravity variables, it would be problematic to include years that where characterized by severe political hardship that distorted the flows of FDI in Croatia and its neighboring countries (Brada et al. 2006). Moreover, Polanec (2004) argues that because of vastly varying initial conditions and transition reforms in the region, only after 1998 did mainstream economic variables begin telling the story of FDI.

The models are specified as follows: first, following Hunya (2000), a basic gravity model using only GDP and geographic distance is run for the dependent variable cumulative FDI 2000–2009. Second, a comprehensive model is run using all nine variables called for by the literature and/or intuitive reasoning. Third, a forward algorithm selects the best variables, justified above, from the dataset. Fourth, the Netherlands and United States are removed in order to control for confusion surrounding the effect of Dutch holding companies, particularly with regard to US firms. Fifth, a forward algorithm is employed using the number of transactions as the dependent variable. Finally, based on the expectation (Alfaro and Chen 2010) that firms from different countries were impacted differentially by the global financial crisis that began in 2007, the dependent variable is altered to new FDI projects during the years 2008–2009. The 190 countries included in the analysis are listed in Appendix A.

Finally, the origin effects examined here can be grouped as follows: those expected to facilitate FDI, and those expected to impede it. Hypothesized facilitators include GDP as a measure of economic power (following Bevin and Estrin 2004), GNI (a measure of relative economic strength), trade (Bandelj 2002; Škuflić and Botrić 2009), personnel in research in technology (Deichmann 2004), agglomeration (Head et al. 1999; Botrić and Škuflić 2006), EU integration (Buch et al. 2003; Deichmann 2004), and historical inertia (Bitzenis 2004). Here, historical inertia (HIST) recognizes longstanding connections enjoyed with Croatia by successor states of the Austro-Hungarian Empire and the former Yugoslavia, favoring FDI from Austria, Hungary, Czech Republic, Slovakia, Serbia, Bosnia-Herzegovina, Montenegro, Slovenia, and FYROM. Although it presently shares no land border with Croatia, Italy is added to this group of expected *border effects* both because the region of Tyrol had been administered by Austro-Hungary and because other parts of the country lie directly across the Adriatic from Croatia (following Ok 2010).

Because transportation costs increase with distance, and operational costs increase across cultures, both are expected to impede FDI. Geographic distance, following Hunya (2000), Zademach and Rodríguez-Pose (2009), and Ok (2010), is measured here between economic epicenters rather than capital cities (for example for Canada, it makes sense to use Toronto rather than Ottawa because it is much larger by population and economic activity, and slightly more central). Cultural distance is also captured differently by Grosse and Trevino (1996), Bandelj (2002), and in the present study. Here, cultural distance is quantified on a continuum ranging from 1 to 5, based upon linguistic and alphabetical affinities with Croatia. For example, Slovenes ("1") use a similar Slavonic tongue and the common Latin alphabet; Russians ("2") use a similar Slavonic tongue and different (Cyrillic) alphabet. English and German being widely spoken in Croatia, all native English and German speaking states are assigned "3", and so on, with China, Japan, and others at the end of the cultural continuum with "5".[1] Other mainstream origin effects such as exchange rate change (Grosse and Trevino 1996), political stability (Brada et al. 2006), and corruption measures (Deichmann 2010) in the origin country have been left out of this analysis to improve parsimony, given that little intuitive justification exists to expect them to impact corporate executives who are considering FDI in Croatia in the present context.

Table 3 summarizes the dependent and independent variables used in the models with their anticipated valence signs. Variables are selected based upon expectations formed from the results of previous studies featured in the literature review. Following Zademach and Rodríguez-Pose (2009), *both* the number of investments *and* the value of investments are considered to be of importance in measuring flows. Each investment transaction represents a *location decision*, but at the same time a wide range exists in the monetary value of each investment, and this is an indication of the *degree* of enablement in the origin country.

4 Analysis

Six models are specified in order to address the questions set forth, and the results are presented in Table 4. The goal of the first iteration is to capture the essence of a very simple gravity model. Model 1 is run by entering the prescribed variables ln (GDP) and GEOG in a stepwise manner, yielding a fundamental but incomplete explanation of the origin effects.

$$\mathbf{FDI}_{ij} = e^{\beta}{}_{0}(\ln\mathbf{GDP}_{i}{}^{\beta}{}_{1} - \mathbf{GEOG}_{ij}{}^{\beta}{}_{2})$$

[1] A full rationale and list of countries and their scores is available directly from the author.

Table 3 List of variables with descriptions and sources

Variable	Definition (units)	Valence	data source
FDI	FDI value 2000–2009 inclusive, thousand €		Croatian National Bank (2010)
FDI0809	FDI inflow during 2008–2009 only, thousand €		Croatian National Bank (2010)
FDI#	Number of FDI transactions from each origin, 2000 = 2009		Croatian National Bank (2010)
ln(GDP)[a]	Gross domestic product, mean 2000–2008, million US$	+	World Bank (2010)
GNI	Gross National Income per capita (mean 2000–2008)	+	World Bank (2010)
AGG	Cumulative Value of FDI at the end of 1999	+	Croatian National Bank (2010)
ln(TRADE)	Imports + Exports with partner $_i$, mean 2000–2008, mil USS	+	Croatian National Bank (2010)
HIST	Dummy for Yugoslavia and Austro-Hungarian Empire	+	www.googlemaps.com
EU	Duration of EU membership for 27 countries, 2000–2009	+	www.europa.eu
TECH	Scientists and engineers per million population	+	World Bank (2010)
CULT	Cultural distance between origin $_i$ and Croatia $_j$	−	Author's calculations
GEOG	Distance between main city of country $_i$ and Zagreb (km)	−	Google distance calculator[b]

[a]The variables GDP and TRADE are transformed to logarithms to control heteroskedasticity
[b]http://www.daftlogic.com/projects-google-maps-distance-calculator.htm

where: FDI = value of foreign direct investment 2000–2009 inclusive
e = constant
lnGDP = Logarithm of GDP (mass)
GEOG = geographical distance (resistance)

Geographic distance, the first variable to be entered performs satisfactorily, but it appears to be confounded by the entrance of economic size, as when ln(GDP) is entered, the constant's p value of the coefficient increases from .000 to .647. The reason, most likely, is that while European economies are generally large, many larger economies (the USA and Japan, for instance) are very distant from Croatia, and their companies have contributed very little investment thus far. Still, the null hypothesis can be rejected based upon GEOG's $p = .004$, and ln(GDP)'s $p = .021$. The exercise of Model 1, therefore provides an excellent basis for enhancement of the gravity model.

Model 1: Simple Gravity Model (ln[GDP] and GEOG, value 2000–2009)
Model 2: Enter Selection (all variables, value 2000–2009)
Model 3: Stepwise Forward Selection, all variables (value 2000–2009)
Model 4: Stepwise Forward Selection, all variables without Netherlands and USA (2008–2009)
Model 5: Stepwise Forward Selection, all variables (transactions 2000–2009)
Model 6: Stepwise Selection, all variables with (2008–2009) as dependent variable

Table 4 Coefficients and significance levels of variables in the models

	Model 1 coefficients	Model 2 coefficients	Model 3 coefficients	Model 4 coefficients	Model 5 coefficients	Model 6 coefficients
Independent variable ↓	FDI	FDI	FDI	FDI	FDI#	FDI0809
Constant (*e*)	76.381	−99.030	−23.907	−12.722	−1.676	−.975
ln(GDP)	23.562[b]	−4.373				
GNI		.003				.0000552[a]
AGG		2.420[a]	2.390[a]	3.404[a]	.488[a]	.003[a]
ln(TRADE)		2.182			2.517[a]	.047[b]
HIST		784.270[a]	742.358[a]	770.767[a]	248.933[a]	2.079[a]
EU		59.396[a]	59.295[a]	28.647[a]	.196[b]	.196[a]
TECH		−.027				
CULT		28.498				
GEOG	−.029[b]	.002				−.0000504[c]
R^2	.086[a]	.558[a]	.553[a]	.682[a]	.691[a]	.679[a]

[a]Statistically significant at the 0.001 level (two-tailed)
[b]Statistically significant at the 0.005 level (two-tailed)
[c]Statistically significant at the 0.05 level (two-tailed)

Model 2 is then an augmentation of the simple gravity model based upon the variables found in the literature, and those such as historical inertial (HIST) and cultural distance (CULT) that make intuitive sense as articulated earlier. The comprehensive equation takes the following form:

$$\text{FDIij} = e + \beta_1\text{GDP}_i + \beta_2\text{GNI}_i + \beta_3\text{TRADE}_{ij} + \beta_4\text{TECH}_i + \beta_5\text{AGG}_{ij} + \beta_6\text{EU}_i + \beta_7\text{HIST}_{ij} - \beta_8\text{CULT}_{ij} - \beta_9\text{GEOG}_{ij}$$

with the following notations:

e = constant for fitting the equation

β_{1}– β_9 = coefficients for each independent variable described in Table 3.

Model 2 includes all of the variables in this equation, and performs quite well with an R^2 of .558. Simple correlations are presented in Appendix B. The three best predictors are AGG (agglomeration), EU (years of membership), and HIST (former states of Austro-Hungary and Yugoslavia), all significant at the .000 level. The marginal effects interpretation of Model 2 is that with respect to the constant of −99,030, every million Euros of FDI in place by 1999 results in 2,420 € at the end of 2009. Further, each year of EU membership has facilitated 59,396 €, and the binary HIST variable favors FDI from other countries in former Austro-Hungary and Yugoslavia at the average starting point of 784,270 €. Because the constant *e* is negative and neither geographic nor cultural distance is significant predictors in this particular model, it is not necessarily problematic that their valence signs are positive. As FDI was shown to be negatively and significantly related to distance in Model 1, a reasonable explanation of its positive and not significant outcome in Model 2 is that distance is being captured by the significant EU and HIST variables. Nevertheless, the variable GNI is problematic in this model because of a low tolerance of .441/high variance inflation factor ("VIF") of 2.268, signaling that the variance of GNI's regression coefficient is too high.

In Model 3, the SPSS forward algorithm is set to enter the variables in order of their explanatory importance, which is as follows: AGG (1999 value of FDI from same origin), EU (years of membership), HIST (Yugoslavia, Austro-Hungary, and Italy). This model with three predictors yields a respectable R^2 of .553, but with the advantage of being much more parsimonious. The first variable entered is AGG, which alone remarkably yields a R^2 of .363. At this point (with only one predictor), as excluded variables the distance variable is negative and significant with a coefficient of −.173 ($p = .003$); likewise, cultural distance is negative and significant at −.128 ($p = .038$). This observation reveals that gravity predictors are indeed at work, and confirms earlier speculation that they are being masked by other variables as the number of predictors increases. Further proof is presented when EU membership and HIST enter Model 3, and the two distance variables become positive (.023 and .045, respectively), and their significance levels explode to .672 and .424, respectively.

Model 3 is completed with the addition of EU and HIST. The coefficients are very similar to those of Model 2, signaling a dramatic drop-off in explanatory power following the first three variables. Given the constant of −23.907, every million Euros of FDI in place by 1999 results in 2.390 € at the end of 2009, each year of EU membership on average yields 59.396 € in FDI, and a shared history with neighbors provides advantages resulting in 742,358 €.

As acknowledged in Sect. 3, some firms from the USA and elsewhere use the Netherlands as a tax haven, registering there in order to benefit from preferential tax treatment in Europe. Model 4 differs from Model 3 with the removal of the Netherlands and USA, leading to interesting results. Probably because the Netherlands is a founding EU member and the second leading origin of FDI in Croatia with 6.156 € billion, with its removal the HIST (Austro-Hungary/Yugoslavia) variable became the second to be selected, ahead of EU membership, and the coefficient dropped from 59.295 to 28.647, but remained positive and significant at the.000 level. The resulting R^2 of this model is .682 (vs. .553 in Model 3).

The number of investment transactions is also intuitively important, because each transaction represents a location decision. Although a simple Pearson correlation of .765 links the number of investments to the total value, the country rankings are quite different. For example, the average investment from Slovenia is worth 1.39 € million, while the average Dutch project is 9.76 € million. Therefore, Model 5 interrogates the earlier findings to test the impact of each determinant on the number of transactions from the 10 years under investigation. Like Model 4, a forward algorithm is used to add variables in order of fit as follows: AGG, HIST, EU, and TRADE. Remarkably, the results are very similar to the findings thus far. All of the variables are significant at the $p = .002$ level, and the R^2 of this "transactions" model is .691, the highest of any model in this exercise. Moreover, because data from the Croatian Central Bank show that firms from 94 countries have invested in Croatia, a great deal of intuitive weight can be placed upon the outcome of this model.

To conclude the exercise, Model 6 is an attempt to explore the origins of FDI using only the two most recent years of available data for capturing any impact of the global financial crisis that began in 2007, and as a means for more generally examining whether the explanatory power of the predictors remain the same. After Alfaro and Chen (2010), it is evident that firms respond very differently to the global financial crisis and how it impacts both host and (in this case) home countries. In short, origins of FDI changed dramatically in 2008–2009, and so did the factors that facilitated FDI.

Model 6 is dramatically different from Models 1–5 because a greater number of variables (six) are identified as significant predictors of FDI inflow into Croatia from 2008 to 2009. In order of importance, these are EU, GNI, HIST, AGG, log (TRADE), and DIST, all with valence signs as predicted. A cursory examination of the dataset reveals the top five origins during this time, which in order are Austria, the Netherlands, Hungary, Germany, and Slovenia, followed by twelve other European countries, ten of them being EU members.

Overall, the models unveil the importance of several enabling factors in origin countries that have facilitated FDI during Croatia's period of transition leading up to its impending EU accession. These factors include agglomeration, European Union membership, historical linkages, and trade links, each of which is found to be significant in at least three of the six models. While this effort makes considerable progress toward better understanding FDI in the context of a gravity model, such manuscripts are limited in scope and further research remains to be done to understand.

Agglomeration, the first determinant to be selected in all of the models, is defined here as the value of FDI in Croatia from each origin at the outset of substantial FDI inflows that began in 1999. Following early observations by Knickerbocker (1973) and in harmony with work in multiple contexts by Head et al. (1999), Botrić and Škuflić (2006), Rodríguez-Pose and Cresenzi (2008), and Deichmann (2010), "herd mentality" plays a role in Croatia, where firms from shared origins tend to follow one another.

FDI in Croatia is dominated by firms from the European Union, and while other predicted explanations including cultural and geographic proximity (which would also favor European countries) were not significant in most models, it is clear that in Croatia, economic integration enables FDI. This finding probably reflects evidence that corporate decision makers from the EU already consider Croatia's accession a *fait accompli*, and they have been proactive in entering the country, in spite of unresolved concerns about bureaucracy (*Croatia Business* 2010) and corruption (Srdoc and Samy 2009).

The findings presented here are particularly robust not only because they are based upon six different models of various intuitive specifications, but also because the dependent variables include the value of FDI from 2000 to 2009, the value of the years 2008–2009 (following the outset of the global economic crisis), and the number of transactions from nearly 100 countries. Given the provision of excellent data from the Croatian National Bank, this analysis therefore follows Zademach and Rodígues-Pose (2009) in examining both the investment decision (number of transactions) and the magnitude of those decisions (the value of investments).

Growth in FDI to Croatia, like other economic activity, took a hit during the global economic crisis that began in 2007, as shown in Fig. 1. As pointed out by Alfaro and Chen (2010), the recession had differential effects on firms according to home country. Model 6 yields the observation that the variables explaining Croatian FDI origins also changed during this time. Specifically, the friction of distance became more important to investors, as it is shown to be a negative and significant predictor of FDI. Moreover, for the first time gross national income, another gravity variable became a significant predictor of FDI. Still, more research is needed to disentangle the complexity of the crisis and how it impacted FDI. Moreover, as the availability of projects, type of investment, and the origins of firms continue to change over time (Hargitai 2010), further inquiry is needed into the dynamics of location factors with reference to other global opportunities. For such an undertaking, certainly, econometric approaches should be complemented by qualitative case-based methodologies.

5 Conclusions

This chapter demonstrates the relevance of the gravity model in FDI research. In the simplest specified model, geographic distance and GDP (log transformation) both prove to be significant predictors of FDI, but not sufficient for a full understanding of the origins. Following Bandelj's (2002) analysis of destinations across Central and Eastern Europe, trade flows are also found here to be a significant origin-effect of FDI in Croatia. In the lean economic circumstances of recent years (2008–2009), gross national income emerged as a (statistically significant) measure of origin mass. Overall, the key lessons learned here result from the observed importance of agglomeration, EU membership, and historical linkages as enablers of FDI into the Republic of Croatia.

Among its main contributions, this research questions and confirms the importance of the historical legacies of the Austro-Hungarian Empire, Yugoslavia, and linkages with portions of Italy. This variable helps to explain the origins of FDI at the $p = .001$ level of significance in five of the six models. With 1,219 firms investing in Croatia, Austria represents the most important origin, followed by Italy with 949. Slovenia is third with 767, Hungary tenth with 213, and Bosnia-Herzegovina twelfth with 123, still more prominent than France in terms of FDI in Croatia. This original finding reflects the importance of longstanding economic ties across present borders, and emphasizes the role of local knowledge in international business first unveiled by O' hUallachaín and Reid (1992) in the United States. To the extent that this variable also captures cultural proximity, the lack of significance of the CULT variable is understandable, as the OLS forward selection algorithm avoids variables that are redundant to those already in the models.

The policy implications of this research are numerous. Clearly, recognizing the importance of follow-the-leader tendencies among firms from shared origins,

Croatia's Trade and Investment Promotion Agency might specifically and actively target additional firms from successful origin countries (particularly those in the European Union and those sharing historical linkages) to undertake the many projects that they list in their "e-book of investments" posted prominently at www.croinvest.org. This agency rightfully markets FDI "success stories" on its web site. However, it could do more to help decision-makers overcome residual uncertainty about instability even long after the Dayton Accords have been signed, and to facilitate navigation through a daunting bureaucracy (*Croatia Business* 2010) and permitting process. In such a direction, lessons might be gleaned from other regional competitors like the Czech Republic, which, according to Benáček (2008) demonstrates "administrative competence". The Czech Republic and its promotion agency Czechinvest have been praised for their transparent investment policies, streamline permitting process, and provision of meaningful aftercare to foreign corporations (Deichmann 2010). Moreover, would-be investors need assurances against globally publicized corruption problems in Croatia (Srdoc and Samy 2009). Transparency International (2010) lists Croatia's corruption perceptions index at 4.3/10, with higher scores representing "very clean". Croatia is therefore viewed as being less corrupt than several of its Balkan neighbors, but more corrupt than regional competitors including the Višegrad Group and Turkey. The burden of overcoming such a reputation falls upon Croatia's government to clarify and enforce its own laws, and upon its outreach agencies to reassure and assist investors.

This chapter on origin-effects of FDI in Croatia contributes to a small but growing literature on the republic's FDI landscape. Filling in what Hunya (2000) and Dunning (1998) consider a neglected aspect of Dunning's (1980) eclectic framework by focusing upon and modeling home country attributes, it complements studies on country-level competition for FDI into Central and Eastern Europe by Deichmann et al. (2003), Borrmann et al. (2005), Botrić and Škuflić (2006), Dabić and Pejić-Bach (2008), and Hunya (2010). These findings can also be considered alongside examinations of FDI's impacts (Hunya and Škudar 2006) which are generally viewed to be positive, and the disparate county-level distribution of FDI (Škuflić and Botrić 2009). Given Croatia's impending 2013 European Union accession, as well as its unique conditions vis-à-vis its neighbors (tourism economy with relatively high property costs and wage rates, for example), a rich number of future research directions remain.

In sum, the present analysis of home country conditions and FDI flows contributes to the collective scholarly understanding of origin-effects, with specific reference to the context of Croatia as it emerges from the rubble of former Yugoslavia and toward integration with the European Union. In this unique context, mainstream explanations of FDI origin such as agglomeration and trade are clearly at work. Additionally legacies of the former Austro-Hungarian Empire and Yugoslavia remain evident, as does growing facilitation of FDI from EU countries in the midst of Croatia's accession preparations. Implications for government policy are presented, mainly with regard to targeting likely investors and streamlining the investment process by promoting transparency and facilitating the permitting process.

Appendix A: Countries in the Dataset (N = 190)

Afghanistan
Albania
Algeria
Andorra
Angola
Antigua and Barbuda
Argentina
Armenia
Australia
Austria
Azerbaijan
Bahamas, The
Bahrain
Bangladesh
Barbados
Belarus
Belgium
Belize
Benin
Bhutan
Bolivia
Bosnia
Botswana
Brazil
Brunei
Bulgaria
Burkina Faso
Burma (Myanmar)
Burundi
Cambodia
Cameroon
Canada
Cape Verde
Central African Rep
Chad
Chile
China
Colombia
Comoros
Congo (Brazzaville)
Congo (Kinshasa)
Costa Rica
Cote d'Ivoire
Croatia
Cuba
Cyprus
Denmark
Djibouti
Dominica
Dominican Republic
East Timor
Ecuador
Egypt
El Salvador
Equatorial Guinea
Eritrea
Estonia
Ethiopia
Fiji
Finland
France
FYROM
Gabon
Gambia
Georgia
Germany
Ghana
Greece
Grenada
Guatemala
Guinea-Bissau
Guinea
Guyana
Haiti
Honduras
Hungary
Iceland
India
Indonesia
Iran
Iraq
Ireland
Israel
Italy
Jamaica
Japan
Jordan
Kazakhstan
Kenya
Kiribati
Korea (North)
Korea (South)
Kuwait
Kyrgyzstan
Laos
Latvia
Lebanon
Lesotho
Liberia
Libya
Liechtenstein
Lithuania
Luxembourg
Madagascar
Malawi
Malaysia
Maldives
Mali
Malta
Marshall Islands
Mauritania
Mauritius
Mexico
Micronesia
Moldova
Monaco
Mongolia
Morocco
Mozambique
Namibia
Nauru
Nepal
Netherlands
New Zealand
Nicaragua
Niger
Nigeria
Norway
Oman
Pakistan
Palau
Panama
Papua New Guinea
Paraguay
Peru
Philippines
Poland
Portugal
Puerto Rico
Qatar
Romania
Russian Federation
Rwanda
Saint Kitts and Nevis
Saint Lucia
Saint Vincent
Samoa
San Marino
Saudi Arabia
Senegal
Serbia/Montenegro
Seychelles
Sierra Leone
Singapore
Slovakia
Slovenia
Solomon Islands
Somalia
South Africa
Spain
Sri Lanka
Sudan
Suriname
Swaziland
Sweden
Switzerland
Syria
Taiwan
Tajikistan
Tanzania
Thailand
Togo
Tonga
Trinidad and Tobago
Tunisia
Turkey
Turkmenistan
Tuvalu
Uganda
Ukraine
United Arab Emirates
United Kingdom
United States
Uruguay
Uzbekistan
Venezuela
Vietnam
Yemen
Zambia
Zimbabwe

Appendix B: Correlation Matrix

	FDI	lnFDI	lnGDP	GNI	lnTRADE	TECH	AGG	EU	HIST	GEOG	CULT
FDI	1.000	.652	.214	.373	.378	.148	.602	.523	.425	−.245	−.309
lnFDI	.652	1.000	.338	.567	.577	.225	.367	.718	.486	−.463	−.506
lnGDP	.214	.338	1.000	.273	.477	.158	.233	.330	.125	−.229	−.302
GNI	.373	.567	.273	1.000	.428	.549	.382	.556	.076	−.247	−.418
lnTRADE	.378	.577	.477	.428	1.000	.170	.337	.469	.304	−.332	−.488
TECH	.148	.225	.158	.549	.170	1.000	.216	.272	.005	−.113	−.183
AGG	.602	.367	.233	.382	.337	.216	1.000	.316	.171	−.126	−.328
EU	.523	.718	.330	.556	.469	.272	.316	1.000	.269	−.421	−.330
HIST	.425	.486	.125	.076	.304	.005	.171	.269	1.000	−.288	−.351
GEOG	−.245	−.463	−.229	−.247	−.332	−.113	−.126	−.421	−.288	1.000	.293
CULT	−.309	−.506	−.302	−.418	−.488	−.183	−.328	−.330	−.351	.293	1.000

References

Alfaro, L, Chen M (2010) Foreign direct investment and establishment performance. USITC working paper, June. Available at: http://www.usitc.gov/research_and_analysis/economics_seminars/2010/Alfaro_and_Chen_GlobalFinancialCrisis.pdf. Accessed 20 Aug

Bandelj N (2002) Embedded economies: social relations as determinants of foreign direct investment in Central and Eastern Europe. Soc Forces 81(2):411–444

Benáček V (2008) Management of the policies of development in the Czech Republic: CzechInvest as an example of public administration competence. In: Proceedings of the 16th NISP acee annual conference. Bratislava. http://www1.ceses.cuni.cz/benacek/Benacek-NISPA_Bratislava.pdf. Accessed 10 Nov 2009

Bevin, Alan A, Saul Estrin (2004) The Determinants of Foreign Direct Investment into European Transition Economies. *Journal of Comparative Economics*. 32, 775–787

Bitzenis A (2004) Explanatory variables for low western investment in Bulgaria. Eastern Eur Econ 42(6):5–38

Borrmann C, Jungnickel R, Keller D (2005) What gravity models can tell us about the position of German FDI in Central and Eastern Europe. Hamburg Institute of International Economics (HWWA), Discussion paper 328, August

Botrić V, Škuflić L (2006) Main determinants of foreign direct investment in the Southeast European countries. Transit Stud Rev 13(2):359–377

Brada JC, Kutan AM, Yigit TM (2006) The effects of transition and political instability on foreign direct investment flows: Central Europe and the Balkans. Econ Transit 14(4):649–680

Brenton P, Di Mauro F, Lücke M (1998) Economic integration and FDI: an empirical analysis of Foreign investment in the EU and in Central and Eastern Europe. Institut fiir Weltwirtschaft. Kiel working paper #890. Available at: http://www.econstor.eu/bitstream/10419/1046/1/252636090.pdf. Accessed 16 Sept 2010

Buch, Claudia, Kokta, Robert, Piazolo, Daniel (2003) Does the East get what would otherwise flow to the South? FDI diversion in Europe. *Journal of Comparative Economics*. 31, 94–109

Croatian Business (2010). More bureaucracy for Foreign property owners in Croatia. http://croatiabusinessreport.wordpress.com/2010/09/30/more-bureaucracy-for-foreign-property-owners-in-croatia/. September 30, accessed 10 Oct

Croatian National Bank (2010) Statistics database. Available at: http://www.hnb.hr/statistika/estatistika.htm. Accessed 10 Oct
Dabić M, Pejić-Bach M (2008) Understanding the foreign direct investment environments in EU 27 + candidate country Croatia: current determinants and patters. Int J Entrepreneurship Innovat Manag (IJEIM) 8(3):254–271
Deichmann JI (2004) Origins of foreign direct investment in Poland, 1989–2001. J Bus Econ Stud 10(1):12–28
Deichmann JI (2010) Origin-effects and foreign direct investment in the Czech Republic: the role of government promotion abroad. Comp Econ Stud 52:249–272
Deichmann JI, Eshghi A, Haughton D, Sayek S, Teebagy N (2003) Foreign direct investment in the Eurasian transition states. Eastern Eur Econ 41(1):5–34
Dunning J (1980) Toward an eclectic theory of international production: some empirical tests. J Int Bus Stud 11:9–31
Dunning JH (1998) Location and the multinational enterprise: a neglected factor? J Int Bus Stud 29(1):45–66
Dunning John (2008) Institutional reform, FDI and the locational competitiveness of European transition economies. In: Dunning J, Gugler P (eds) Progress in international business research, vol 2, Foreign direct investment, location and competitiveness. Elsevier, Boston, pp 175–201
EBRD (European Bank for Reconstruction and Development) (2010) Transition report. EBRD, London
Grosse R, Trevino L (1996) Foreign direct investment in the United States: an analysis by country of origin. J Int Bus Stud 27(1):139–155
Hargitai Z (2010) Informational interview with European Bank for reconstruction and development's Director for Croatia. Zagreb, 2 November
Head CK, Ries JC, Swenson DL (1999) Attracting foreign manufacturing: investment promotion and agglomeration. Reg Sci Urban Econ 29:197–218
Hunya G (2000) Home country patterns of foreign direct investment in Central and East European countries. Russ E Eur Financ Tr 36(2)
Hunya G, Škudar A (2006) The role of foreign direct investment in the Croatian economy (final report) A study prepared for the investment compact project "Investment and trade liberalization, strengthening development and implementation of investment and trade policy in the Western Balkans" http://www.oecd.org/dataoecd/55/33/37707398.pdf. Accessed 10 Sept 2010
Hunya G (2010) Database on foreign direct investment in Central, East and Southeast Europe, 2010: FDI in the CEECs hit hard by the global crisis. Vienna Institute for International Economic Studies. http://publications.wiiw.ac.at/files/pdf/FDI/fdi_may10_contents.pdf
Knickerbocker F (1973) Oligopolistic reaction and multinational enterprise. Harvard University, Boston
Lewer J, Van den Berg H (2008) A gravity model of immigration. Econ Lett 99(1):164–167
O'hUallacháin B, Reid N (1992) Source country differences in the spatial distribution of foreign direct investment in the United States. Prof Geogr 44:272–285
Ok ST (2010) What determines intra-EU trade? The gravity model revisited. Int Res J Financ Econ 39:244–250
Polanec S (2004) Convergence at last? Evidence from transition economies. Eastern Eur Econ 42(4):55–80
Redžepagić S, Richet X (2009) Attractivity of the FDI in Western Balkans: evidence from the Central and Eastern European Countries (CEEC). Working paper. Available at: http://oliver.efri.hr/~euconf/2009/docs/Session7/3%20Redzepagic%20Richet.pdf. Accessed 20 Dec 2010
Rodríguez-Pose A, Crescenzi R (2008) Mountains in a flat world: why proximity still matters for the location of economic activity. Cambridge J Reg, Econ Soc 1:371–388
Škuflić L, Botrić V (2009) Foreign direct investment in Croatia: regional perspective. Ekonomska Istraživanja 22(3):9–28

Srdoc N, Samy JA (2009) Corruption in Croatia: despite the EU's assurances, Zagreb is no role model for the region. Wall Street Journal Europe. May 19. Available at: http://online.wsj.com/article/SB124267799642331663.html. Accessed 4 Nov 2010

Tinbergen J (1962) Shaping the world economy: suggestions for an international economic policy. Twentieth Century Fund, New York

World Bank (2010) Key development data and statistics. http://web.worldbank.org/, data obtained from the World Bank web site on 20 July

Transparency International (2010) Corruption perceptions index. Available at http://www.transparency.org/policy_research/surveys_indices/cpi/2010. Accessed 27 Oct

Zademach H-M, Rodríguez-Pose A (2009) Cross-Border M&As and the changing economic geography of Europe. Eur Plann Stud 17(5):765–789

Zhao H, Zhu G (2000) Location factors and country-of-origin differences: an empirical analysis of FDI in China. Multinatl Bus Rev 80:60–73

Balkan Area and EU-15: An Empirical Investigation of Income Convergence

Eftychia Tsanana, Constantinos Katrakilidis, and Panagiotis Pantelidis

This paper empirically explores the issue of income convergence of the Balkan economies with the European Union's-15 average (EU-15) over the period 1989–2009. The adopted econometric methodology has been suggested by Nahar and Inder (2002) and is considered more efficient in detecting possible catching up effects compared to the relevant conventional methods. The findings of this paper point out the existence of dissimilarities among the examined Balkan economies in the process to catch up with the EU-15. In particular, the results support income convergence with the EU-15 only for Greece and Slovenia.

1 Introduction

The German reunion and the breakup of Yugoslavia and the Soviet Union invoked the dramatic change of the socialistic schemes of Central and Eastern Europe (CEE). In 1989, two contradictory trends appeared in the Balkan zone. The first concerned the openness to the West leaving back the communist regimes. Besides, the reawaken nationalism among the nations of Yugoslavia resulted in conflicts and created a new framework for the future relations between the Balkans and the international community (Papasotiriou, 1994).

E. Tsanana (✉) • C. Katrakilidis
Department of Economics, School of Law, Economics and Political Sciences, Aristotle University of Thessaloniki, Thessaloniki, Greece
e-mail: etsanana@econ.auth.gr; katrak@econ.auth.gr

P. Pantelidis
Department of Business Administration, School of Economics and Business Administration, Serres, TEI of Serres, Serres, Greece
e-mail: pan@teiser.gr

A. Karasavvoglou and P. Polychronidou (eds.), *Balkan and Eastern European Countries in the Midst of the Global Economic Crisis*, Contributions to Economics,
DOI 10.1007/978-3-7908-2873-3_2, © Springer-Verlag Berlin Heidelberg 2013

Over the last decades the Balkans' future in Europe has attracted the interest of the academic community and the European Commission. Despite the past tendencies, the European Union (EU) considered the Balkans and the CEE countries as a matter of priority and developed the conditions for its enlargement towards the Easter Bloc. The first enlargement, though not in terms of GDP, took place in 2004 by including eight CEE countries. According to Gros and Steinherr (2001), the transition of the CEE countries was completed in 1997 though some differences remained between the states of Central Europe and the Baltic region and the rest of the countries. Cavenaile and Dubois (2011) supported that there has been still a long way for the CEE countries towards income convergence. These countries, though aiming at joining the EU were not forming a homogenous group of economies with similar characteristics. The events of 1989 shocked the CEE economies resulting in significant drawbacks in production (Rosenberg 2000).

The notion of convergence has been a subject of discussions and theoretical analyses since the eighteenth century. Convergence is inherent to the theory of economic growth, as it describes a process within which a certain level of growth defined as target is approached. It is also refers to the narrowing of the difference between two values over time.

The roots of convergence are found to the neoclassical growth model of Solow, a mathematical approach aimed at explaining convergence. Modern growth theory has been grounded on Solow's dynamic model (Solow 1956). However, the neoclassical theory was initially presented by Sala-i-Martin (1996) as a methodology to bibliography. The main idea was that poor economies tend to grow faster than the rich ones. The movement of a country towards a group leader addresses the topic of catching up.

Regarding the empirical evidence on convergence, the relevant research efforts appeared during the last decades when larger data sets became available (Baumol 1986). Concerning the literature for the Balkan economies in particular the majority of the research efforts used samples that included only a limited number of countries from the full Balkan group (Amplatz C. (2004), Baldwin et al. (1997), Bjorksten (2000), Bonetto et al. (2009), Breuss (2001), European Commission (2001), Del Bo et al. (2010), Doyle et al. (2001), Figuet and Nenovsky (2006), Lejour et al. (2001), Martín et al. (2001), Marini (2003), EEAG (2004), Kutan and Yigit (2004), Fidrmuc and Korhonen (2004), El Ouardighi and Somun-Kapetanovic (2007, 2009), Sarajevs (2001), Sideris (2010), Szeles and Marinescu (2010), Zbigniew and Prochniak (2004, 2007)).

This paper aims at detecting possible income catching up between the Balkan economies and the EU-15 average. The contribution of this paper lies in the use of a recent testing methodology for convergence, suggested by Nahar and Inder (2002). The adopted time series methodology is less restrictive as far as it allows non stationary processes to converge. Besides, a researcher is allowed to identify countries within a group that may not be converging. A further contribution could be the enrichment of the relevant literature by testing the full set of countries in the Balkan area.

The paper is structured as follows: Sect. 2 provides a short description of the examined Balkan economies over the period 1989–2009. Section 3, illustrates the background of the adopted empirical methodology. Section 4, presents the data used and the results of the empirical analysis. Finally, Sect. 5 summarizes and concludes.

2 Economic Performance of the Balkan Zone

The Balkan area is situated in the Southeastern Europe and consists of 13 countries, which are either fully, or partially or outside this area: Albania, Bosnia and Herzegovina, Bulgaria, Croatia, FYROM, Greece, Kosovo, Montenegro, Slovenia, Serbia and further times Romania. Four of them (Bulgaria, Greece, Romania and Slovenia) have already gained their membership to the EU and have reached a higher level of growth closer to the EU. The rest of the countries are either candidates (FYROM) or, potential candidates (Albania, Bosnia and Herzegovina, Serbia) or in negotiations (Croatia). Each one of these countries has particular characteristics along with dissimilarities in the growth process.

The participation of the Balkan countries in international organizations has strengthened their international presence. Their performance in terms of per capita income is plotted in Fig. 1, using the GDP_{PC} series in natural logs:

The first impression is that all countries are below the EU-15 average with the income gap from EU being obvious. According to Fig. 1, Greece and Slovenia move closer to the EU-15 average while Albania and Bosnia and Herzegovina present the lowest income levels and are placed last. The period until 2000 is clearly characterized by several fluctuations that smooth over after 2000, as it can be observed from Fig. 2 below. Furthermore, there is an obvious decrease in the GDP differentials from the EU-15 average providing a more clear evidence of convergence.

Albania. Albania is a potential candidate for EU accession since 2009 and is already member of the United Nations (UN), North Atlantic Treaty Organization (NATO), Organization of Security and Co-operation in Europe and other international organizations. The most important problems of Albania are the huge informal economy and the lack of energy and transportation infrastructure. The basic economic activity seems to be agriculture as it occupies more than half of the population but surprising represents only the one-fifth of GDP. In addition, the economy is based a lot on remittances from abroad. The global crisis has severely affected growth in Albania decreasing from the 6% during 2004–2008 to a 3% in 2009–2010.

Bulgaria. Bulgaria is one of the oldest countries in Europe in the heart of the Balkan Peninsula that participated in the Eastern Bloc[1] until 1989. Bulgaria joined NATO in 2004, the EU in 2007 and is also a member of the UN, the World Trade Organization (WTO), the Organization for Security and Co-operation in Europe and is one of the founders of the Organization of the Black

[1] A union of the former Communist states of Eastern and Central Europe.

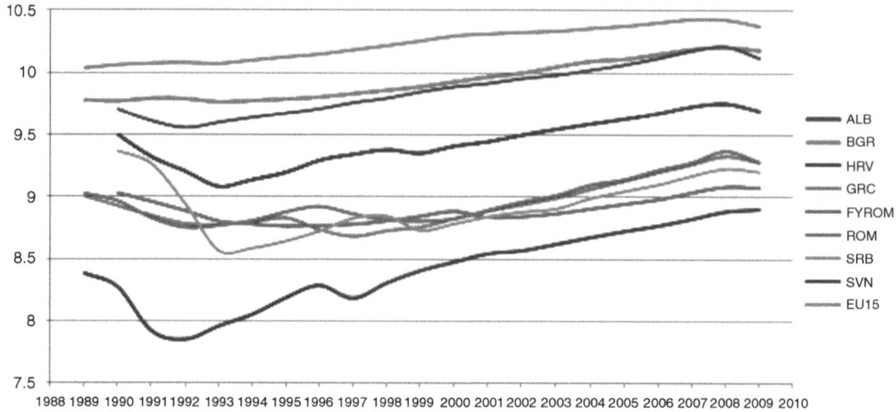

Fig. 1 The performance of GDP_{PC} series over 1989–2009

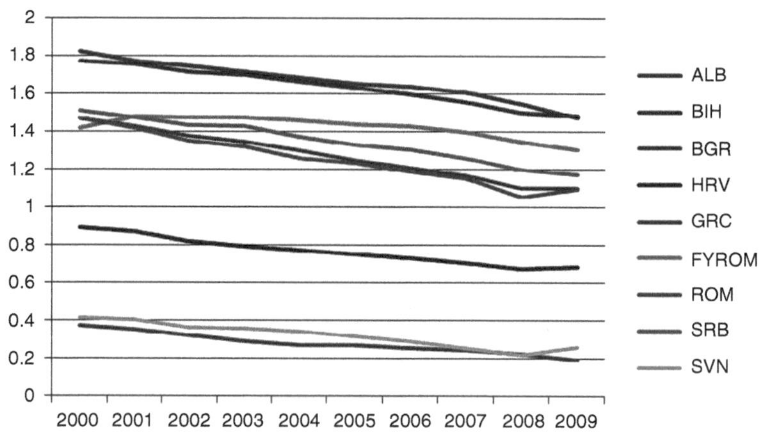

Fig. 2 The performance of the GDP_{PC} differentials from EU15 average

Sea Economic Cooperation. Concerning the economic activity, Bulgaria is an industrialized economy with an extremely good performance recently. However, the recent global crisis has had a negative impact on its economy especially in oil industry.

Croatia. After the Second World War, Croatia became part of Yugoslavia. Nationalism and conflicts were usual due to the population mixture. In 1992, Croatia won its independence and in the same year became a member of the UN. Since 2009, Croatia has the biggest biogas plant in Europe. Over the period 2000–2007 Croatia showed signals of improvement holding a steady rate of growth. Croatia has participated in international organizations and is going to be a member of the EU on July the 1st 2013.

FYROM. FYROM became an independent nation in 1991 and since 2005 has applied for joining the EU. The majority of its trade relations are among the other countries of the former Yugoslavia. It keeps on having one of the lowest per capita GDP in Europe. Regarding the economic structure, services' sector has the largest share in GDP while industry follows with textiles, iron, and steel being the basic exports goods. Agriculture represents only a small part of GDP though wine and vegetables are significant export goods. Its macroeconomic stability was achieved after 1996 and managed to record a positive growth rate in 2010.

Greece. Greece is the country with the longest history in Balkans. Right after the world war, Greece joined NATO[2] and since then was settled the basis of its economic stabilization. During the period 1953–1972 the Greek economy developed rapidly and structured within international events. In 1981, Greece joined the European Community (EC) being the tenth member and the first among the Mediterranean countries after Italy. A new phase for Greece came with the Cold War's ending and Greece oriented to the West located in a really advantageous position. It was the most developed country in economic terms and had the most homogeneous population among the Balkan countries. However, Greece's progress was not the expected mainly due to bad governmental choices. Greece entered the euro zone in 2001. The recent global crisis revealed a number of serious problems of the Greek economy and in 2010 the government signed a memorandum with International Monetary Fund in order to cover its borrowing needs and face with the difficulties more efficiently.

Romania. Romania has been a member of the EU since 2007 and of NATO since 2004. It gained its independence from the Ottoman Empire in 1877. After 1989, the country had a large period of economic imbalance. There was a need of structural reforms and industrial renewal. From 2000, the Romanian economy showed macroeconomic stability expressed through high growth rates, low unemployment and low inflation rates. The global crisis affected the economy and a decline in growth rate was marked down. It should be mentioned that Romania has significant natural resources and important industrial activities such as metallurgy, petrochemicals and machinery.

Serbia. In 1989, Slobodan Milosevic became president of Serbia's Republic and aimed at following the dream of "Great Serbia". His desire of Serbian domination ended up to the violent breakup of Yugoslavia. As a result, Croatia, FYROM and Slovenia declared their independence in 1991 and Bosnia and Herzegovina in 1992. Since 1992, Serbia remained united only with Montenegro but in a new state union, under the name new Federal Republic of Yugoslavia (FRY). As it was expected, Serbia faced with ethnic campaigns and as a result FRY was expelled from UN. The leadership of Milosevic did not change its direction not even in 1998, when it was obliged to face an Albanian insurgency in the province of Kosovo. Serbia indicated a non international reaction by rejecting a proposed settlement. This situation led to NATO's intervention with the well known consequences.

[2] It has to be mentioned that in 1974 Greece retired its military participation to NATO in order to protest against the Turkish advance in Cyprus and rejoined in 1980.

Slovenia. Slovenia became a member of EU in 2004. It used to be also a part of Yugoslavia since 1929. In 1991, Slovenia managed to win its independence. Its secession from Yugoslavia was easier because there were not any Serbian minorities living in the state and besides, it was the first one reacting. Slovenia faced with a lot of economic problems and nowadays its economy is oriented to the services' sector and especially in the field of information technology. The basic and most developed economic sectors are pharmaceutical, automobile industry, food industry, and industry of electrical devices, metal processing and chemicals.

3 Methodological Issues

The selected method that was recommended by Nahar and Inder (2002), examines convergence as a movement of a set of countries with similar characteristics toward a group leader. It is oriented to the creation of a time trend function. Following Nelson and Plosser (1982), the selected time series convert to stationaries after removing their trend. A researcher is allowed to identify countries within a group that may not be converging. The adopted methodology is less restrictive as far as it concerns stationarity in comparison with the unit root tests as it allows non stationary converging processes. Nahar and Inder (2002) pointed out with this test that it is more appropriate for a set of countries that have the same steady state to have as point of reference the output level of the leader. They also denied connecting stationarity with convergence as they supported that several times it is rejected convergence when it really exists. It is assumed also that the technical change among the economies of the sample is common through the following analysis.

Let y_{it} be the logarithm of GDP_{PC} for any economy $i(i = 1, 2 \ldots N)$ during $t(t = 1, 2 \ldots T)$ period of time. Taking into consideration the neoclassical growth model we should underline for economy i that:

$$\lim_{n \to \infty} E_t \left(y_{it+n} - a_{t+n} \right) = \mu_i \tag{1}$$

where a_{t+n} is a common parameter determined as benchmark, μ_i is a balanced growth path of economy i. μ_i is non zero except from the case of similar countries. In case of absolute convergence, the relation (1) is written as follows:

$$\lim_{n \to \infty} E_t \left(y_{it+n} - a_{t+n} \right) = 0 \tag{2}$$

that is, the long run average of the difference $y_{it+n} - a_{t+n}$ should converge to zero through time. In addition, the group leader can be the country or the group of countries with the best per capita economic performance. Therefore, the other countries should converge to the leader. The leader in our case is the average of EU-15. This average results from a group of developed economies that have high growth rates.

Firstly, we will define as d_{it} the per capita output gap:

$$d_{it} = y_{it} - \overline{y}_{EU15,t} \tag{3}$$

where $\overline{y}_{EU15,t}$ represents the steady state of the countries in the EU-15 area. As the output per capita's (GDP_{PC}) distance between a country and the EU-15 group (which is set as the steady state) declines and approaches zero through time, convergence is noticed. When d_{it} heads towards to zero during time, the rate of change in d_{it} has to be positive for convergence to hold:

$$\frac{\partial}{\partial t} d_{it} > 0 \tag{4}$$

The definition of absolute convergence in (2) is transformed based on (3) as follows:

$$\lim_{n \to \infty} E_t\,(d_{it}) = 0 \tag{5}$$

since $d_{it+n} > 0$ and its rate is positive with $d_{it+n} \to \infty$ as $n \to \infty$. The positive average slope function $\left(\frac{\partial}{\partial t} d_{it} > 0\right)$ is used to determine convergence. In order to calculate $\frac{\partial}{\partial t} d_{it}$, the d_{it} should be expressed as a function of time trend t:

$$d_{it} = f(t) + u_{it} \tag{6}$$

The general equation (6) is analyzed:

$$d_{it} = \theta_0 + \theta_1 t + \theta_2 t^2 + \theta_3 t^3 + \cdots + \theta_{k-1} t^{k-1} + \theta_k t^k + u_{it} \tag{7}$$

where $\theta_0,\ \theta_1,\ \theta_2,\ \theta_3,\ \cdots \theta_{k-1},\ \theta_k$ factors are situated in front of each trend and u_{it} is the error term whose mean is equal to zero. There is one function for every country of the sample. The estimation is done using Ordinary Least Squares (OLS). The Akaike Information Criterion (AIC) was chosen to find the optimal time trend polynomial.

Moreover, in order to test the convergence's hypothesis the rate of change in d_{it} should be positive:

$$\frac{1}{T} \sum_{t=1}^{T} \frac{\partial}{\partial t} d_{it} > 0 \tag{8}$$

Analyzing further (7), the following equation comes out:where r_k is defined as follows:

$$r_k = \frac{k}{T} \sum_{t=1}^{T} t^{k-1} \tag{9}$$

Convergence is tested posing the following pair of hypotheses:

$$H_o : r'\theta \leq 0 \sim \textit{no catching up}$$
$$H_1 : r'\theta > 0 \sim \textit{catching up}$$

To answer the question of catching up, we can perform a Wald test and determine the statistical significance.

4 Data and Empirical Results

4.1 Data

The data used in this empirical analysis were downloaded from the World Bank's database. The sample used includes eight Balkan countries: Albania, Bulgaria, Croatia, FYROM, Greece, Romania, Serbia and Slovenia. The analysis uses GDP_{PC} series, expressed in PPP, in US Dollars and in constant prices of 2005. When GDP_{PC} (GDP_{PC} = GDP/population) is equivalent to PPP a common background for the countries' set is established as all currencies' matters are solved. Following Maddison (2001), it is the best indicator to compare the economic performance of countries in an international level. The period examined is 1989–2009 and as benchmark is set the EU-15 average of the same indicator. It should be mentioned that not all the countries of our sample have data available for the entire period. Actually, Albania, Bulgaria and Greece have data from 1989, Croatia, FYROM, Serbia and Slovenia from 1990.

4.2 The Results of the Empirical Investigation

This paper follows the methodology of Nahar and Inder (2002) to test convergence. The analysis is performed for eight countries of the Balkan area and the dataset covers the period 1989–2009. First of all, we create the variable d_{it} and we determine a model for every country based on the relation (7). We estimate several models including dummy variables in order to reach the appropriate number of time trends t variables by means of AIC. Next, we calculate the r_k index and in conjunction with the estimated coefficients of the time trends we perform a Wald test to conclude over the existence of convergence. Table 1 summarizes the chosen polynomial order of time trend variables, the average slopes, the results of the convergence test based on the output gap values and the period examined:

The findings for Slovenia and Greece indicate convergence for both countries since they present a positive average slope and the Wald tests suggest the rejection of the null hypothesis of no convergence. In the cases of Bulgaria and Romania, we

Table 1 Results of Nahar and Inder methodolology

Leader: EU-15					
Countries	Order of t	Average slope	Wald test	P-value	Period
Albania	5	−0.003072955	0.27447	0.600	1989–2009
Bulgaria	2	0.0012302	0.98657	0.321	1989–2009
Croatia	5	−0.035741786	73.1448	0.000	1990–2009
FYROM	4	−0.02576585	414.3412	0.000	1990–2009
Greece	2	0.0037518	51.5021	0.000	1989–2009
Romania	2	0.000306	0.024158	0.876	1989–2009
Serbia	4	−0.05776455	49.1172	0.000	1990–2009
Slovenia	3	0.00537568	9.7465	0.002	1990–2009

find a positive average slope for both countries though statistically insignificant. Therefore, we conclude in favor of no convergence for these two countries.

Similar conclusions are provided for Albania, Croatia, FYROM and Serbia. These countries present negative average slopes hence supporting evidence in favor of no convergence with the EU-15 average. The lack of convergence in these countries could be also explained through the regional disparities. As Petratos (2009) mentioned *...a significant part of regional inequalities is due to the inability of the least advanced regions to close the development gap and converge towards the national average.*

5 Summary and Concluding Remarks

In this paper the issue of catching up between the Balkan countries and the EU-15 average is investigated. The analysis has been performed for eight Balkan countries during the period 1989–2009. The data set has been downloaded from the World Bank's database. In the context of the empirical analysis, the methodology of Nahar and Inder is performed to investigate catching up convergence. The results revealed the existence of dissimilarities among the examined Balkan economies in the catching up process towards the EU-15. It seems that the performance of the examined Balkan economies has been negatively affected by the political and economic conditions of the recent past as many conflicts and populations' movements along with political instability had occurred. The Balkan wars and the trade embargo imposed on Yugoslavia affected the whole region and the economic reform policies were not well appeared (Sarajevs, 2001). More particularly, the empirical evidence supported convergence with the EU-15 only for the cases of Greece and Slovenia. An obvious explanation is that these two countries have already joined EU and EMU. Our findings are partially in line with Sarajevs (2001), Bonetto et al. (2009), Szeles and Marinescu (2010) and Del Bo et al. (2010). In the above studies convergence with EU was confirmed for certain Balkan economies being a small club of countries within a wider sample used for the empirical analysis. However, Estrin and Urga (1997) found no evidence of convergence between the communist block and the West.

The first indications of development at the end of 1990s along with the stability after 2000, only helped towards reducing the disparities among Balkan countries. However, the income gap relative to the EU-15 for a considerable number of Balkan economies remained significant. In this direction, our results argue that EU integration process is one of the main driving forces for reforms aiming at growth and development. Concluding, it seems necessary for a number of Balkan Countries and especially for the ones that are candidates and potential candidates for further policy actions such as convergence in monetary policies (Brada and Kutan 2002) and financial systems (Bonetto et al. 2009), in order to establish and strengthen a more feasible catching up effort and thus to prepare effectively the accession in the EU.

References

Amplatz C (2004) The economic convergence performance of Central and Eastern European countries. Econ Plan 36:273–295

Baldwin R, Francois JF, Portes R (1997) The costs and benefits of enlargement: the impact on the EU and Central Europe. Econ Policy 24:127–176

Baumol W (1986) Productivity growth, convergence and welfare: what the long-run data show. Am Econ Rev 76:1071–1085, European Economic Review 40, no. 6: 1325–52

Bjorksten NJ (2000) Real convergence in the enlarged Euro area: a coming challenge for monetary policy. Bank of Finland Economics Department. Working paper no. 1/2000. Available at SSRN: http://ssrn.com/abstract=233888 or doi:10.2139/ssrn.233888

Bonetto F, Srdjan R, Tykhonenko A (2009) Balkan countries: catching up and their integration in the European financial system. Panoeconomicus 4:475–489

Brada J, Kutan AM (2002) Balkan and Mediterranean candidates for European Union membership: the convergence of their monetary policy with that of the European Central Bank. Eastern Eur Econ 40(4):31–44

Breuss F (2001) Macroeconomic effects of EU enlargement for old and new members. WIFO working paper 143

Cavenaile L, Dubois D (2011) An empirical analysis of income convergence in the European Union. Appl Econ Lett 18:1705

Del Bo C, Florio M, Manzi G (2010) Regional infrastructure and convergence: growth implications in a spatial framework. Transit Stud Rev 17:475–493

Doyle P, Kuis L, Jiang G (2001) Real convergence to EU income levels: Central Europe from 1990 to the long term. IMF working paper 01/146

EEAG (2004) Report on the European economy 2004. CESifo, Munich

European Commission (2001) The economic impact of enlargement. Enlargement paper 4

Fidrmuc J, Korhonen I (2004) The euro goes East: implications of the 2000–2002 economic slowdown for synchronisation of business cycles between the euro area and CEEs. Comp Econ Stud 46:45–62

Figuet JM, Nenovsky N (2006) Convergence and shocks in the road to EU: empirical investigations for Bulgaria and Romania. William Davidson Institute Working Paper, No. 810

Gros D, Steinherr A (2001) The first ten years of transition: planting the seeds of economic reform in Central and Eastern Europe. MIT Press, Cambridge, MA

El Ouardighi J, Somun-Kapetanovic R (2007) Do Balkan countries have a European future? An analysis of real economic convergence 1989–2005. South East Eur J Econ Bus 2:23–30, ISSN:1840-118X

El Ouardighi J, Somun-Kapetanovic R (2009) Convergence and inequality of income: the case of Western Balkan countries. Eur J Comp Econ 6(2): 207–225, ISSN 1722–4667. Available online at http://eaces.liuc.it

Estrin S, Urga G (1997) Convergence in output in transition economies central & Eastern Europe 1970–1995. CEPR Discussion Papers, 1616

Kutan AM, Yigit TM (2004) Nominal and real stochastic convergence of transition economies. J Comp Econ 32:23–36

Lejour AM, De Mooij RA, Nahuis R (2001) EU enlargement: economic implications for countries and industries. CBP document no. 011

Marini M (2003) Convergence of candidate countries to European Union: an analysis on industrial production index using dynamic factor model. Paper presented at the Eurostat Colloquium on modern tools for business cycle analysis, Luxembourg

Martín C, Velazquez FJ, Funck B (2001) European integration and income convergence. Lessons for Central and Eastern European countries. World Bank technical paper 514

Maddison A (2001) The world economy: a millennial perspective. OECD, Paris

Nahar S, Inder B (2002) Testing convergence in economic growth for OECD countries. Appl Econ 34:2011–2022

Nelson C, Plosser C (1982) Trends and random walks in macroeconomic time series: some evidence and implications. J Monet Econ 10:139–162

Papasotiriou H (1994) The Balkans after the cold war. Library of the International Relations' Institution/Papazisi, Athens

Petratos G (2009) Regional growth and inequalities in the European Union. Discussion paper series, 15(2):23–44. Available online at: http://www.prd.uth.gr/research/DP/2009/uth-prd-dp-2009-2_en.pdf

Szeles MR, Marinescu N (2010) Real convergence in the CEECs, euro area accession and the role of Romania. Eur J Comp Econ 7(1):181–202, ISSN 1722–4667

Rosenberg D (2000) Eastern enlargement of the European Union: problems of convergence. Massachusetts Institute for Social and Economic/University of Massachusetts-Amherst/ Institute for International Economic and Political Studies/Russian Academy of Sciences, Moscow

Sala-i-Martin X (1996) Regional cohesion: evidence and theories of regional growth and convergence. Europ Econ Rev 40(6):1325–1352

Sarajevs V (2001) Convergence of European transition economies and the EU: what do the data show. Bank of Finland, Institute for Economies in Transition. Discussion paper no. 13 (all opinions expressed are the author's and do not necessarily reflect bank's opinion)

Sideris D (2010) The Western Balkans on the road to the EU: an assessment of their integration with the euro zone using the generalized purchasing power parity approach. Bank of Greece. http://economics.soc.uoc.gr/macro/docs/Year/2010/papers/paper_1_67.doc

Solow RM (1956) A contribution to the theory of economic growth. Q J Econ 70:65–94

Zbigniew M, Prochniak M (2004) Economic convergence between the CEE-8 and the European Union. East Eur Econ 45:59–76

Zbigniew M, Prochniak M (2007) Real economic convergence in the EU accession countries. Int J Appl Econ Quant Stud 1–3 www.europa.eu

The Economic Relations of Bosnia–Herzegovina and FYROM with the Other States that Emerged from the Breakup of Yugoslavia Considering the Ohrid and Dayton Agreements: The Phenomenon of Yugonostalgia in Trade and Economic Relations of Those Countries

George D. Borovas

1 Introduction

Since the establishment of Tito's Yugoslavia, its multicultural, multiethnic structure constituted the key feature in shaping domestic policy. Ethnic relations continued to concern the Yugoslav Communist Party, which in the subsequent years invented, formed and tried to impose the so-called Yugoslav identity to solve the national issue (Stanimirović 1987; Hristidis 2003). Within the ideological framework of the Yugoslav Identity what was also formed was the slogan 'Brotherhood and Unity' (Bratstvo i Jedinstvo), as well as the position of the party concerning the antifascist struggle, according to which all nations of the Yugoslav Federation equally contributed to the fight against the conqueror (Lampe 2000).

Constant efforts were made to create the principles according to which the country would be ruled. From its inception in 1945 to its breakup in 1989 the country was governed by four institutional – constitutional frameworks, which in fact constituted a continuous effort to resolve problems, maintain balances and bridge differences among nations and in particular between Serbs and Croats (Hristidis 2003).

A period characterized by the expansion of democratization was inaugurated in 1960 and in 1963 a new constitution was passed that instituted the 'Socialist Democracy', granting greater autonomy to the Republics and introducing the country's political life into the term 'Socialist Self-Management'. The purpose of these changes was to create a governance model different from that of the Soviet Union, attempting to reduce tensions between the numerous nationalities that constituted to the multicultural society of the country (Ivanović 2002).

The decentralization policy implemented by Yugoslavia, particularly during the 1960s, led to the strengthening of national identities, the separation into different

G.D. Borovas (✉)
Department of Balkan Studies, University of Western Macedonia, 3rd klm Florinas – Nikis, 53100 Florina, Greece
e-mail: gborovas@uowm.gr

A. Karasavvoglou and P. Polychronidou (eds.), *Balkan and Eastern European Countries in the Midst of the Global Economic Crisis*, Contributions to Economics,
DOI 10.1007/978-3-7908-2873-3_3,

ethnic groups and the reduction of tolerance towards members of different ethnic groups (Kuzmanović 1995). As a result, national identities were strengthened over the collective – Yugoslav identity that the Communist Party of Yugoslavia attempted to promote and impose during the first period of Tito's Yugoslavia (Stanimirovic & Stanisavic 1987).

In 1974, a new constitution was established which essentially constituted a new attempt to solve the problems among the Yugoslav Republics, although in the end it actually exacerbated them. Through this Constitution, the provinces of Kosovo and Vojvodina were transformed into de facto Republics adopting behaviors, which simulated the ones of the official Republics. That is to say, they gradually began to act and behave as independent states (Borovas, 2008).

These developments significantly reduced the capacity of Serbia to exert influence and interference on the other Republics, leading to the expansion of discontent among Serbs throughout the country. The idea of the Serbian leadership received a severe blow, forcing Serbia to limit itself to a secondary role in the management of central authority, thereby contributing to the growing nationalism within its interior and to the gradual weakening of the Yugoslav consciousness of the Serbian population of Yugoslavia.

Eventually, the implementation of Tito's governance program resulted in the excitement of nationalism, undermined the country's unity in the long term and led to its breakup in 1989, since, after Tito's death in 1980, certain politicians appeared into the politics of the country with a speech more of a nationalistic and disruptive tone than a unifying one (Ivanović 2002). The strong presence of nationalistic forces was culminated in 1986 when Slobodan Milosevic became the leader of the Serbian Communist Party in the eighth session of the Central Committee of the Serbian Communist Party.

During the period 1987–1991, obvious changes became apparent into the society of Yugoslavia which were characterized by the end of the one-party governance system, the magnification of nationalistic demands and the claims raised by Croatia and Slovenia as well.

The core choices in the following years substantially contributed to the outbreak of the Yugoslav crisis. In the 23rd Congress of the Communist Party of Yugoslavia there were serious reactions by other Confederate Republics as their nationalism and the fear of returning to forms of governance of the interwar period were made active, due to the pressure exerted by the Milosevic's policy in the autonomous region of Kosovo. These disagreements eventually led to the breakup of the Communist Union of Yugoslavia in the early 1990, which marked the beginning of the dissolution of Yugoslavia.

Clearly, the constant internal problem of Yugoslavia throughout its existence from 1945 to 1990 was the formation of interethnic relations among its ethnic communities as well as the stabilization of its society, a problem faced by all pluralistic societies (Borovas 2008).

After the breakup of Yugoslavia, the international community was called upon to confront this problem into the countries that were formed, particularly in Bosnia – Herzegovina, FYROM and Serbia, where armed conflicts broke out among ethnic groups. In these cases there were two kinds of responses by the international community; the diplomatic one in the cases of Bosnia – Herzegovina and FYROM and the military one in the case of Serbia – Kosovo.

2 The Dayton and Ohrid Agreements, Lijphart's Theoretical Model of Consociational Democracy and Yugonostalgia

The Dayton and Ohrid Agreements constitute two interventions made by the international community: on the one hand, with the purpose peace to be achieved and on the other, the territorial integrity of the other two countries, Bosnia – Herzegovina and FYROM to be safeguarded through bridging the ethnic differences of the ethnic group residents in their territories. (Ni Aiolain 2001, p. 63) To meet their objectives, the agreements had to manage to reconstruct the multiethnic societies of the countries whose coherence had received a keystroke by the armed transnational conflicts that had taken place particularly in the case of Bosnia, where the methods followed as well as the severity of conflicts caused the reaction of the international public opinion.

To reconstruct the coherence of multiethnic societies of both countries, the method chosen to be implemented through the Agreements was based on 'power sharing' among the ethnic groups involved in the conflict, which was described by Lijphart as 'Consociational democracy' in his work entitled 'Democracy in plural societies' with variations in the case of each country.

Lijphart's approach is based on four principles (Lijphart 1977), namely the following:

(a) The creation of large government coalitions: In this way, the ability to express the views of the largest possible part of society in shaping the government's work is ensured.

(b) The possibility of exercising mutual vetoes during the decision-making process: According to this principle, all groups are able to exercise veto during decision-making, as Lijphart believes that in this way the stability of the system is ensured. But this is contrasted by the fact that this ability may lead to the failure of exercising policy and ultimately to political stagnation in the countries, since many decisions may touch on privileges or acquired rights of various population groups.

(c) The principle of proportionality: According to this principle, the country's citizens are represented through proportional representation of population groups in the parliament, which is then proportionately represented in the country's government. This enables policy and decision-making to take place behind closed doors in the light of mutual concessions and compromises among the political leaders of various groups which substantially constitute the country's government, preventing, thus, social – nationalistic tensions in the country that would not possibly appear if the decisions were made by a broad representative institution such as the Parliament. This principle along with the principle of creating large coalitions has caused the exercise of intense criticism since these considerations made by Lijphart are considered to be particularly undemocratic as it has been pointed out that: on the one hand, there is enforcement of decisions made by the political elite of the country to the parliamentary groups; on the other hand, there is substantial weakness to invert the weak opposition, the negative vote of which plays in fact no role, forcing it toward political allegiance to the system according to which the country has been structured. At the same time, in this way the electoral process leads to a process resembling an inventory of powers shared by the numerous groups that make up the society of the country.

(d) Federalism or partial autonomy: Under this principle, the numerous population groups are separated into independent administrative structures within the state structure of the country. This principle, although not mentioned by him, constitutes the essential precondition for the exercise of mutual vetoes since in this manner it is ensured that this process will not lead to deadlocks and inefficiency.

At this point we should refer generally to the positions put forward by Lijphart considering the speculation for a solution in countries with deep ethnic ruptures. According to his positions, there are three ways to resolve ethnic – political problems of a divided society without overthrowing democracy:

- The first way is by assimilation, which according to Lijphart may occur in cases that there is a large dominant ethnic group in the edges of which there is another smaller one; due to cohabitation and through interaction ultimately the dominant ethnic group assimilates the smaller one.
- The second way is Consociational Democracy.
- Finally, the third method which should be applied, if no solution is reached by means of the two previous methods and which is eventually the only way to avoid bloodshed is the separation into national states as in the case of Czechoslovakia. However, this solution presents a major problem in its implementation, as members of ethnic groups do not live in separate areas which are ethnically homogenized to allow for a separation into homogeneous states. This is absolutely clear in the case of Yugoslavia, especially Bosnia – Herzegovina.

It is obvious, even from Lijphart's theoretical approach, that there was difficulty in solving ethnic differences in the former Yugoslavian area as, on the one hand, the effort to assimilate different ethnic groups into the Yugoslavian context through the creation of a common national identity, Yugoslavism, had failed and, on the other hand, the effort towards a definitive solution through national sharing instead of bloodshed brought the opposite result.

For these reasons, a different approach should be sought in order to solve ethnic differences in the former Yugoslavia; a solution which at first was sought in haste under the pressure from the international public opinion to resolve the conflict in Bosnia and which subsequently, after updating of proposals, was selected for the FYROM and showed that it could lead to peaceful coexistence of the ethnic groups that resided in these two areas.

Another factor affecting the selection of theoretical model of Consociational Democracy as a model for resolving ethnic differences in the area of Yugoslavia was also the commitment not to change the existing borders (Owen 1995). As a national sharing both Bosnia and FYROM would change the existing borders since the Croat-Bosnians would pursue the annexation of their territories in Croatia and so would the Bosnian-Serbs who had a clear position on this for the creation of Great Serbia. Similar goals were shared by the Albanians of FYROM whose positions seemed to be common with the positions held by the Albanians in Kosovo for the creation of Great Albania.

During this period, Consociational Democracy appears to be a good approach to the solution of this very complicated problem in the former Yugoslavia, since it answers the key question of how to restore social cohesion in an area suffering so many wounds by armed conflicts, and therefore the territorial integrity of both countries to be achieved.

Lijphart's model of consociational democracy seems to be similar to the Socialist self-management model, which had been implemented after 1960, in Yugoslavia (see Table 1). This is why the particular model is regarded as the most appropriate for achieving social coherence while ensuring the territorial integrity of both countries as it could create a system of governance familiar to the citizens that could be accepted and create a feeling of security.

It is possible that the familiarity shown by the structured governance system of the two framework agreements in Bosnia – Herzegovina and FYROM with the former system of governance in Yugoslavia provided the grounds for the Yugonostalgia phenomenon that emerged in a part of their societies.

When the Yugonostalgia phenomenon initially appeared, it took everyone by surprise as it was considered to pose on the one hand nostalgia for the communist governance system of Yugoslavia and on the other hand nostalgia for the common national identity "Yugoslav", which was a complicated fact especially after the deadly conflicts in Croatia and Bosnia – Herzegovina. However, this phenomenon deals with social factors rather than political and national ones. As Tanja Petrović in her work "Nostalgia for Space" mentions "...ex-Yugoslavs lost a great deal of space when Yugoslavia broke apart. In Yugoslavia, a Serb could easily travel and have vacation on the coast, but, now, the coast is no longer too viable an option..." (Petrovic 2007), that is, in essence Yugoslavia may not have been better than today's countries but this does not mean that life in them is better. For this reason, when former Yugoslavs talk about Yugoslavia they enter a secure area in which they felt most comfortable, shared values and lived with dignity during the time they lived united (Petrovic 2007) as unemployment rates were low, and people used to live in a stable, rich country that had a good educational system. These features are essentially reproduced through the collective memory of the former Yugoslavs and manifest the Yugonostalgia phenomenon. For this reason, this phenomenon is in no way related to the reconstitution of Yugoslavia and its political system but only to the reconstruction of lost social structures and values in the countries that emerged from the breakup of Yugoslavia.

Table 1 Cumulative summary of the principles of consociational republic, the Dayton and Ohrid agreements and socialist self-management

Consociational democracy	Dayton agreement	Ohrid agreement	Socialist self-management
Large governmental coalitions	Creation of a government scheme in which all nations of the country participate	Participation of all ethnicities of the country in the government scheme	Participation of all ethnicities of the country in the government scheme
Ability to Exercise mutual veto in the decision-making process	Right of mutual veto	Mutual veto on decisions relating to the nationalities of the country	
Principle of Proportionality	Proportional representation of all ethnic groups in the country	proportional representation of recognised nationalities in all structures of the country	Proportional representation of all nationalities and all citizens of the country at various levels of decision making (collective presidency)
Federalism or partial autonomy	National autonomy with the creation of two entities	Strengthening local government and allowing the dominant ethnic group to use its language and national symbols	Federalism or partial autonomy

3 The Formation Conditions of the Economic Cooperation of Bosnia–Herzegovina and FYROM with the Former Yugoslav Republics

Yugoslavia was the only country of central financial planning that had close commercial ties with Western countries as it was not a member of COMEKON. As a result, the EU countries constituted its most important economic partners, with its total import and export activities with them amounting to 40% of total business (Papazoglou 2005; Udovicki 1996). At the same time, it was also an exception compared to the other countries of central financial planning in its trade structure as trade in processed products, machinery and equipment constituted the bulk of all its commercial transactions (Papazoglou 2005) (Table 2).

After the breakup of Yugoslavia and during the transition period of the countries that emerged, FYROM and Bosnia – Herzegovina (BH) exhibited similar characteristics to other countries in the region (Uvalic 1992; Hinic (1994)). FYROM, like Croatia, had the smallest initial fall in exports but then they showed a more modest increase while the case of FYROM followed a highly unstable

Table 2 Some indicators on SEE countries in 1989

	Area (in 000sqarekm)	Population (mln 1990)	GDP/cap (1989 US$)	Exports to CMEA (%)	Imports from CMEA (%)	Exports to SEE (%)	Imports from SEE (%)
Albania	28.7	3.2	723	46.3	44.8	na	na
Bulgaria	110.9	8.9	2,320	83.0	71.5	13.4	6.5
Romania	237.5	23.2	1,730	40.5	38.5	3.2	4.4
SFRY	255.8	23.8	2,490	29.9	26.3	2.1	2.2

Source: Uvalic (1997b) based on various sources (World Bank (2002), OECD, UNECE, IMF, EIU)

Table 3 Trade by destination of Yugoslav republics in 1987 (in % of GMP)

Republics of SFR Yugoslavia	Deliveries to the local market	Deliveries to markets of other republics	Deliveries abroad (exports)
Bosnia and Herzegovina	56.1	24.2	19.8
Croatia	67.0	18.7	14.3
FYROM	60.8	21.4	17.8
Montenegro	57.5	25.0	17.5
Serbia (with K and V)	69.0	13.4	17.6
Serbia proper	62.3	17.4	**20.3**
Kosovo	64.6	24.0	11.4
Voivodina	58.1	28.8	13.1
Slovenia	57.5	20.3	**22.2**

Source: Uvalic (1993), based on data of the Serbian Institute of Statistics

course (Uvalic 2002a, b). As opposed to the FYROM, BE showed a dramatic and phenomenal increase in its exports which was a result of the very limited export base due to the war, and which amounted to 36 million dollars (Papazoglou 2005). In contrast, while imports initially declined, afterwards they increased at a much faster pace especially for BE, while FYROM along with Bulgaria constituted the countries with the smallest trade deficit in the region (Papazoglou 2005). This fact indicates the lack of competitiveness in the economies of both countries but in fact the widening of the trade deficit reflects the collapse of their productive systems and hence the ability to face international competition in product markets (Uvalic 1997; Jovicic et al. 2001). Both the slow pace of reforms and the outbreak of several military conflicts in the region contributed to this outcome (Uvalic 1992; 2001b) (Table 3).

The common feature of FYROM and BE during the period 1993–2006 remains the high proportion of commercial transactions with the countries of SE Europe while they continue the tradition of extensive trade with the former Yugoslav republics, even though the increased rate of commercial transactions with EU countries is increased, with the FYROM being the only country to increase the share of intra-regional transactions (imf 2003; wiiw 2003; Anastasakis & Dzelilovic 2002) (Table 4).

More specifically, in 2003 BH was the country with the most intra-regional transactions focused on two countries, Serbia – Montenegro (S&M) and Croatia, while trade with other countries were at low levels (Bartlett 2001, 2003; Central Bank

Table 4 EU and SEE shares in total trade of SEE countries (in %) – 1998

Country (and sources)	EU share in exports	EU share in imports	SEE share in exports	SEE share in imports
Albania (IMF; BH excluded)	88.8	77.9	3.0	7.2
Bosnia and Herzegovina (BH Central Bank and IMF)	21.9	29.5	***66.6***	***52.8***
Bulgaria (IMF)	51.7	46.5	7.7	3.4
Croatia (IMF; Albania and FRY excluded)	48.7	62.6	25.2	12.2
FYROM (IMF)	50.3	46.4	23.4	32.8
Romania (IMF; FRY excluded)	64.6	57.9	1.9	1.0
Slovenia (IMF; FRY and Croatia excluded)	65.5	69.5	15.1	1.9
FR Yugoslavia (Yugoslav statistics and IMF)	32.9	38.7	***35.1***	16.3

Source: Uvalic (2001). Whenever available, data of the IMF have been used (*IMF Direction of Trade Statistics Quarterly,* September 1999). Given that for Bosnia and Herzegovina and FR Yugoslavia IMF statistics were rather incomplete, they have been integrated with national sources: for Bosnia, unpublished data on foreign trade of both entities obtained directly from the Central Bank of Bosnia and Herzegovina in mid-January 2000; and for FR Yugoslavia, *Index* no. 1, 1999, Federal Statistical Office

of Bosnia). This is noteworthy as it demonstrates the trade relations between the two entities which make up the country and which were formed through the Dayton agreement (Cristie 2001; Damijan and Masten 2002). The FYROM also displayed much intra-regional trade, which, however, was mainly directed towards S&M in 2003 (wiiw 2003; Economist intelligent unit). What indicates intra-regional trade between the two countries is the increase in the volume of trade between S&M and the FYROM and BH, which from 155 million dollars in 2003–2004 reached 190 million U.S. dollars showing, thus, an increase equal to 6% (Miljković 2006) (Tables 5 and 6).

On June 27, 2001, a memorandum was signed in Brussels which laid the groundwork for a free trade zone in Southeast Europe by the following countries: Albania, Bosnia – Herzegovina, Bulgaria, Croatia, Serbia – Montenegro, the FYROM, Moldova and Romania (Commission of European Communities 2002). This memorandum provided for the liberalization of trade to the level of 90% by 2008. In late January 2006, the European Commission presented a series of measures that would promote economic cooperation among countries of the Western Balkans. This supported the signing of a free trade agreement among S&M (including Kosovo) BH, Albania, Croatia and FYROM, which would replace the former 32 individual trade cooperation agreements between these countries. On December 19 of the same year, the Framework Free Trade Agreement (CEFTA) was signed in Bucharest which would include, along with the present parties, Croatia and FYROM, from May 1, 2007, Albania, BH, Montenegro, Serbia and UNIMIK which represented Kosovo. The signing of the CEFTA was a positive experience for the participating countries since it revitalized their economies through trade, giving them the opportunity for economic development while at

Table 5 EU shares in total trade of the SEE-8 (in %), 1999–2003

EU shares in exports						EU shares in imports					
	1999	2000	2001	2002	2003		1999	2000	2001	2002	2003
Albania	93.64	93.34	90.96	92.14	93.35	Albania	80.18	74.81	74.70	70.72	68.22
B and H	46.70	53.06	56.82	51.42	57.17	B and H	38.62	39.99	39.00	37.75	36.42
Bulgaria	54.20	51.74	55.19	56.13	57.09	Bulgaria	50.01	44.93	49.77	50.53	49.82
Croatia	49.09	53.43	52.55	50.52	52.92	Croatia	56.49	55.76	55.47	55.54	56.00
FYROM	44.72	42.58	48.75	42.99	48.93	FYROM	40.14	38.13	42.74	54.76	51.60
Moldova	20.56	21.66	21.29	22.36	23.36	Moldova	26.65	29.10	27.42	26.41	28.38
Romania	65.48	63.95	67.95	67.29	67.90	Romania	60.49	56.68	57.42	58.65	57.86
S and M	36.40	36.80	41.46	39.12	41.28	S and M	41.50	36.89	36.88	37.26	40.62

Sources: Calculated on the basis of data of the IMF (2004), *Direction of Trade Statistics – Yearbook 2004*, supplemented in a few cases by national statistics of FR Yugoslavia, Croatia, and Bosnia and Herzegovina (see note 16). Data for Serbia and Montenegro do not include Kosovo

Table 6 SEE countries shares of intra-regional trade (in % of total)

SEE shares in exports						SEE shares in imports					
	1999	2000	2001	2002	2003		1999	2000	2001	2002	2003
Albania	2.91	4.24	5.30	3.88	3.16	Albania	6.68	7.15	5.86	7.18	6.10
B and H	38.94	30.76	29.77	36.39	29.56	B and H	32.11	28.36	29.18	31.02	32.58
Bulgaria	10.42	13.09	10.19	9.58	9.90	Bulgaria	2.23	4.48	3.03	2.85	3.33
Croatia	15.15	15.64	16.67	19.32	19.52	Croatia	2.73	2.44	2.90	3.25	3.94
FYROM	30.70	33.74	32.38	35.85	35.36	FYROM	19.85	17.60	19.43	20.35	21.31
Moldova	10.17	8.84	7.48	9.53	12.40	Moldova	15.83	17.55	13.18	11.10	9.52
Romania	4.28	6.04	4.59	3.55	4.25	Romania	1.,58	1.62	1.53	1.29	1.53
S and M	34.36	30.71	27.40	29.70	31.46	S and M	24.15	22.03	14.93	12.24	9.01

Sources: Calculated on the basis of data of the IMF (2004), *Direction of Trade Statistics – Yearbook 2004*, supplemented in a few cases by national statistics of FR Yugoslavia, Croatia, and Bosnia and Herzegovina (see note 16). Data for Serbia and Montenegro do not include Kosovo

the same time it created the framework for economic – commercial cooperation with the EU countries as they constitute their main trade partner (Table 7).

The signing of the CEFTA affected the trade of BH and FYROM respectively and was a favorable factor for the development of their transactions with both their neighboring countries and in particular with the countries which were former Yugoslav Republics. For this reason, as shown in the following financial reports of the corresponding Greek embassies, the trade of BH and FYROM with the former Yugoslav Republics constitute a significant part of their international commercial transactions (UNECE). However, it was not only the existence of CEFTA that contributed to this fact but there were other factors as well, such as low-cost of goods, the ability to communicate through a common language, that is, Serb-Croatian, etc. At the same time, FYROM and BH signed bilateral agreements to avoid double taxation in the following countries: Croatia, Serbia, Slovenia, and Bosnia-Herzegovina (Uvalic 2003a, b) (Table 8).

Table 7 SEE countries regional trade, as % of total trade, 2000

Country group	Exports	Imports	Exports and imports
SEE-5			
Trade with other countries in the SEE-5 group (mln. $)	1671.2	1823.2	3494.4
SEE-5 total world trade (mln. $)	6885.5	14652.6	21538.1
Share of SEE-5 trade in total trade (in %)	24.3	12.4	16.2
SEE-7			
Trade with other countries in the SEE-7 group (mln. $)	2762.2	2260.2	5022.4
SEE-7 total world trade (mln. $)	22012.5	32882.6	54895.1
Share of SEE-7 trade in total trade (in %)	12.5	6.9	9.2

Source: Calculated on the basis of data provided in the IMF Direction of Trade Statistics Yearbook 2001, except for Bosnia and Herzegovina and FR Yugoslavia, for which national statistics have been used

Table 8 Exports of FYROM by destination country 2007–2009 (in million us dollars)

	Country	2007	% 2007/06	2008	% 2008/07	2009	% 2009/08	% Exports 2009
1	Germany	484.0	28.7	563.2	16.4	450.4	−20.0	16.7
2	Serbia*	639.4	14.6	934.7	46.2	337.6	−53.9	12.5
3	Kosovo	–	–	–	–	314.5	–	11.7
4	Greece	420.4	16.4	535.0	27.3	290.0	−45.8	10.8
5	Italy	346.8	46.5	321.0	−7.4	218.0	−32.1	8.1
6	Bulgaria	242.5	85.3	376.6	55.3	217.0	−42.4	8.1
7	Croatia	163.9	32.0	229.0	39.7	152.7	−33.3	5.7
8	Bosnia-Herzegovina	88.0	36.0	104.8	19.1	86.6	−17.0	3.2
9	Albania	72.7	79.1	106.8	45.9	83.9	−17.4	3.1
10	Holland	71.8	29.6	70.6	−1.7	51.5	−12.9	2.3
11	U.K.	75.1	104.6	70.0	−5.8	42.9	−38.7	1.5
12	Turkey	53.2	−3.6	31.6	−40.6	40.8	29.1	1.5
13	Slovenia	68.7	65.7	65.1	−5.2	34.3	−47.3	1.3
14	Russia	23.6	−7.9	32.7	38.6	22.5	−31.2	0.8
15	Romania	19.3	44.2	33.5	73.6	20.0	−40.3	0.7
16	Others country	586.8	106.8	503.6	−14.2	318.8	36.7	11.9
	Total	3356.2	39.0	3978.2	18.5	2691.5	32.3	100.0

Source: State Statistical Office of FYROM
Note: Up to 2006 Serbia and Montenegro
* Serbia with and without Kosovo

For these reasons, the composition of the countries the FYROM deals with remained the same from 2006 up to 2009. These include Western European countries and the neighboring former Yugoslav Republics, particularly in the context of the preferential conditions of the CEFTA agreement and the bilateral agreements, which had been signed for the avoidance of double taxation of goods. Something similar has taken place from 2006 onwards in the trade of BH as well (Table 9).

Table 9 Imports of FYROM by country of origin 2007–2009 (in million us dollars)

	Country	2007	% 2007/06	2008	% 2008/07	2009	% 2009/08	% Imports 2009
1	Germany	525.3	42.2	650.3	23.8	517.5	−20.4	10.3
2	Russia	643.3	12.9	930.9	44.7	495.0	−46.8	9.8
3	Greece	413.4	29.2	510.8	23.6	439.2	−14.0	8.7
4	Serbia*	448.4	58.6	532.0	18.6	397.1	−25.4	7.9
5	Italy	303.5	33.8	382.9	26.2	361.7	−5.5	7.2
6	China	242.7	74.1	314.8	29.7	289.4	−8.1	5.7
7	Turkey	194.8	57.2	268.7	37.9	250.7	−6.7	5.0
8	Bulgaria	267.1	6.7	327.1	22.5	242.6	−25.8	4.8
9	Slovenia	154.5	19.4	203.4	31.7	190.9	−6.1	3.8
10	Switzerland	114.3	93.4	292.7	156.1	123.1	−57.9	2.4

Source: State Statistical Office of FYROM
Note: Up to 2006 Serbia and Montenegro
* Serbia with and without Kosovo

The Stabilization and Association Process (SAP) launched by the EU in mid-1999, offered the SEE-5 generous trade preferences, contractual relations through the signing of Stabilization and Association Agreements, a new programme of financial assistance (CARDS), and for the first time since the beginning of the transition, prospects of future EU membership (Milikovic and Vladimir 2006). Today, regional co-operation has become one of the main pillars of both the SAP and the Stability Pact for SEE, as both initiatives emphasize the importance of regional co-operation for achieving more permanent peace, stability and development for the SEE countries such as FYROM and BH.

4 Conclusions

The large volume of trade between FYROM and BH with the Republics that emerged from the breakup of Yugoslavia is not a fact which could be interpreted in a one-dimensional way, as it is a combination of many factors (Gligorov 1999).

At first, to explain this phenomenon, the common past shared with the other countries, which were parts of Yugoslavia, should be referred to. This has created a common code of trade strengthened by the existence of common consumer habits that had been developed during the period of their coexistence within the uniform state structure of Yugoslavia (Gligorov 1997). In no way does this fact render the transactions in the commercial – financial sector a part of the Yugonostalgia phenomenon since it is limited to the social components of their citizens' life which mainly deal with social factors such as sense of security.

A second factor that affects trade in these two countries is directly linked to the features of their economies, as these were formed during the transition. The lack of competitiveness in their overall economy combined with low-wage workers made consumers turn to the market of low cost products, many of which were produced in countries that emerged from the breakup of Yugoslavia (Gligorov 1998). Especially in the case of BH, what played an important role in shaping the balance of trade was the violent armed conflicts, which devastated the country's production structure and led to products imported from Serbia and Croatia due to political beliefs (Kaminski and de la Rocha 2002).

The third but most important factor lies beneath the two framework agreements, the Dayton and Ohrid ones, which were in fact imposed by the international community to resolve the ethnic conflicts that had arisen. As a continuation of these agreements, what was also signed within the framework of economic cooperation is the memorandum in 2001 for the creation of a free trade zone as well as the CEFTA (Messerlin and Miroudot 2003). If we examine the relationship between the framework agreements for the settlement of ethnic disputes and the agreements for the creation of free trade, it is obvious that the latter are a natural continuation of the former in the field of interstate trade as they construct an environment that simulates the framework existed during the Yugoslav period regarding trade among the then-existing republics and today's independent states (Michalopoulos 2002).

The high volume of trade of BH and FYROM with the former Yugoslav Republics is mainly due to political planning that has taken place within the achievement of lasting peace and stability in the region (Miljovski and Uzunov 2001). The political feasibility of creating free trade areas is presented in papers by both Uvalic on 'Regional Cooperation in Southeast Europe' in 2001, and Anastasakis and Bojicic – Dzelilovic in the 'Balkan Regional Cooperation and European Integration' in 2002 (see Uvalic 2001a; Anastasakis 2002). These papers present in detail the arguments according to which political integration in Southeast Europe assists in resolving the political and security problems of the region as it promotes the ideas of stability, peace and development, while at the same time the reasons for which the EU and the international community promote economic cooperation in the region are analyzed (Muco and Fresher 2003).

Therefore, we understand that high volume trade of BH and FYROM is based mainly on planning policy to achieve lasting peace and stability in the region.

References

Anastasakis, O, Vesna Bojicic-Dzelilovic (2002) Balkan Regional Cooperation & European Integration. London, The Hellenic Observatory, The European Institute, The London School of Economics and Political Science: 86

Bartlett W (2001) Regional co-operation in South-East Europe: panacea or dysfunction? Banka Mag, Zagreb, January

Bartlett W (2003) Regional cooperation and economic development in South East Europe: obstacles and opportunities. Paper presented at the Second EACES Dubrovnik conference, Inter-University Centre, 10–12 Apr

Bianchini S, Uvalic M (eds) (1997) The Balkans and the challenge of economic integration – regional and European perspectives. Longo Editore, Ravenna

Borovas G (2008) 'Οι συμφωνίες Dayton και Αχρίδας ως μοντέλα επίλυσης εθνοτικών συγκρούσεων. Αξιολόγηση και σύγκριση [The Dayton and Ohrid agreements as models to resolve ethnic conflicts. Evaluation and comparison] (University of Western Macedonia)

Central Bank of Bosnia and Herzegovina, Foreign Trade Statistics of Bosnia and Herzegovina, unpublished material, Sarajevo, 12 Jan 2000

Christie E (2001) Potential trade in Southeastern Europe: a gravity model approach, Vienna, WIIW projects on 'Long-Term Development in Southeast Europe' and 'Regionalism in Southeast Europe' (http://www.wiiw.ac.at/balkan/)

Commission of the European Communities (2002) 'Report from the commission – the stabilisation and association process for South East Europe – first annual report', Brussels, 4 Apr, COM (2002) 163 Final

Commission of the European Communities (2003) Report from the commission – the stabilisation and association process for South East Europe – second annual report', Brussels, 26 Mar, COM (2002) 139 Final

Damijan J, Masten I (2002) Time-dependent efficiency of free trade agreements: the case of Slovenia and the CEFTA agreement. LICOS discussion paper no. 117/2002, Katholieke Universiteit Leuven, LICOS Centre for Transition Economies

Economist Intelligence Unit, Country Forecast – Economies in Transition – Eastern Europe and the former Soviet Union – Regional Overview, London, various issues

European Bank for Reconstruction and Development (2003) Transition report 2003. Integration and regional cooperation, London

Gligorov V (1997) Trade in the Balkans. WIIW Monthly Report no. 3, Vienna

Gligorov V (1998) Trade and investment in the Balkans. In: Vladimir G, Vidovic H (eds) On the way to normality – the states on the territory of former Yugoslavia in the Postwar period. WIIW Paper no. 250, October

Gligorov V, Kaldor M, Tsoukalis L (1999) Economic reconstruction and European integration. Paper presented at the LSE – WIIW conference reconstruction and integration in Southeast Europe – economic aspects, Vienna, WIIW, November

Hinic B (1994) Ekonomski tokovi na prostoru SFRJ i modaliteti njihovog obnavljanja ('Economic flows in the area of SFR Yugoslavia and means for their renewal'). In: Tomislav P (ed) Strategija povratka Jugoslavije na svetsko trziste (Strategy for Yugoslavia's return to the world market). Institut ekonomskih nauka, Belgrade, pp 88–115

Hristidis G (2003) Τα κομμουνιστικά Βαλκάνια. Εισαγωγή στην εσωτερική και εξωτερική πολιτική στην Αλβανία, Βουλγαρία, Γιουγκοσλαβία και Ρουμανία την περίοδο 1945–1989 [The communist Balkans. Introduction to domestic and foreign policy in Albania, Bulgaria, Yugoslavia and Romania in the period 1945–1989]. Thessaloniki Vanias (in Greeks)

Ivanović N (2002). Vlast i drzava. Beograd. s.n

(IMF) I. M. F. (2003) International Monetary Fund (IMF). From http://www.imf.org/external/

(wiiw), T. V. I. f. I. E. S. (2003) The Vienna Institute for international economic studies (wiiw). From http://www.wiiw.ac.at/

(I.M.F.) Direction of trade statistics yearbook, Washington, various issues

(I.M.F.) Direction of trade statistics quarterly, Washington, various issues

Jovicic M, Zdravkovic M, Dragutinovic Mitrovic R (2001) Federal Republic Yugosalvia: trade potentials and comparative advantages, Vienna, WIIW projects on 'Long-Term Development in Southeast Europe' and 'Regionalism in Southeast Europe' (http://www.wiiw.ac.at/balkan/)

Kaminski B, de la Rocha M (2002) Policy-induced integration in Balkans: policy options and their assessment, in World Bank (2002), June

Kuzmanović B (1995) Social distance towards individual nation: ethnic distance. Society in crisis: Yugoslavia in the early 90s. L. Mladen. Beograd, Višnjić

Lampe JR (2000) Yugoslavia as history. Twice there was a country. Cambridge University Press, Cambridge

Lijphart A (1977) Democracy in plural societies. Yale University Press, New Haven

Messerlin P, Miroudot S (2003) Trade liberalisation in South East Europe: from a network of 23 FTAs to a full free trade area? A summary. Paper presented at the WIIW conference, 21 Nov

Michalopoulos C (2002) The Western Balkans in world trade – an sesay in memoriam of Bela Balassa. World Bank, Washington, DC

Miljovski J, Uzunov V (2001) International and regional economic integration in South East Europe – the case of Macedonia', Vienna, WIIW projects on 'Long-term development in Southeast Europe' and 'Regionalism in Southeast Europe' (http://www.wiiw.ac.at/balkan/)

Miljković D, Vladimir Vučković (2006) Serbian Foreign Trade, Competitiveness and Exchange Rate Policy. Agora without frontiers **12**(2):13

Muço M, Frasheri A (2003) Does economic cooperation in the Balkans follow ethnic lines? An alternative. In: Franicevic V, Kimura H (eds) Globalisation, democratization and development – European and Japanese views of change in South East Europe. Masmedia, Zagreb, pp 325–348

Ni Aiolain F (2001) The fractured soul of the Dayton peace agreement: A legal analysis. *Reconstructing multiethnic societies: The case of Bosnia – Herzegovina*. D. Š. F. Bieber. Hampshire, Ashgate Publishing Limited

Owen D (1995) Balkan odyssey. Gollancz Victor, London

Papazoglou C (2005) Οι οικονομίες της Νότιο-Ανατολικής Ευρώπης [The economies of Southeast Europe]. s.i., Kritiki Publication (in Greek)

Petrovic T (2007) The territory of the former Yugoslavia in the mental maps of former Yugoslavs: Nostalgia for space. Sprawy Narodowościowe, Seria Nova

Stanimirović BM, Stanisavić (1987) *Marksizam i Socijalisticko Samoupravljnje (Marxism and Socialist self-management)* Beograd, Naučna Knjiga in Serbian

Udovicki K (1996) Market forces and economic integration: lessons from Yugoslavia, 1970–1987. In: Crnobrnja M, Papic Z, Bogetic Z (eds) The cost of war in former Yugoslavia. Peace and Crisis Management Foundation/Europa Press, Paris and Belgrade

UNECE, Economic survey of Europe, Geneva, various issues

Uvalic M (1992) Investment and property rights in Yugoslavia – the long transition to a market economy. Cambridge University Press, Cambridge

Uvalic M (1993) The disintegration of Yugoslavia: its costs and benefits. Communist Econ Ec Trans 5(3):273–293

Uvalic M (1997a) European economic integration – what role for the Balkans? In: Bianchini, Uvalic (eds) pp 19–34

Uvalic M (1997b) Economic problems and prospects of the successor states of former Yugoslavia. In: Bianchini, Uvalic (eds) pp 161–184

Uvalic M (2001a) Regional co-operation in Southeastern Europe. In: Veremis T, Daianu D (eds) Balkan reconstruction. Frank Cass, London

Uvalic M (2001b) Regional co-operation in Southeast Europe. J Southeast Eur Black Sea Stud 1(1):23–40

Uvalic M (2002a) Economic integration in Southeastern Europe. Ekonomski Anali XLVI:121–147, October 2002

Uvalic M (2002b) Regional cooperation and the enlargement of the European Union: lessons learned? Int Polit Sci Rev 23(3):319–333

Uvalic M (2003a) Trade liberalisation in Southeastern Europe – recent controversies and open questions. In: Proceedings of the conference organised by the Peace and Crisis Management Foundation, Cavtat, Croatia, May

Uvalic M (2003b) Trade liberalisation in the Balkans – a blessing in disguise? In: Conference on trade & economic integration of the Western Balkan countries in the European Union organised by the Albanian Center for International Trade (ACIT) in cooperation with the Ministry of Economy, Tirana, ACIT Research Paper, Tirana, 12–13 Dec 2003 (www.acit-al.org/publications/Research_papers/dec_2003).

World Bank (2002) Trade policies and institutions in the countries of South Eastern Europe in the EU association and stabilization process – regional report, Washington, 28 June

The Impact of Inflation Targeting Policy on the Inflation Uncertainty in Turkey

Özcan Karahan and Olcay Çolak

1 Introduction

A growing number of developed and developing countries have adopted Inflation Targeting (IT) Policy as a monetary regime since the early 1990s because of the perceived failure of previous policies, namely money supply and exchange rate targets. Compared to other strategies, "IT Policy can be characterized by the public announcement of official quantitative targets for the inflation rate over one or more horizons, and by explicit acknowledgment that low and stable inflation is monetary policy's primary long-term goal. Other important features of IT Policy are vigorous efforts to communicate with the public about the plans and objectives of the monetary authorities, and, in many cases, mechanisms that strengthen the central bank's accountability for attaining those objectives" (Bernanke et al. 1999, p. 4). Thus, the fundamental criteria for inflation targeting are the public announcement of a numerical target for inflation, the commitment to price stability as the overriding goal of monetary policy, the use of an information-inclusive strategy and the adoption of transparency and accountability in monetary policy actions. (Amato and Gerlach 2002, p. 782).

There are various debates on the effects and performance of inflation targeting indicated basic properties above in the economic literature. Most significant discussion has been made about the effect of inflation targeting programs on inflation uncertainty. Having chosen inflation targets as the nominal anchor, the central bank commits to a pre-specified target in this monetary policy strategy and such a

Ö. Karahan (✉)
Bandırma Faculty of Economics and Administrative Sciences, Balıkesir University, 10100 Bandırma-Balıkesir, Turkey
e-mail: okarahan@balikesir.edu.tr

O. Çolak
Department of Economics, Rize University, 53100 Rize, Turkey
e-mail: olcay.colak@rize.edu.tr

A. Karasavvoglou and P. Polychronidou (eds.), *Balkan and Eastern European Countries in the Midst of the Global Economic Crisis*, Contributions to Economics, DOI 10.1007/978-3-7908-2873-3_4, © Springer-Verlag Berlin Heidelberg 2013

commitment rule has the potential to eliminate the uncertainty about price level. From this point of view, it can be argued that IT increases transparency since the price level or inflation rate is better understood by the public (Bernanke and Mishkin 1997, p. 6).

Indeed "transparency" is the most significant fact provided by IT Regime in order to decrease uncertainty. This fact makes much clearer the future path of monetary policy by making explicit the purpose of the central bank. Especially, putting a formal target for future inflation level by Central Bank in the framework of IT Policy increases transparency and thus decreases inflation uncertainty since it helps towards anchoring expectations in the face of inflationary shocks. Central Bank of Turkey (CBT) has adopted Inflation Targeting (IT) as a monetary regime after 2001 – between 2002 and 2006 implicitly and then explicitly. Following the collapse of the stabilization policy based on a Crawling Exchange Rate Peg in 2001, implicit IT Policy has been firstly preferred until a reasonable set of conditions were satisfied in 2006 (Kara 2006, p. 3). Thus, Turkey represents a good case study opportunity for determining effectiveness of the IT Policy on inflation uncertainty. From this perspective, our study tries to analyze whether there is a decline in inflation uncertainty after the adoption of inflation targeting in Turkey. Finally the success of Turkish experience concerning with IT Policy in decreasing inflation uncertainty has been examined.

The paper proceeds as follows. Section 2 describes the literature. Section 3 presents the data, methodology and empirical results and finally Sect. 4 concludes.

2 Literature Review

There are numerous studies in the literature examining the effect of IT Policy on inflation uncertainty. While determining the impact of IT Policy on inflation uncertainty, expected inflation is measured or created using data getting from either survey responses of professional forecasters or time series. Researchers previously measured inflation uncertainty as the standard deviation of inflation and the cross-sectional dispersion of inflation forecast from surveys of professional forecasters. More recently GARCH Models to account for time-varying inflation volatility or uncertainty have become popular. Empirical results are generally ambiguous concerning the effect of IT Policy on inflation uncertainty although some studies find favorable indication related to the issue.

In general framework, Evans and Wachtel (1993) analyze the relation between monetary policy change and inflation uncertainty. Using survey data, authors develop a model of the inflation process from which they can derive measures of inflation uncertainty that account for the prospects of changing monetary regimes. This model allows for showing structural change arising in switching monetary regimes in inflation uncertainty from 1953 to 1993 in the United States. They showed that variations in the inflation uncertainty on inflation expectation closely match the movements in the regime uncertainty components of inflation's conditional variance. Thus, they suggested that uncertainty concerning the monetary regime may be the underlying source of the observed volatility of inflation.

Johnson (2002) also uses inflation surveys of experts in targeting and non-targeting countries to measure the expected inflation and variability of inflation and estimates the impact of IT on the consensus of professional inflation forecasts. The author shows that an inflation targeting regime decreases the level of expected inflation; however, the variability of inflation forecast errors (change in inflation variability) does not decrease significantly in the targeting countries (Australia, Canada, New Zealand, Sweden, the UK) compared to not targeting countries (France, Germany, Italy, Japan, Netherlands, the US). In another study, Johnson (2003), again producing the level of expected inflation from survey responses of professional forecasters, measures the effect of the announcement of inflation targets on the level of expected inflation in five countries (Australia, Canada, New Zealand, Sweden, the United Kingdom). The results show that after the announcement of targets the level of expected inflation decreased in Australia, Canada, New Zealand and Sweden but not United Kingdom.

Capistran and Ramos-Francia (2010) also examine the effect of having an inflation targeting framework on the dispersion of inflation forecasts from professional forecasters. Using a panel data set of 25 countries – 14 of those are inflation targeting countries – with 16 years of monthly information, they find that the dispersion of long run inflation expectation is smaller in targeting regimes after controlling for country-specific effects. When separating the effects between developed and developing countries, the dispersion of inflation expectations after inflation targeting is smaller and statistically significant only in developing countries. Using monthly inflation data from 1957 to 1997, Dittmar et al. (1999) argue that inflation variability (as the standard deviation of inflation) decreases after the adoption of inflation-targeting programs giving evidence from G-10 countries. The authors have found that the magnitudes of uncertainty about inflation are the expected consequence of commonly proposed inflation-targeting regimes. The adoption of inflation-targeting regimes around the world has been associated with lower inflation and less variable inflation.

Besides the studies depending on survey or variability based measures of inflation uncertainty, more recently GARCH techniques have become popular. Kontonikas (2004) analyzes the impact of IT Policy, using British time series data over the period 1972–2002 and implementing GARCH methods to model inflation uncertainty. Uncertainty is a proxy using the estimated conditional volatility from symmetric, asymmetric and component GARCH-M models of inflation. The results indicate that the adoption of an explicit target eliminates inflation persistence and reduces long-run uncertainty. Ertürk and Özlale (2004), also using a time-varying parameter model with GARCH specification, try to test whether there has been a structural break in expected inflation and inflation uncertainty after the implementation of inflation targeting in five industrialized countries: Australia, Canada, New Zealand, Sweden and the United Kingdom between 1980 and 2003. Test results indicate that the inflation targeting regimes are particularly successful in reducing expected inflation while there is less evidence that implementation of inflation targeting reduces inflation uncertainty significantly.

More recently, Berument and Yuksel (2007) try to investigate whether inflation targeting programs have altered the pattern of inflation variability for five developed countries (Australia, Canada, New Zealand, Sweden, the UK) and four emerging economies (Brazil, Chile, Colombia, South Africa) implementing inflation-targeting programs. A GARCH specification was used to model inflation variability and they could not find lower conditional inflation expectations except for Australia, Chile and Sweden under various specifications. Therefore, their empirical support for the lower inflation and variability for the inflation targeting regimes is limited. Miles (2008) particularly examines the impact of inflation targeting on inflation uncertainty, as well as inflation persistence in Canada using GARCH-M and T-GARCH Methods. He indicates that inflation targeting lowers inflation persistence, but surprisingly increases uncertainty. He stresses on the failure of IT to lower uncertainty and also argues that such an effect may be due to the failure of the previous formal target, the M_1 money supply, to successfully combat inflation. The author argues that, for the case of Canada, IT has actually raised inflation uncertainty, given the past level of inflation, although it has helped lower the persistence of inflation shocks, and was followed by a lower level of inflation. Payne (2009) examines the impact of inflation targeting on inflation volatility in Thailand within the context of an ARIMA-GARCH Model. He argues that the implementation of inflation targeting for Thailand in May 2000 marginally reduced the degree of volatility persistence in response to inflationary shocks (i.e. inflation uncertainty). Taş (2009) implements a conditional variance (PARCH) approach to investigate the performance of IT on inflation uncertainty in 19 countries. Both individual and panel data analyses conclude that IT countries have significantly lowered inflation variances after inflation targeting. Also, the decrease in inflation uncertainty is significantly higher in emerging economies compared to developed countries.

3 Data, Methodology and Empirical Results

Monthly Consumer Price Index (CPI) data has been obtained from Turkish Statistical Office (TURKSTAT) for Turkey from 1990:1–2011:2. To see the impact of IT Policy on inflation uncertainty we separate the data set in two periodical groups which are pre-inflation targeting period – Pre-IT Period – (1990:1–2001:12) and inflation targeting period – IT Period – (2002:1–2011:2). For the first sub-period our data set of CPI is based on 1987 = 100 and for the second sub-period is based on 1994 = 100. We take the logarithm of CPI and calculate the monthly time series of inflation, LINF1 for 1990:1–2001:12 and LINF2 for 2002:1–2011:2.

The Central Bank of Turkey (CTB) has adopted Inflation Targeting (IT) as a monetary regime after 2001, from 2002 to 2006 implicitly and then explicitly. Thus, the years after 2002 can be called IT Period for Turkey. Table 1 presents the

Table 1 Summary statistics of inflation series in pre-IT Period and IT Period

Summary statistics	Pre-IT Period (1990:1–2001:12)	IT Period (2002:1–2011:2)
Number of observation	144	110
Mean	4.58 %	0.89 %
Median	4.43 %	0.79 %
Maximum	22.07 %	3.41 %
Minimum	−0.92 %	−0.73 %
Standard deviation	2.51 %	0.88 %
Skewness	2.391443	0.551300
Kurtosis	17.82175	3.007707

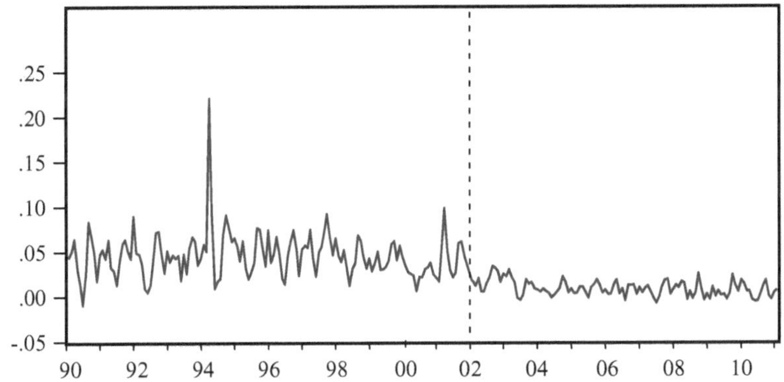

Fig. 1 The path of inflation series pre-IT Period (1990–2001) and IT Period (2002–2011)

summary statistics for Pre-IT Period (1990–2001) and IT Period (2002–2011). It can be indicated from Table 1 that the IT Period in Turkey after 2002 resulted in the mean inflation rates decreasing as much as nearly 80 % (from 4.58 % to 0.89 %). Also standard deviation is reduced as much as 65 % relative the Pre-IT Period (from 2.51 % to 0.88 %). The degree of Skewness and Kurtosis was reduced as well as in the IT Period. The results presented with summary statistics are also confirmed by Fig. 1, which shows that inflation (as monthly percentage change in CPI) in the IT Period exhibits less mean and volatility compared to Pre-IT Period. To sum up: the observed reduction in mean and standard deviation in summary statistics show that in the post-targeting period inflation in Turkey is substantially less persistent and less variable.

In order to determine the effect of IT Policy on inflation uncertainty, besides the summary statistics above, we should derive the new inflation uncertainty data within the context of a time varying parameter model with GARCH (Generalized Autoregressive Conditional Heteroskedasticity) specification. Since Engle's (1982) paper on ARCH and the subsequent GARCH extension by Bollerslev (1986), many studies have used the estimated one-step ahead conditional variance from GARCH models of inflation to proxy inflation uncertainty. (Taş 2009, p. 4).

While modeling the conditional variance, or the volatility, of a variable, Engle postulated the following relationship:

$$\sigma_{ut}^{2} = \alpha_0 + \alpha_1 u_{t-1}^2 + \ldots + \alpha_p u_{t-p}^2 \tag{1}$$

Volatility from the previous period is measured by the lags of the squared residuals. The conditional disturbance variance is the variance of u_t, conditional on information available up to time $t-1$. This is written by the following equations:

$$\sigma_u^2 = \mathrm{Var}(u_t | u_{t-1} \ldots u_{t-p}) \tag{2}$$

$$\sigma_u^2 = \mathrm{E}(u_t^2 | u_{t-1} \ldots u_{t-p}) \tag{3}$$

Recent disturbances influence the variance of the current disturbance and thus the variance of the dependent variable. The process described above is called an ARCH (p) process. On the other hand, the unit variance is not a restriction as any other variance can be rescaled to unity by suitable adjustment of the other parameters. We go on, for reasons of simplicity, to study the properties of an ARCH (1) model. This model is written as:

$$Y_t = \beta_1 + \beta_2 X_{t2} + \ldots + \beta_K X_{tK} + u_t \tag{4}$$

$$u_t = \varepsilon_t \sqrt{\alpha_0 + \alpha_1 u_{t-1}^2} \tag{5}$$

In both equations the disturbance term u_t, is normally distributed by 0 mean and $\alpha_0 + \alpha_1 u_{t-1}^2$ variance (Vogelvang 2005, p. 193). Since its "discovery" in 1982, ARCH modeling has become a growth industry, with all kinds of variations on the original model. One that has become popular is the generalized autoregressive conditional heteroskedasticity (GARCH) model, originally proposed by Bollerslev. The simplest GARCH model is the GARCH (1, 1) model, which can be written as:

$$\sigma_t^2 = \alpha_0 + \alpha_1 u_{t-1}^2 + \alpha_2 \sigma_{t-1}^2 \tag{6}$$

Equation 6 says that the conditional variance of u at time t (σ_t^2) depends not only on the squared error term in the previous time period (u^2_{t-1}) but also on its conditional variance in the previous time period (σ^2_{t-1}). This model can be generalized to a GARCH (*p*, *q*) model in which there are *p* lagged terms of the squared error term and *q* terms of the lagged conditional variances (Gujarati 2004, p. 862). According to the GARCH equation stated above (6), the moving average component (ARCH term) is u^2_{t-1} and represents inflation volatility from the previous period. The autoregressive component (GARCH term) is σ^2_{t-1} and

Table 2 ADF unit root test

	Level	First diff.	MacKinnon critical values		
LINF1	−0.8202	−8.3569	1 %	−3.47	−4.02
			5 %	−2.88	−3.44
			10 %	−2.57	−3.14
LINF2	−2.4115	−5.8218	1 %	−3.49	−4.04
			5 %	−2.88	−3.45
			10 %	−2.58	−3.15

represents the forecast variance of inflation from previous period. The sum of the coefficients $(\alpha_1 + \alpha_2)$ in the conditional variance equation determines volatility persistence (uncertainty) due to inflationary shocks. If the sum of α_1 and α_2 gets closer to one, then the shock becomes more persistent (Payne 2009, p. 235).

Thus, the GARCH time series estimation provides a more sophisticated method of estimating time-varying uncertainty or modeling changes in variance. Most modern investigations of inflation uncertainty employ GARCH models. Indeed, GARCH techniques are popular in empirical investigations of the inflation uncertainty since the estimated conditional volatility can serve as a proxy for uncertainty. In other words, the GARCH Model of inflation is estimated and the conditional variance from this estimation is used as inflation uncertainty. Moreover, since GARCH models provide a parametric measure of inflation uncertainty, an explicit test can be conducted to determine whether the conditional variance is statistically significant.

Before GARCH, the primary descriptive tool to capture time-varying conditional standard deviation and conditional variance was the rolling standard deviation or the rolling variance. This is the standard deviation or variance calculated using a fixed number of the most recent observations. The idea behind this assumes that the variance changes slowly over time and is approximately constant on short rolling-time windows. However, the assumption of equal weights seems unattractive in modern variance modeling. GARCH Models allow the data to determine the best weights to use in forecasting the variance.

In this paper we use a time series of Turkish Inflation producing from Consumer Price Index in a GARCH Model to create a measure of inflation uncertainty. At first step, ADF Unit Root Test is employed on the inflation series for stationary condition. Then, best inflation models are specified using Autoregressive Models, for both terms pre-IT Period and IT Period. Later, we employ ARCH-LM test in order to examine the ARCH effects in the residuals of the models. Finally, we derive variance equation from GARCH Model (1, 1) specification and analyze the effect of IT policy on inflation uncertainty.

3.1 ADF Unit Root Test

The unit root test is employed on the series for stationary condition and the results of Augmented Dickey-Fuller (ADF) test are given in Table 2 for both pre-IT Period

Table 3 The results of inflation model for pre-IT Period

Dependent variable: DLINF1 method: least squares				
Variable	Coefficient	Std. error	t-statistic	Prob.
C	0.045596	0.002074	21.98209	0.0000
AR(1)	0.895460	0.081533	10.98276	0.0000
AR(2)	−0.852160	0.071093	−11.98655	0.0000
MA(1)	−0.633025	0.111467	−5.679015	0.0000
MA(2)	0.691539	0.097692	7.078769	0.0000
R-squared	0.243089	Mean dependent var		0.045802
Adjusted R-squared	0.220827	S.D. dependent var		0.025328
S.E. of regression	0.022357	Akaike info criterion		−4.728532
Sum squared resid.	0.067978	Schwarz criterion		−4.623966
Log likelihood	338.3615	F-statistic		10.91944
Durbin-Watson stat	1.743826	Prob (F-statistic)		0.000000

and IT Period. Our null hypothesis for the unit root test is, Ho: $\delta = 0$ or time series of inflation are non stationary.

By including intercept into the model at level, the value of ADF-test statistics is less than MacKinnon critical values at each significance level and indicates that the acceptance of the null hypothesis series is non stationary. The result of ADF unit root test indicates that series of LINF1 for the periods of 1990:1–2001:12 and LINF2 for 2002:1–2011:12 become stationary after taking the first difference of the series, DLINF1 and DLINF2 respectively.

3.2 *Autoregressive Inflation Model Specifications*

For fitting the best inflation models, the correlogram of the residuals was checked and the following criterions were considered: (1) significance of the parameters, (2) high determination coefficient, (3) minimum of Akaike (AIC) and Schwarz information criteria (SIC), (4) maximum Log-likelihood ratio and (5) significance of F-test statistics.

Under these circumstances, concerning with pre-IT period, the most suitable case is the ARMA (2, 2) model of inflation that meets the criterions stated above. For the pre-IT period, the ARMA (2, 2) model of inflation is estimated and the results are given in Table 3. As we see for the pre-IT period, the ARMA (2, 2) model of inflation is estimated and the results are given in Table 3, all coefficients of the parameters of ARMA (2, 2) are significant at each significance level. Even determination coefficient which indicates the explanatory power of the model seems to be low; it is the highest among the other models. The value of F-statistics is the most significant, the value of the log likelihood ratio is the maximum, AIC and SIC information criterions are the lowest among the other models.

Table 4 The results of inflation model for IT Period

Dependent variable: DLINF2 method: least squares				
Variable	Coefficient	Std. error	t-statistics	Prob.
C	0.009075	0.000942	9.633054	0.0000
AR(1)	1.002657	0.0465995	21.51647	0.0000
AR(2)	−0.914793	0.044427	−20.59086	0.0000
MA (1)	−0.687876	0.007960	−86.41626	0.0000
MA (2)	0.994985	0.007627	130.4500	0.0000
R-squared	0.434536	Mean dependent var		0.008807
Adjusted R-squared	0.412361	S.D. dependent var		0.008868
S.E. of regression	0.006798	Akaike info criterion		−7.098784
Sum squared resid.	0.004714	Schwarz criterion		−6.973885
Log likelihood	384.7849	F-statistics		19.59569
Durbin-Watson stat	1.614662	Prob (F-statistics)		0.000000

Table 5 ARCH-LM test for pre-IT Period

ARCH test				
F-statistics	0.106974	Probability		0.744111
Obs*R-squared	0.108441	Probability		0.741926
Dependent variable: RESID^2				
Method: least squares				
Variable	Coefficient	Std. error	t-statistics	Prob.
C	0.000498	0.000209	2.385779	0.0184
RESID^2(−1)	−0.027832	0.085095	−0.327069	0.7441

For IT Period, the most suitable case or inflation model is selected as ARMA (2, 2) by considering the criterions stated above. Looking at the Inflation Model for IT Period in Table 4, the selected model meets all the criterions stated above and inflation series follows an ARMA (2, 2) process. It is superior to the others in meeting most of the criterions stated above; the coefficients of the parameters of the model are significant at each significance level, determination coefficient of the model is 43 % and highest among the others, AIC and SIC information criterions are minimum and Log likelihood ratio is the maximum among the other models. Also the value of F-statistics is the maximum and the most significant one.

3.3 ARCH-LM Tests

Before estimating the uncertainty of inflation we should check whether the residuals of the inflation series from the model display ARCH effect or not. In this context, the ARCH-LM test is performed and the results of the test are given in Tables 5 and 6 for pre-IT Period and IT period respectively.

Table 6 ARCH-LM test for IT Period

ARCH test:				
F-statistics	2.934463	Probability		0.089687
Obs*R-squared	2.908819	Probability		0.088096
Dependent variable: RESID^2				
Method: least squares				
Variable	Coefficient	Std. Error	t-statistics	Prob.
C	3.69E-05	6.74E-06	5.469792	0.0000
RESID^2(−1)	0.165934	0.096866	1.713027	0.0897

The ARCH-LM test is performed by estimating residuals ($\hat{e}_t$) from mean equation and obtaining the squares of the residuals ($\hat{e}_t^2$). The null and alternative hypotheses are: $H_0 : \gamma_1 = 0$ and $H_1 : \gamma_1 \neq 0$.

If there is no ARCH effect, then $\gamma_1 = 0$ and the fit of mean equation will be poor and the equation R^2 will be low. If there are ARCH effects, we expect the magnitude of $\hat{e}_t^2$ to depend on its lagged values and the R^2 will be relatively high. If the null hypothesis is true, then the test statistics (T-q) R^2 distributed (in large samples) as X^2_q; where q is the order of lag, and T-q is the number of complete observations. If (T-q) $R^2 \geq X^2_{1-\alpha,\, q}$ then we reject the null hypothesis that $\gamma_1 = 0$ and conclude that ARCH effects are present (Hill et al. 2008, p. 369). For the pre-IT period in Table 5, LM-test statistic is 0.10 less than the table values of χ_1^2 at all significance level, so the null hypothesis that indicates no ARCH effects on residuals is not rejected and inflation model for pre-IT period does not contain ARCH effect. In the case of IT period in Table 6, the test statistic is 2.90 greater than the table value of χ_1^2 at 10 % significance level, so the null hypothesis that indicates no ARCH effects on residuals is rejected and means that residuals of the ARMA (2, 2) model of inflation contains ARCH effect.

3.4 GARCH (1, 1) Model Specifications

After detecting the ARCH effects in each model, we can proceed to fit the GARCH model to create the inflation uncertainty for pre-IT Period and IT period. The GARCH technique is popular in empirical investigation of the inflation uncertainty since the estimated conditional volatility can serve as a proxy for uncertainty. The advantageous of using GARCH (1, 1) model in creating the inflation uncertainty series is to display the ARCH effects in the main equation of GARCH model. In this context, the equations of inflation and conditional variance are presented in Tables 7 and 8 for pre-IT Period and IT period respectively.

When we look at the parameters of the variance equation in Table 7, they are significant, while the parameters of variance equation in Table 8 are insignificant except the GARCH term in IT period. In variance equations, the coefficients of ARCH, that is RESID (−1) ^2, give the degree of inflation uncertainty, while the coefficients of GARCH indicate the persistence of this volatility. The sum of the

Table 7 The results of GARCH (1, 1) model for pre-IT Period

Dependent variable: DLINF1

Method: ML – ARCH (Marquardt) – Normal distribution

GARCH = C(6) + C(7)*RESID(−1)^2 + C(8)*GARCH(−1)

	Coefficient	Std. error	z-statistics	Prob.
C	0.046229	0.000806	57.38153	0.0000
AR(1)	0.881082	0.058862	14.96857	0.0000
AR(2)	−0.829007	0.049337	−16.80312	0.0000
MA(1)	−0.631780	0.088382	−7.148272	0.0000
MA(2)	0.653772	0.074109	8.821732	0.0000
Variance equation				
C	−2.61E-06	9.67E-07	−2.697371	0.0070
RESID(−1)^2	−0.011657	0.001112	−10.48367	0.0000
GARCH (−1)	1.030550	0.002688	383.4066	0.0000
R-squared	Mean Dep. Var	S.D Dep. Var.	AIC	SIC
0.240088	0.045802	0.025328	−4.808307	−4.641002
Adj. R-squared	Sum Squ. resid	Log likelihood	F-Stat.	DW-Stat.
0.200093	0.068248	346.987	6.002898	1.707901

Table 8 The results of GARCH (1, 1) model for IT Period

Dependent variable: DLINF2

Method: ML – ARCH (Marquardt) – Normal distribution

GARCH = C(6) + C(7)*RESID(−1)^2 + C(8)*GARCH(−1)

	Coefficient	Std. error	z-statistics	Prob.
C	0.008171	0.000840	9.732335	0.0000
AR(1)	0.985270	0.040633	24.24811	0.0000
AR(2)	−0.950760	0.041738	−22.77897	0.0000
MA(1)	−0.699619	0.038987	−17.94477	0.0000
MA(2)	0.919654	0.038415	23.93968	0.0000
Variance equation				
C	5.13E-06	8.23E-06	0.623882	0.5327
RESID(−1)^2	0.179655	0.139536	1.287520	0.1979
GARCH(−1)	0.706046	0.252747	2.793488	0.0052
R-squared	Mean Dep. Var	S.D Dep. Var.	AIC	SIC
0.370946	0.008807	0.008868	−7.046583	−6.846745
Adj. R-squared	Sum Squ. resid.	Log likelihood	F-Stat.	DW-Stat.
0.326467	0.005244	384.9922	8.339883	1.464351

ARCH and GARCH coefficient in pre-IT Period exceeds one, indicating that volatility shocks are quite persistent compared to same value 0.87 in IT-Period. Consequently, the decreasing rate of inflation uncertainty by the implementation of IT policy in Turkey after 2002 is supported by the values of the coefficients of the variance equations in GARCH Models.

The decreasing volatility persistence of inflation or inflation uncertainty is also obtained from the trend in GARCH series displayed in Fig. 2. The left side panel in

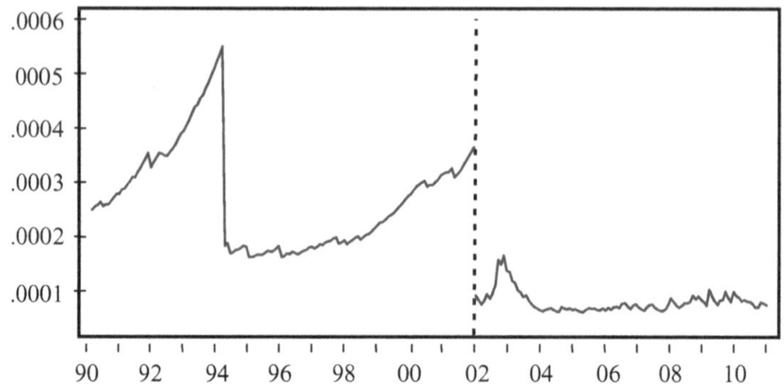

Fig. 2 Inflation uncertainty generated by GARCH model from 1990 to 2011

Fig. 2 shows the trend of inflation uncertainty for pre-IT period from 1990 to 2002 while right side the panel for IT period. Figure 2 also indicates that inflation uncertainty decreases by the implementation of IT Policy after 2002 in Turkey. Inflation uncertainty or the volume of volatility decreases and follows a stable path around 0.0001 in IT period which is quite low when it is compared to the trend in pre-IT period. Thus, it is obviously seen that inflation uncertainty clusters around lower rates in magnitude in IT Period. In conclusion IT policy managed to decrease the inflation uncertainty in Turkey.

4 Conclusion

Inflation Targeting Policy has become increasingly popular and is offered as a means to achieve price stability. In this context, many countries that have adopted this regime are believed to stabilize their economies with the help of a monetary discipline satisfied by the features of inflation targeting. It can also easily be claimed that these regimes could also lower the uncertainties that may emerge from the inflation process.

Using a GARCH Method to model inflation uncertainty based on monthly Consumer Price Index, this paper examines whether Inflation Targeting Policy implemented after 2001 altered the pattern of inflation variability for the Turkish Economy. The empirical analysis of the data set shows that inflation uncertainty is significantly lower after the Central Bank of Turkey has adopted Inflation Targeting as a monetary regime after 2001 – between 2002 and 2006 implicitly and then explicitly. In other words, our findings support the view that IT Policy is successful in reducing inflation uncertainty.

References

Amato JD, Gerlach S (2002) Inflation targeting in emerging market and transition economies: lessons after a decade. Eur Econ Rev 46:781–790

Bernanke B, Mishkin F (1997) Inflation targeting: a new framework for monetary policy? National Bureau of Economic Research Work Pap, 5893

Bernanke B, Laubach T, Mishkin F, Posen A (1999) Inflation targeting: lessons from the international experience. Princeton University Press, USA

Berument H, Yuksel E (2007) Effects of adopting inflation targeting regimes on inflation variability. Physica A 375:265–273

Bollerslev T (1986) Generalized autoregressive conditional heteroskedasticity. J Econ 31:307–327

Capistran C, Ramos-Francia M (2010) Does inflation targeting affect the dispersion of inflation expectations? J Money Credit Bank 42:113

Dittmar R, Gavin WT, Kydland FE (1999) Price-level uncertainty and inflation targeting. Fed Reser Bank of St Louis Rev 81:23–33

Engle R (1982) Autoregressive conditional heteroskedasticity with estimates of the variance of UK inflation. Econometrica 50:987–1008

Ertürk B, Ozlale U (2004) Do inflation targeting regimes reduce inflation uncertainty: evidence from five industrialized countries. Mimeo/Bilkent University, Ankara

Evans M, Wachtel P (1993) Inflation regimes and the sources of inflation uncertainty. J Money Credit Bank 25:475–511

Gujarati D (2004) Basic econometrics. McGraw-Hill, New York

Hill C et al (2008) Principles of econometrics, 3rd edn. Wiley, New York

Johnson DR (2002) The effect of inflation targeting on the behavior of expected inflation: evidence from an 11 country panel. J Monet Econ 49–8:1521–1538

Johnson DR (2003) The effect of inflation targeting on the level of expected inflation in five countries. Rev Econ Stat 85–4:1076–1081

Kara HA (2006) Turkish experience with implicit inflation targeting. Resear and Monet Pol Dep Work Pap, 06/03, Central Bank of Turkey, Ankara

Kontonikas A (2004) Inflation and inflation uncertainty in the UK evidence from GARCH modeling. Econ Model 21–3:524–543

Miles W (2008) Inflation targeting and monetary policy in Canada: what is the impact on inflation uncertainty? North Amer J Econ Fin 19:235–248

Payne EJ (2009) Inflation targeting and the inflation-inflation uncertainty relationship: evidence from Thailand. Appl Econ Lett 16–3:233–238

Taş KO (2009) Inflation targeting and inflation uncertainty. TOBB University of Economics and Technology, Department of Economics Work Pap, No.: 09–07, Ankara

Vogelvang B (2005) Econometrics: theory and applications with EViews. Financial Times, London

Fiscal Policy Under the EMU: Facts and Prospects

Georgios Makris and Konstantinos Filippidis

1 EMU: The Historical Background

Europe's EMU is unlike any other case of monetary unification in history. In the EU sovereign countries retain a large degree of fiscal autonomy while monetary policy is centralized and entrusted to an independent central bank – the ECB – with a clear mandate to preserve price stability.

The treaty of Rome, which established the European Economic Community (EEC), did not contain any explicit call for a single currency. The first debate on a project for the establishment of a monetary union and a common currency began in the 1960s. One of the reasons that could explain the interest of the European leaders in the monetary union has been the need to protect the European economies from the strong exchange rate fluctuations, as a result of the prevailing imbalances in the international monetary system.

At the time of the of Bretton Woods system breakdown, in 1971, many European countries tried to stabilize their exchange rates. The next effort was the creation of the European Monetary System in 1979 which, according to Helleiner (2004), established a kind of "mini Bretton Woods". It was an arrangement by which most nations of the EEC linked their currencies to prevent large fluctuations greater than 2, 25%, related to one another, stabilize foreign exchange rates and counter inflation among members. The main elements of this arrangement were the "currency snake", the Exchange Rate Mechanism (ERM), the extension of European credit facilities and the creation of the European Monetary Cooperation Fund.

By the second half of the 1980s, European leaders began to consider the EMU project. At the European Council in Hanover, in June 1989, Jacques Delors, the President of the European Commission, was entrusted with developing a plan for

G. Makris (✉) • K. Filippidis
Department of Balkan Studies, University of Western Macedonia, 3rd km N. Rd, Florina, Niki 53100, Greece
e-mail: gmakris@uowm.gr; kost_philip@hotmail.com

A. Karasavvoglou and P. Polychronidou (eds.), *Balkan and Eastern European Countries in the Midst of the Global Economic Crisis*, Contributions to Economics,
DOI 10.1007/978-3-7908-2873-3_5, © Springer-Verlag Berlin Heidelberg 2013

economic and monetary union. This was an important conclusion that resulted in the establishment of the subsequent Treaty on European Union (TEU).

The publication of the "Delors' Plan", in April 1989, set the target of the EMU, by adopting, initially, the stability of exchange rate mechanisms and, later on, of the common currency itself. It was a proposal that eventually led to the signing of the Maastricht Treaty in February 1992 (in force since 1993) and to the determination of the currency and fiscal criteria, necessary for the success of the EMU. The TEU clearly defined the monetary and financial principles underlying the EMU. According to this Treaty, EU member-states are required to meet specific criteria, in order to successfully achieve the EMU. These criteria require by the economies of the member-states to "converge" on low rates of inflation, similar interest rates, stable exchange rates, and to display stringent fiscal responsibility measured by public deficit no greater than 3% of Gross Domestic Product (GDP).

The official adoption of the single currency in January 1999, with a 3-year transition period before the introduction of notes and coins, by 11 EU member-states (Greece adopted the euro in 2001, Slovenia in 2007, Cyprus and Malta in 2008, Slovakia in 2009 and Estonia in 2011) was as a key step in the process of economic and political integration in Europe. In this sense the EMU is not only a step in the process towards a "closer union" but probably the most daring so far (Ballabriga and Martinez-Mongay 2002).

The potential cost of monetary integration led economists, as well as politicians, to agree on the need for articulating some sense of prior "convergence" among candidate EMU member-countries. Moreover, to ensure lasting fiscal convergence of the countries which participate in the EMU, a SGP was adopted at the Amsterdam European Council in June 1997, through which all member-states acknowledge the need for a sound and effective fiscal policy for the smooth operation of the EMU. The introduction of the SGP was the answer to the reservations concerning monetary and budgetary discipline in the EMU. The basic reason for the implementation of the SGP was to strengthen the provisions of the TEU on fiscal discipline in the EMU. The SGP is the fiscal pillar of the EMU, with a series of institutional arrangements supplementing this, rules-based, framework, in order to achieve the medium-term fiscal targets, for the member-states having adopted the euro. This reflects the need for monetary policy to have a forward-looking, medium-term orientation. It also acknowledges the existence of short-term volatility in prices, which cannot be controlled by monetary policy.

Although the EMU at the moment of its creation did not meet the criteria of the optimum currency area (Bukowski 2011), it is now a reality, constituting the third step of a long process with the establishment of a common currency in 2002. The EMU is not only the adoption of a common currency for the European citizens. It is a process with many different aspects, among them the orientation and luck of independence of the national fiscal policies which depend a lot on the priorities and the rules set by the SGP.

Nowadays, the ECB, created in 1998, still conducts the monetary policy while the fiscal policy is in the national governments' authority. This rules-based framework is complemented by a series of institutional arrangements in order to achieve the medium-term fiscal targets for the member-states that have adopted the euro. This reflects the need for monetary policy to have a forward-looking, medium-term orientation. It also acknowledges the existence of short-term volatility in prices, which cannot be controlled by monetary policy.

Fiscal policies drawn, according to the criteria of the SGP, by the ECB, ensure fiscal sustainability and a stable monetary union. The strictness of the SGP was probably prompted by short-term goals for dealing with the unstable situations in the public finances in many member-states.

2 Fiscal Policy Versus Monetary Policy and the SGP Rules

The SGP had two aspects: a preventive, early-warning system for identifying and correcting budgetary slippages before they drive the deficit above the 3% of GDP, ceiling set by the EU Treaty (European Commission 2002), and a dissuasive set of rules, to put pressure on member-states to avoid excessive deficits and to take measures to correct them quickly if they occur.

The principal concern of the SGP was to enforce fiscal discipline as a permanent feature of the EMU, although the guardian of monetary stability that sets the monetary rules is the ECB. Within that framework, the EMU was strengthened with the establishment of the European System of Central Banks (ESCB). This system was made up of the participating countries' national central banks and the EECB. The central banks would continue to exist as members of the ESCB, following the policy of the ECB.

In the past two decades, there has been an increasing consensus in the EU on the existence of a stable macroeconomic framework, which means price stability and central bank independence. According to this opinion the price stability was a necessary requirement for sustainable economic growth. At the same time the European Union, by underlying the emphasis on price stability, creates the belief that monetary policy can have an influence on real economic variables. Furthermore, the creation of the ECB had effects on policy making at a European and a national government level.

In order to understand the relation between fiscal and monetary policy, it is necessary to understand, on the one hand, the basic reasons behind the establishment of the SGP and, on the other, the desire of the member-states to follow their own fiscal policies. At the same time, a strong interdependence exists between fiscal authorities and the ECB. Moreover, a particular vexing issue that remains on the table is the interplay between fiscal authorities of the EMU, and the single monetary policy. The consequences of this fact have exercised serious tensions between centralized and national control in governance and economic policy-making within the EU (McNamara 2002).

The primary role of the ECB is to set the rules and to construct the plan of monetary policy inside the euro-zone. The official strategy and the main aim of the ECB, is to stabilize inflation indicators at a low level over the medium term.

The implementation of monetary policy by the ECB relies on two sets of economic indicators: (1) monetary aggregates and (2) a series of other variables – GDP growth, unemployment, wage growth, etc. (European Parliament 1999). The ECB sets the goal of low inflation rate in order to achieve a low interest rate that will contribute to the economic growth in the euro area. The contribution of fiscal stability and the role of the SGP are very important in this field. SGP' rules are necessary in a monetary union, such as the EMU, to prevent what economists call "free rider" behaviour by individual countries (Tanzi 2003). Interest rates tend to be the same for all countries of the EMU and if a member-state has fiscal deficits and especially large public debts, this situation affects the level of interest rates throughout the union. In other words, a country that runs a large fiscal deficit, and accumulates a large public debt, will impose higher interest costs on all the members of the union and this cost will be shared with the other member-states (Tanzi 2003).

The adoption of the common currency has provided the opportunity for a wide debate between the supporters of euro and its opponents. This dialogue does not focus only on the adoption of euro but also in the medium and long term effects of the EMU. Many neo-liberals see the abandonment of the national currencies as a way to import price stability. Advocates of the euro have also argued that it will help to insulate countries from speculative financial flows and will attract stable long term foreign investments. In order to preserve financial liberalization and exchange rate stability the EMU members abandoned the independence of the domestic monetary policy. A Following the adoption of the euro, in 2002, the euro area countries have one of the strongest monetary units and a stable economic path against the speculators.

At the beginning of the 1990s neo-liberal policy makers perceived the EMU as a way to set their convictions on the fiscal policy and also as a way to prevent national policy makers from pursuing "old" (Keynesian) macroeconomic policies. They have also argued that it will help to insulate countries from speculative financial flows and will attract stable long term foreign investments. The reason is clear: the adoption of the SGP. The national governments agreed to the elimination of their national currencies and set their national fiscal policies under the SGP. This Pact, according to neo-liberals, eliminates the possibility of national devaluations. Some left wing politicians have also expressed their concerns about the project. They have been worried about the cutbacks to the welfare state, the domestic deregulation and the inability of the state to address employment and other social and economic problems, as the Pact reduces the freedom of governments to conduct their own fiscal policies. The SGP eliminates the opportunities for more flexible policies by penalizing countries that run fiscal deficits of more than 3% of the GDP in periods that are not considered exceptional (Tanzi 2003).

On the other hand, the creators of the SGP seemed to be particularly concerned by deficits and the stabilizing role of fiscal policy. Effectively, fiscal policies of the EU member-states were frequently characterized as pro-cyclical, creating growing deficits and exerting pressures on debt ratios. These high deficits appeared to be a major concern for the Europeans, when the solution is putting a limit for these deficits. The adoption of the EMU fiscal-policy framework would impose a strict sufficient condition for sustainability.

The Pact's strictness, although beneficial for the implementation of monetary policy, has a negative influence in the ability of public authorities to create and implement their fiscal policy. From the very beginning the SGP was criticized. Firstly, there was concern whether the member-states would manage to attain a budgetary position that would meet the rules of the Pact, and secondly, whether the implementation of the SGP itself would have benefits for the EMU and the member-states. The answer provided by Eichengreen and Wyplosz (1998) is that benefits are probably minimal, and could have been achieved in other ways. Five years later, Walter (2002) argued that it would be wrong to embark upon far reaching changes in euro area monetary and fiscal policy but asks for some improvements of the existing EMU framework. The Pact has also been criticized as being insufficiently flexible and needing to be applied only over the economic cycle (Graue 2005).

The idea that fiscal policy cannot escape from the limitations set by monetary policy, is not without critique. Fiscal policies drawn, according to the criteria of the SGP, by the ECB, ensure fiscal sustainability and a stable monetary union. Ballabriga and Martinez-Mongay (2005) argue that the strictness of the SGP, set up at the beginning of the 1990s, was probably prompted by short-term goals for dealing with unstable situations in the public finances in many member-states. In some euro countries, the empirical results indicate that the EU public finance was strengthened from the fiscal provision of the Maastricht Treaty and the SGP. Some argue that this notion is valid in only few euro area countries.

Uhlig (2002) also suggests that the SGP is influenced by the different fiscal policies in the member-states and there are differences b between the member-states in the implementation of the strategic aim of the Pact. This happens because currently the SGP relies on Ecofin, i.e. the meetings of the finance ministers of the EU, to reprimand a country or to impose penalties in case of excessive deficits. The Ecofin according to Uhlig (2002) dealt with leniency with the first few violators of the SGP. This seems to be the case when we see the public debt to GDP ratio in three euro-zone countries: when in 2004 the average public debt for the euro-zone countries had reached 70.7%, it was 106.2% in Italy, 109.9% in Greece and 100.7% in Belgium, clearly a case that supports the previous point.

Uhlig (2002) has suggested that there is a need to keep the rules of the SGP more coherent to the fiscal policies of the national governments in order to achieve a stable EMU. It could be argued however, that the implementation of the SGP is better applied with some degree of flexibility. This flexibility can allow some countries to bend the rules; this has been the case in the past. The SGP worked well in the run-up to the euro as an orientation for sound fiscal policy. Despite that, in 2001 and 2002 France, Germany, Portugal and Italy had trouble to comply with the deficit limit of 3% of GDP (Walter 2002). But should we create a system which is not able to adapt the national special conditions?

Helleiner (2004) and Ballabriga and Martinez-Mongay (2005) agree that the monetary policy did not manage to subordinate fiscal policy inside the EMU. As Uhlig concludes (2002), the national regulatory bodies have to become parts of a larger agreement and network targeting the maintenance of fiscal stability.

It can be argued that the EMU implies the loss of the sovereign interest rate and exchange rate instruments. Some argue that this argument is valid but is irrelevant because of the potential cost for the member-states when joining a monetary union. The primary objective of monetary policy is price stability and with that kind of stability, monetary policy can support a general macroeconomic policy.

Moreover, there is a need to consider the effectiveness of monetary and fiscal policy. According to Lane (2002), on the one side monetary policy has significant real effects on macroeconomic variables such output and employment, and the evidence can be seen in the reports of the ESCB. Nevertheless, the effectiveness of fiscal policy on macroeconomic variables has not been substantiated by empirical research. According to Bukowski (2011), fiscal policy in the medium and long run fails to ensure macroeconomic stabilization as it may possibly lead to internal and external disequilibria as well as to monetary distortions. As to fiscal policy, budgetary discipline is necessary to support the monetary policy of the ECB (Walter 2002). Apart from these facts, the overall performance of macroeconomic policy is affected by the interactions between fiscal and monetary policy.

3 The Aftermath of the Economic Crisis

3.1 The Strengthening of Institutions

Almost immediately after the events of the world economic crisis of 2008 and its negative effects on EU economies, there was a huge concern about economic governance in the EU, initiating a widespread dialogue about its improvement. This crisis revealed additional, important, structural problems in the operation of the EU institutions. The external debt of many member-states, the structural and budgetary deficits and the fragility of their banking system had not been dealt with the required severity in the framework of the SGP. Furthermore, the crisis added one more problem: the need for liquidity and a bail out mechanism which would not only prevent attacks from speculators but would also guarantee a viable debt restructuring.

The EU tried to respond to these challenges by creating new institutions, like the European Financial Stability Facility (EFSF) and the European Financial Stabilization Mechanism (EFSM). Through this framework and with the contribution and collaboration of the International Monetary Fund (IMF) countries which were affected heavily from the consequences of the economic crisis (Greece, Portugal and Ireland, mainly) were forced to borrow from these mechanisms in order to overcome the deterioration of their structural problems. In order for the assistance to be effective, the countries were obliged to implement strict budgetary programs and structural reforms. On the other hand, the ECB bought Greek, Irish and Portuguese government bonds. Nevertheless, this response was considered inefficient and delayed due to the size of the crisis and the complexity of the interdependence of the banking system.

Continuing the effort for more effective economic governance, the European Committee and the Ecofin Council of the 27 finance ministers endorsed the Good Economic Governance six draft regulations package to make sure that EU countries – mainly euro-zone members – would avoid, in the future, irresponsible fiscal behavior and restrict public debt to manageable levels. In March 2011, following the outbreak of the 2008 global financial crisis and the pressing fiscal problems faced by countries like Greece, Portugal and Ireland, a Competitiveness Pact was proposed, eventually to be adopted as "Euro Plus Pact". It was the EU's response to the consequences of the crisis, seeking to defend the euro and to set the foundations for further growth. Under these last developments and the debate that followed on the fiscal problems faced by members of the euro, problems which threatened the stability of the euro-zone, there is much more emphasis placed on stricter fiscal policy measures and rules. To what extend however, those new rules and policy measures can guarantee economic growth and the convergence of the EU member-states? On 15 March 2011, Ecofin reached agreement on the six following measures to strengthen economic governance:

1. To adopt a draft regulation amending regulation 1466/97 on the surveillance of member-states budgetary and economic policies;
2. To draft a new regulation amending regulation 1467/97 on the EU's excessive deficit procedure;
3. To draft a new regulation on the enforcement of budgetary surveillance in the euro area;
4. To draft a regulation on the prevention and correction of macroeconomic imbalances;
5. To draft regulation on enforcement measures, correcting excessive macroeconomic imbalances in the euro area;
6. To draft a directive on requirements for the member-states' budgetary frameworks (New Europe 2011).

It was a proposal attempting to impose neoliberal values in all fields. Apart from the proposed regulations, the most important measures were on: the constitutional consolidation on budgetary balance, deregulation of wage indexation, increase of age retirement limits and tax harmonization of companies.

Furthermore, the common proposal made by France and Germany, the so-called "Pact for Competitiveness", which was adopted, in its less heavy form as "Euro Plus Pact" (EPP), on 25 March by the euro-zone member-states plus Denmark, Poland, Bulgaria, Romania, Lithuania and Latvia, belongs to the same context. The Pact constitutes a renewed effort for stronger economic policy coordination for competitiveness and convergence and rests on four guiding rules:

1. It will be in line with and strengthen the existing economic governance in the EU;
2. It will be focused, action-oriented, and cover policy areas fostering competitiveness and convergence;
3. Each year, concrete national commitments will be undertaken by each Head of State or Government;
4. The Pact will fully respect the integrity of the Single Market.

In addition to these issues, attention will be paid to tax policy coordination and the development of a common corporate tax base.

The objectives of the EPP are to foster competitiveness and employment, to contribute further to the sustainability of public finances and to reinforce financial stability. In order to demonstrate a real commitment for change and ensure the necessary political impetus to reach common objectives, each year participating member-states will agree at the highest level on a set of concrete actions to be achieved within 12 months (European Council 2011). The selection of the specific policy measures to be implemented will remain the responsibility of each country, but the choice will be guided by considering in particular the issues mentioned above. These commitments will also be reflected in the National Reform Programs and Stability Programs, submitted each year, which will be assessed by the Commission, the Council, and the Euro-group. The creation of the European Stability Mechanism (ESM) is also foreseen, and will come into force after June 2013 to replace the EFSF and the EFSM.

3.2 Theoretical Concerns

The theoretical background of these measures is based on the idea that the absorption of macroeconomic imbalances between member-states can be achieved with the reduction of labor cost in countries that face permanent structural deficits of their commercial balances. In this way, the "asymmetric shocks" might be faced via the flexibility of markets and not via the structural funds. On the other hand, the Community budget, which should not be overloaded furthermore, will be also financed by Euro bonds that will allow the financial support of the EU's long term goals and will protect from speculative attacks against member-states.

Nevertheless, the EU has entered in a new phase of stricter economic governance in order to eliminate the effects of the economic crisis, strengthen the Euro, but also having the purpose of improving competitiveness and growth. Many questions arise concerning the accuracy of the theoretical approach, supporting such a policy option. On the practical side, there are serious concerns relating to the ability of the member-states to reach an agreement for the resolution of acute problems, like sovereign crises, despite the punishment supposedly imposed on those states that deviate from the limits of fiscal discipline. Greater emphasis would also be placed on the debt criterion of the SGP, with member-states whose debt exceeds 60% of GDP required to take steps to reduce their debt at a pre-defined pace, even if their deficit is below 3% of GDP. To determine whether the debt ratio is sufficiently diminishing toward the 60% of GDP threshold, a numerical benchmark would be introduced. On the other hand, the delayed reaction that has been observed in asymmetric shocks is possible to constitute a risk for speculative attacks against the countries that are exposed at high risks.

Examining the question from a theoretical point we can realize the danger of negative macroeconomic repercussions from the implementation of common budgetary discipline and other measures for the national economies. This danger could arise from the reduction of domestic demand and cause cumulative negative effects on productivity and employment. Furthermore, these negative effects may become stronger if these countries fail to achieve their short and mid-term financial goals and create a vicious circle of a persistent increase in government lending that can become a dept trap.

There is a risk that the negative pressures faced by peripheral economies, like those of south, central and southeastern Europe, which are already members of the EU, would become even greater. Of course these divergent groups of countries were facing different problems at the start of the crisis: structural problems of the developed or peripheral capitalist economies for the one group, problems relating with the way the transition from a centrally planned to a market economy took place for the other. In particular for the latter, the convergence with the European average in a globalized environment took place in the context of a rapid economic expansion, characterized by inflationary pressures and external imbalances (Makris 2009). Inflationary pressures which, following the initial stage of transition, were caused by the increase in financing, as a result of capital inflows and the operation of Western European banks, Foreign Direct Investments (FDI) (Lane and Milesi-Ferretti 2002) and quite often the pro-cyclical economic policy of governments, in combination with the exchange rate regimes. In addition, we should not ignore the Balassa-Samuelson effect, which although not universally accepted (see, Cheung and Lai 2000; Égert 2002a, b; Mihaljek and Klau 2003), has contributed to the development of inflationary pressures; factors which, on the eve of the crisis, led many economies in the region to overheat. If we add the rise in the labor cost that took place in many countries, the loss of export competitiveness – with obvious consequences for the trade balance – became acutely felt.

The crisis, which had initially spread from the euro zone, sharply deteriorated as a result of those structural problems in transition economies. As the analysis has attempted to show, we believe that the crisis was spread in the national economies as a result of:

- The reduction of exports mainly to the EU (the main trade partner), causing a reduction in demand, proportional to the size of the export sector, a reduction in investments and employment.
- The high volatility of capital flows which caused important capital outflows and the reduction of capital inflows corresponding to FDI, in a period when investors avoid "high risk" investments; a situation that undermined even further the capacity to preserve external imbalances.
- The withdrawal of the borrowing capacity in currency of the private sector, because of the cautiousness of the parent banking sector, businesses and households alike, but also as a result of the devaluation tendency of the national currencies under a fluctuating exchange rate regime.

Concluding, the proposed "toughening" of the Pact, will strengthen the pro-cyclical nature of fiscal policy, undermining the social protection net of societies, but at the same time obstructing the operation of the automatic fiscal stabilizers. It's a phenomenon that is threatening to become intense in the fragile economies of south, central and southeastern Europe. The policy of reducing wages, one of the measures included in the EPP, aims at improving export competitiveness and increasing the EU's share in world exports. At the specific juncture however, when at a European level production does not correspond to the capacity of production capacities, such a policy will result in the further reduction of demand and in recession (Jones 2011). After all, competitiveness is affected more by differences at the level of productivity (Jamet 2007) than by the level of labor costs. As for competitiveness, "labor" is only one of the defining factors affecting the competitiveness of states and businesses (Prokopenko 1998); and specifically it's the "quality of human resources" that relates positively with policy actions for its development. Besides, apart from the exchange rate currency factor, competitiveness's relation to productivity at a macroeconomic level depends also on other factors, such as the way a country has been integrated into the global economy, the benefits of technological progress, the structural adjustments or the increasing demand for a sustained development.

4 Epilogue

The events of the world economic crisis in 2008 had important consequences on the economic governance of the EU. The SGP, which had been adopted in 1997, to strengthened the budgetary discipline in the framework of the EMU, proved unable to manage immediately and effectively the post crisis events. The 2010 European sovereign debt crisis was the starting year for a revised plan on EMU. These concerns led to the creation of new institutions and mechanisms, thus the first reaction led to the adoption of the EPP on 25th of March 2011, aiming to support competitiveness and employment. According to the rules of the new Pact, the 17 member-states of the euro-zone, as well as other six countries of the EU, will have to implement strict budgetary discipline. The neo-liberal argument that is central in the logic characterizing the Pact, i.e. macroeconomic imbalances that must be restored through the flexibility of labor market, is open to criticism because of the possibility to generate, in combination with the followed fiscal policy, conditions of recession as a result of falling domestic demand. Irrespective of the debate concerning the defining factors for the increase of productivity and competitiveness, the risk of a failed convergence between the member-states of the Pact becomes increasingly possible, involving especially the fragile economies of south, central and southeast European countries.

References

Ballabriga F, Martinez-Mongay C (2002) Has EMU shifted policy? Resource document. European Commission, Directorate-General for Economic and Financial Affairs, Economic paper 166, http://europa.eu.int/comm/economy_finance. Accessed 3 Apr 2011

Ballabriga F, Martinez-Mongay C (2005) Sustainability of EU public finances. Resource document. European Commission, Directorate-General for Economic and Financial Affairs, Economic paper 225. http://europa.eu.int/comm/economy_finance. Accessed 3 Apr 2011

Bukowski S (2011) Economic and Monetary Union – current fiscal disturbances and the future. Int Adv Econ Res. doi:10.1007/s11294-011-9310-7

Cheung YW, Lai KS (2000) On cross-country differences in the persistence of real exchange rates. J Int Econ 50(2):375–397

Égert B (2002a) Estimating the impact of the Balassa – Samuelson effect on inflation and the real exchange rate during the transition. Econ Syst 26(1):1–16

Égert B (2002b) Investigating the Balassa – Samuelson hypothesis in the transition: do we understand what we see? A panel study. Econ Transit 10(2):273–309

Eichengreen B, Wyplosz C (1998) The stability pact: more than a minor nuisance? Economic Policy 13(26):65–104

European Council (2011) Conclusions. Resource document. Brussels, EUCO 10/1/11 REV 1. www.cosilium.europa.eu/uedocs/cms_data/docs/pressdata/en/ec/120296.pdf. Accessed 22 Apr 2011

European Commission, Directorate General for Economic and Financial Affairs (2002) Co-ordination of economic policies in the EU: a presentation of key features of the main procedures. Resource document. Euro papers, 45. ec.europa.eu.int/comm/economy_finance/publications/publication1022_en.pdf. Accessed 2 Apr 2011

European Parliament, Commitee on Monetary and Economic Affairs (1999) An analysis of rhe ECB's monetary strategy and its contribution to growth and employment. Resource document. Project No.: IV/99/32a. http://www.europarl.eu.int/comparl/econ/pdf/emu/speeches/991129/gros/default_en.pdf. Accessed 2 Apr 2011

De Graue P (2005) Economics of monetary union, 6th edn. Oxford University Press, Oxford

Helleiner E (2004) The evolution of the international monetary and financial system. In: Ravenhill J (ed) Global political economy. Oxford University Press, Oxford, pp 213–240

Jamet JF (2007) La compétitivité des entreprises européennes. Resource document. Fondation Robert Schuman, Les policy papers de la Fondation. http://www.robert_schuman.eu/question_europe.pho?num=qe-60. Accessed 17 Apr 2011

Jones E (2011) Euro Plus: old wine in old bottles, Public Service Europe. http://www.jhubc.it/facultypages/ejones/2011_04_07_Public_Service_Europe.pdf. Accessed 17 Apr 2011

Lane P (2002) Monetary-fiscal interactions in an uncertain world: lessons for European policymakers. http://www.Economics/TEP/2002_papers/TEPNo13PL22.pdf. Accessed 20 Mar 2011

Lane PR, Milesi-Ferretti GM (2002) External wealth, the trade balance, and the real exchange rate. Eur Econ Rev 46:1049–1071

Makris G (2009) Mondialisation et la crise financière internationale actuelle: une approche théorique de leurs liens. In: Les Annales de l'Université Valahia de Targoviste-Section Sciences Economiques. Bibliotheca, Targoviste, pp 83–92

McNamara KR (2002) Managing the Euro – The European Central Bank. In: Peterson J, Shackleton M (eds) The Institutions of the European Union. Oxford University Press, Oxford

Mihaljek D, Klau M (2003) The Balassa – Samuelson effect in Central Europe: a disaggregated analysis. Bank for International Settlements, Working papers, 143

New Europe (2011) Securing euro-zone's financial future. The six new regulations are the only tangible new measures. http://www.neurope.eu/articles/105316.php. Accessed 10 Apr 2011

Prokopenko J (1998) Mondialisation, compétitivité et stratégies de productivité. Organisation Internationale du Travail, Document de Travail, EMD/22/F. http://www/ilo-mirror.library.cornell.edu/public/french/employment/ent/papersemd22/htm. Accessed 22 Apr 2011

Tanzi V (2003) Critics of EU budgetary limits are wrong. www.european institute.org/20030602380/Summer/Fall-2003/critics-of-eu-budgetary-limits-are-wrong.html. Accessed 10 Mar 2011

Uhlig H (2002) One money, but many fiscal policies in Europe: what are the consequences? CEPR, Discussion paper series, 3296

Walter N (2002) EMU Pact: no big bang reforms, but more flexibility, http://www.euractiv.com/euro/emu-pact-big-bang-reforms-flexibility/article-117014. Accessed 2 Apr 2011

Part II
Finance and Banking

Central Banks Between Classicism and Modernity

Felix-Constantin Burcea, Victor Bălău, Cristina Bâldan, Tiberiu-Cristian Avrămescu, and Emilia Ungureanu

1 Introduction

The functions and character of modern central banks, to some extent, reflect history. The main older functions of central banking, such as monetary policy, started to be somewhat different than they were in the early days of central banking. In the beginning, central banks were the dominant issuers of banknotes and bankers to the government. Indeed, most of the time these functions went hand in hand. The dominance over note gave to central banks sufficient scale to be the natural choice for government banking business. The initial function of National Banks from Austria, Denmark, France, Spain, among others, was to restore monetary stability and the credibility of banknotes after periods of over issuance and collapses of convertibility.

Pursuit of monetary stability and a credible currency system lay at the heart of early central banks, though to some extent in a different manner than now. Interest rates were adjusted by these banks to preserve stability, but the motivation was survival rather than some wider macroeconomic interest.

Over time, these dominant banks became bankers to the banking system. For commercial reasons, the dominant bank would occasionally lend to customer banks to cover temporary shortfalls in liquidity, an activity that brought with it a natural interest in the health of the customer banks.

Before the twentieth century, central banks were all established as profit-making entities. The potential for conflict between public policy objectives and financial interests was clear. Last resort lending raised the issue of neutrality in dealing with one's commercial rivals. Similar issues arose in terms of monetary management, as it became evident that the dominant banks were usually more profitable during periods of monetary and financial instability.

F.-C. Burcea (✉) • V. Bălău • C. Bâldan • T.-C. Avrămescu • E. Ungureanu
University of Pitesti, Pitesti, Romania
e-mail: felixburcea@yahoo.com; victorbalau_200x@yahoo.co.uk; baldan.cristina@gmail.com; cristiavr@yahoo.com; emiliaungureanu@yahoo.com

A. Karasavvoglou and P. Polychronidou (eds.), *Balkan and Eastern European Countries in the Midst of the Global Economic Crisis*, Contributions to Economics,
DOI 10.1007/978-3-7908-2873-3_6,

Prompted by economic crises between the wars, the breakdown of the gold standard and changes in thinking about the role of government in economic management, the transformation of central banks into public policy agencies was completed by the early twentieth century.

As the public policy focus came to predominate, the breakdown of the gold standard caused the nature of the monetary policy function to change. Without convertibility rules or limits, countries came to have the choice – through their central banks – of how best to maintain internal and external values of their national currencies. How that choice is exercised is at the core of the modern central bank.

The oversight and regulation function became increasingly formalised and direct, pushed also by shifting attitudes towards the role of government in intervening to regulate and guide economic activity. Changing attitudes towards the role of government and of direct intervention also led to the acquisition of an economic development function. Both directly and via the banking system, many central banks began to subsidise the financing of economic sectors that were targeted by governments seeking more rapid industrialisation. Often, preferential treatment involved the direct provision of banking services – especially capital and trade financing – to enterprises in targeted sectors and in particular, state-owned enterprises.

2 The Role of Monetary Policies

In all market oriented economies, the monetary policy represents only one component of economic policy of the state. In essence, the monetary policy is composed by a set of influencing measures on the aggregate demand in the economy, with effects on consumption and investments. The monetary policy objectives are realized through means and specific instruments, which influences the money offer in economy.

Taking into consideration the extremely unfavorable effects of the inflation on the macroeconomic variables, the monetary authorities from the majority of the countries consider that the maintenance of inflation under control represents the main objective of the monetary policy. The problem is formulated with more acuity for a transition economy, more possible when this starts from a very unfavorable situation: structural economic imbalance, chronic generalized penury, distortional system of prices, unsustainable payment balance (Isarescu 2003).

Starting from this situation, it is necessary that, through its objectives, the monetary policy must act for the correction of those imbalances created by the financial-monetary system. In this case, we talk about the excess of money supply without cover, the imbalance between the money demand and offer, the distortions of exchange mechanism. These can be influenced by specific levers available for the monetary authority.

Retrospectively analyzed, the monetary policy of the National Banks followed the same objectives: limiting the increase of monetary supply, equilibrating the money demand and offer by using interest rate policies, realizing the extern equilibrium by correcting the currency exchange mechanism.

External imbalances are usually generated by an unfavorable context, and also by the impossibility of currency mechanism to fast adapt to the new market conditions. Also, usually in emerging economies, it is hard to realize a perfect synchronization of monetary policy with the other components of economic policy.

For example, in Romania, in the external commerce domain, the measures adopted by the government for protecting the internal market have been delayed. Consequently, in the conditions of liberalizing the access for currency resources and the maintenance of price distortions, one part of the resources was for imports with a marginal importance in the given situation.

In the short run, the price evolution is subjected to multiple influences, generated by factors derived from the national economy and from the external environment, which influence the aggregate offer and demand. But, on medium or in the long run, the monetary policy conduits have a fundamental role for assuring the prices stability. The transmission mechanism of monetary policy represents the total number of channels through the central bank, utilizing a set of instruments of monetary policy that can influence the dynamic of aggregate demand of prices in the economy.

From the channels (or specific mechanism) of transmission for monetary policies identified in the economic literature, the practice economy revealed the great importance of: the channel of interest rates practiced by the financial institutions; the credit channel; the exchange rate channel; the channel for effects on welfare and balance; the channel of economic agents anticipating inflation (Bernanke et al. 1999).

At the level of central banks and economic agents, there is a consensus according to which price stability is beneficial, and the monetary policy has the privilege to realize it. This general recommendation is valid for the industrialized economies, but also for the emergent ones, although in the latter, the national banks could confront a more difficult mission, that of responding to real and nominal shocks, as the financial markets are not sufficiently mature and operate with less diversified instruments.

Those kinds of shocks can be generated by unanticipated variances of aliments, energy and administrated prices and, not least, by the massive fluxes of capital. Those limitations at addressing the monetary policy efficiently make the necessity of coherent mix of policies implementation in the case of emerging economies more important. Without the support of other economic policies, the monetary policy could have big difficulties in assuring a reduced inflation in a sustainable manner (Atuk and Ozmen 2009).

3 Stabilization Based on Exchange Rate

The primary force behind the big falls of real exchange rates that have been noticed after big devaluations is the slow adjustment of non-tradable goods and services prices (Burstein et al. 2007). We can analyze data from four important episodes: Mexico (1994); Korea (1997); Brazil (1999) and Argentina (2001). The "discoveries" made on the changes of exchange rate can be resumed as follows: in the first 3 months from the start of an exchange rate crisis, the price of non-tradable goods and services calculated in dollars were reduced with approx. 45% in Korea, Brazil and Mexico. In Argentina, the price has been going down dramatically, with 85%. (Ca'Zorzi et al. 2007).

In sharp contrast, there have been small relative changes of import goods prices expressed in dollars, measured "in port", varying from a decrease of 18% in Argentina, to an increase of 6% in Brazil. Even on medium run (1–2 years), the rate modifications for non-tradable goods in Korea, Brazil and Argentina are very low.

Taking into account the higher importance of emerging economies in the global commerce, precise estimations of the exchange rate modification degree and the market price in emerging economies are of an increased political importance for three main reasons. First of all, the price elasticity compared with the exchange rate determines the potential role of exchange rates in solving global imbalances, because it influences the commercial balance (Betts and Devereux 2000).

Secondly, the exchange rate modification degree and the trade price on the market in emerging economies is a very important parameter when it comes to evaluate the emerging economies role in the global inflation (Vigfusson et al. 2007).

Specifically, the increased share of emerging markets in the global commerce could be associated with the ongoing decline in the modification degree of exchange rate pass through in most of advanced economies. Especially, it was explained that the decrease of exchange rate pass through in the USA comes from an increase of market prices, in more emerging countries, especially in Asian countries affected by the financial crises from 1998 (Bussière and Peltonen 2008).

The third motivation is that the export and import prices elasticity reported to exchange rate pass through in emerging economies is an essential parameter in order to monitor and forecast the real production that can be substantially affected by the condition fluctuations of global exchange (Campa and González 2002). Distribution costs are very high for consumption goods: it represents more than 40% from the selling price in the USA and approximately 60% from the selling price in Argentina (en-detail). The distribution services need local labor force and land so that these ones would lead to a natural differentiation between prices in different countries.

Introducing a distribution sector in a standard model, based on exchange rate stabilization, highly improves its capacity to rationalize by observing the exchange rates dynamics (Ihrig et al. 2006).

There are various studies which approach the macroeconomic impact based on exchange rate stabilization. The specialized literature made substantially progresses in explaining the consumption behavior, investments and current account during its time (Burstein et al. 2003).

The economic behavior of Argentina after the Convertibility Plan is very much alike with typical models based on exchange rate stabilization: it is an economic expansion which brings a preeminent consumption boom and a deterioration of current account.

The costs modification with which companies confront, have direct implications on price – marginal cost level. Knowing the way in which the prices respond to such cost changes, it is essential to understand the way individual markets work and afterwards to understand macroeconomics.

The majority of studies about the exchange rate influence have as a hypothesis that companies behave symmetrically regarding their changing direction. They can give more explanations for which companies can behave asymmetrically. As part of a strategy for establishing the market prices, companies, trying to increase their market share, can make the range higher when the importer's currency is appreciated and decrease the range when the importer's currency is devaluated (Chari et al. 2000).

Firms which utilize local or important inputs can act in similar ways. On the other hand, firms which operate under quantitative constraints, because of commercial restrictions or production ones, can increase their range when the importer's currency is devaluated and can reduce the rage when the importer's currency is appreciated. (Pollard and Coughlin 2004). Companies can also respond asymmetrically at the modifying dimension of exchange rate, adjusting invoiced prices only when there are very big changes in it. In this case, the asymmetry direction depends on the way in which the firms invoice their prices: in national currency or in import currency.

The internal prices hadn't always followed the tendencies of exchange rate variations. Thus, in 1986, we can remark the fact that, although the dollar was strong, the imported good prices hadn't decreased. The biggest example is the one of luxury cars which, despite of dollar's appreciation in comparison with European currencies, have considerably overcome their value in the continent. The phenomenon is recognized as market price fixation.

The following problem is the effect of the dollar devaluation above inflation. Although many economists affirm that the national currency devaluation is transmitted in inflation, there are also opponents to this idea. The main argument is the one that prices haven't decreased once the internal currency strengthens, although their elasticity compared with the exchange rate is low (Krugman 1986).

Fixing prices according to the market must be understood through differences that appear between economies, as far as imbalance competition and a specific dynamic of each case in part is concerned.

According to Paul Krugman, the import prices fall to a small extent in the case in which the national currency is appreciated. Average estimations shows that about 35% and 40% from the dollar's appreciation in the period 1980–1986 was absorbed by increased prices used by exporters to the USA compared to exports to other economies.

The most appropriate interpretation of market price fixation comes from the imbalance competition, with a highlighted importance of demand dynamics, resulting from the costs of market adjustment and infrastructure distribution in order to sell certain imports, as well as offer's dynamics, resulting from the companies' need to invest in reputation.

As a result of national currency appreciation, economic agents exporting in that country find the stock market less attractive, preferring to increase the profit quantity. Moreover, the expectation that national currency will devaluate time affects future incomes, making foreign companies increase the prices in that currency.

On the other side, a permanent appreciation is not generating actions able to bring the future incomes nowadays. Prices may decrease as consequence of bigger competition between exporters to the same country. Studies research suggest that once that internal currency appreciation is finalized, any devaluation perceived as permanent will lead to an increase of passing the exchange rate in prices and to a faster improvement of the countries' commercial balance.

The studies show that the market share evolution of a company determines the way in which exchange rate variation influences prices. The investments which a company makes in order to win the market share are according to the expectation regarding exchange rate variations.

Thereby, it is considered that the foreign economic agents have the tendency to fix low prices on the internal market in order to win a bigger part of it, in the condition in which national currency is foreseen to have a permanent appreciation. Reversely, if it is considered that exchange appreciation is of temporary nature, foreign companies can even increase prices in internal currency. Also, an unsure evolution of the exchange rate increases the value of the market share held by a company.

Moreover, in the USA of the years 1981–1985 pure temporary dollar's appreciation was associated to an import prices increase. Dollar depreciation predictions have played an important role in exporters' decisions to increase prices in American market relative to other markets (Froot and Klemperer 1988).

Exchange rate variations can have different impact according to every economic agent policy: the variations can entirely be transferred in prices (total passing); they can be fully supported by the economic agent in order not to modify prices (zero passing) or an intermediary interpretation (partial passing) (Mishkin 2008).

It is generally admitted the fact that acting in one of the directions mentioned above represents a time consuming process and is different both from one country to another, and between industries. Exchange rate variation effect on the internal prices depends on factors as market structure, companies' behavior and macroeconomic conditions (Lian 2006).

Knowing the internal prices elasticity compared to exchange rate is essential for setting monetary policies, as well as for the annual inflation projection (Freedman and Laxton 2009).

According to the researches of An Lian, the total passing cases of the exchange rate variation in prices are rare. Also, the increased elasticity of the internal prices compared with the exchange rate is associated with small economies with considerable import contacts, having strong monetary shocks and high inflation.

4 External Shocks and Inflation from Euro Zone. The Case of Romania

It is very important to investigate the way of passing from external shocks (petrol prices shocks brought by exchange rate oscillation, to shocks of non-oil import prices to inflation from Euro Zone), in different distribution moments (import prices, producer prices and consumption prices) (Hahn 2003).

External shocks can explain a big part of price indices variation. They might have contributed considerably to inflation in Euro Zone from the beginning of European Monetary Union. Results regarding dimension and passing speed to Euro Zone seem to be robust in time.

Knowing in depth the relation from the base of exchange rate and prices, meaning the passing exchange rate as well as its speed, is essential to evaluate accordingly the monetary policy transmission over the prices, as well as for inflation forecasting. Taking into account the volatility of euro exchange rate from European Monetary Union launch (EMU) in 1999, this subject became a priority for the monetary policy of European Central Bank (ECB) (Coricelli et al. 2006).

In addition to the strong depreciation of Euro currency beginning with 1999, Euro Zone was also hit by external shocks, namely shocks due to prices, and import prices shocks of non-oil goods. For a straight evaluation of price evolution and of risks at the price stability address, also, dimension and passing speed of these shocks over inflation in Euro Zone seems to be of great interest.

In Romania, exchange rate and prices have a direct connection. Contouring in what measure national currency devaluation is transformed in inflation is creating the premises of monetary policy decisions.

Internal price elasticity compared with the exchange rate was high and quite fast in Romania before the adhesion to European Union. It reaches a maximum of 59.72% from rate variation for production prices and 27.43% from the consumption ones. At the same time, the exchange rate variation determines 40–60% from consumption price inflation and even more in production prices.

Small rate variations influence over the inflation was achieved by adopting the monetary basket of 60/40 Euro/Dollar (Gueorguiev 2003). Inflation in an economy has a considerable influence on the elasticity (Taylor 2000). Taylor argues that by a staggered price model and monopoly competition elasticity can decrease once with the inflation. More than that, Choudhri and Hakura (2001) are extending the analysis for more countries and they reached the conclusion that between average inflation and elasticity there is a strong correlation.

Thereby, in an economy dominated by accentuated inflation imbalances, passing the exchange rate variation in internal prices is higher. Price elasticity compared with exchange rate is correlated with the economy's opening degree, economic cycle and inflation level. In developing countries, as well as in emerging markets, passing the exchange rate difference in internal prices was more accentuated than in developed countries.

If we consider the interval 1997–2002, according to Gueorguiev, exchange rate pass-through was affecting to a great extent and very fast prices in Romania, with a value of 60% and 70% for production prices and 30–40% for consumption prices. Usually, the peak of the effect is felt after 12–15 months. Because such a period is considered too short for monetary policies to modify inflation through reference interest rate by influencing crediting, the only alternative for disinflation in the analyzed period was exchange rate balancing.

The option for adopting further on the monetary policy of inflation targeting was justified by the necessity of realizing a sustainable disinflation (Canova and De

Nicolo 2002). The implementation of inflation targeting strategy was not an easy task even before the start of the financial crisis and the fiscal dominance, the massive entrances of capital, the net debtor position of NBR from the banking system and the transmission mechanism of monetary policy combined. Therefore, between 2005 and 2007, we can notice periods in which both inflation anticipations and accentuated appreciations of the national currency coexisted.

This thing raised a serious dilemma for the national bank. Raising interest rates, necessary for bringing the anticipations at the same level as target of inflation, attracted more and more foreign capital, appreciating unsustainably our national currency (Uhlig 2006).

Once the financial crisis started in July 2007, a part of those conditions disappeared. Today, NBR tends to be net creditor of the banking system, and the entrances of foreign capital are now considerably reduced. But this thing does not simplify the implementation of monetary policy. On the contrary, the financial crisis increased the volatility on the monetary and exchange rate markets and tends to amplify the slowdown of the economic activity.

On the one hand, the reduction of external funding and the existence of big external imbalances led to currency depreciation, which feeds the inflation and makes necessary relatively high interest rates. Moreover, economic agents with debts in Euro and other foreign currencies, and consequently the financial system, are vulnerable to a high depreciation of the national currency.

On the other hand, higher interest rates can tend to slow down the economic growth, and, even more, can create bigger costs for those with debts, risking to destabilize the financial sector.

In these conditions emerges the delicate problem of compromise between the monetary policy objectives: assurance of price stability or assurance of financial stability.

5 Conclusion

Even if in some cases central bank policies from different countries have failed, mainly because of the political or transition problems, their role in modern economy is of high importance, especially through actual global economic conditions.

In the last two decades of the past century and during the beginning of our century, the global economy has confronted with major events which irreversibly influenced the approach mode of macroeconomic stability and put the National Central Bank importance in first plan using the available instruments, have conceded in the majority of cases to correct existent imbalances and created the premises of a healthy and durable economic increase.

The monetary policy, especially the inflation policy and the exchange rate policy applied in post December Romania showed that Romanian National Bank has a very important role concerning the macroeconomic and monetary stabilization.

All these policies are detached from the classical functions of Central Banks, marking a necessary evolution to approach new challenges of national economy correlated with the European and global space.

References

Lian An (2006) Exchange rate pass-through: evidence based on vector autoregression with sign restrictions. MPRA paper, 527

Atuk O, Ozmen U (2009) Design and evaluation of core inflation measures for Turkey. IFC working paper, 3

Bernanke BS, Laubach T, Mishkin FS, Posen AS (1999) Inflation targeting: lesson from the international experience. Princeton University Press, Princeton

Betts C, Devereux M (2000) Exchange rate dynamics in a model of pricing-to-market. J Int Econ 50:215–244

Burstein A, Neves J, Rebelo S (2003) Distribution costs and real exchange rate dynamics during Exchange Rate Based Stabilizations. Journal of Monetary Economics, 50, p. 1189–1214

Burstein A, Eichenbaum M, Rebelo S (2007) Modeling exchange rate passthrough after large devaluations. J Monet Econ 54:2

Bussière M, Peltonen T (2008) Exchange rate pass-through in the global economy The role of emerging market economies. ECB working paper, 951

Canova F, De Nicolo G (2002) Monetary disturbances matter for business fluctuations in the G-7. J Monet Econ 49:1131–1159

Ca'Zorzi M, Hahn E, Sanchez M (2007) Exchange rate pass-through in emerging markets. ECB working paper, 739

Campa J, González J (2002) Differences in exchange rate pass-through in the Euro area. CIIF research paper, 479

Chari VV, Kehoe P, McGrattan E (2000) Can sticky price models generate volatile and persistent exchange rates? NBER working paper No. 7869

Choudhri EU, Hakura D (2001) Exchange rate pass-through to domestic prices: does the inflationary environment matter? IMF working papers 01/194, International Monetary Fund

Coricelli F, Jazbec B, Masten I (2006) Exchange rate pass-through in EMU acceding countries: empirical analysis and policy implications. J Bank Finance 30:1375–1391

Freedman C, Laxton D (2009) Why inflation targeting? IMF working paper, 86

Froot K, Klemperer A (1988) Exchange rate pass-through when market share matters. NBER working paper series, 2542

Gueorguiev N (2003) Exchange rate pass through in Romania. IMF working paper, 130

Hahn E (2003) Pass-through of external shocks to Euro area inflation. ECB working paper, 243

Ihrig JE, Marazzi M, Rothenberg A (2006) Exchange rate pass-through in the G-7 countries. Board of Governors of the Federal Reserve System, International Finance discussion papers, 851

Isărescu MC (2003) Reflecţii economice, vol III. Contribuţii la teoria macrostabilizării

Krugman P (1986) Pricing to market when the exchange rate changes. NBER working paper series, 1926

Mishkin F (2008) Exchange rate pass-through and monetary policy. NBER working paper series, 13889

Pollard P, Coughlin C (2004) Size matters: asymmetric exchange rate pass-through at the industry level. Federal Reserve Bank of St. Louis, Working papers 2003–029

Taylor JB (2000) Low inflation, pass-through, and the pricing power of firms. Eur Econ Rev 44(7):1389, Elsevier

Uhlig H (2006) Sign restrictions and Bayesian VARs. Bonn University, ZEI

Vigfusson RJ, Sheets N, Gagnon J (2007) Exchange rate pass-through to export prices: assessing some cross-country evidence. Board of Governors of the Federal Reserve System, International Finance discussion papers, 902

Credit Risk in the Romanian Banking System: Evidence from an ARDL Model

Eftychia Nikolaidou and Sofoklis D. Vogiazas

1 Introduction

Central Banks in South Eastern Europe (SEE) are mandated to foster stability in their respective banking systems as financial stability is considered a sine qua non of sustainable economic progress. The investigation of banking sectors' vulnerability has gained even greater prominence on central bankers' agenda after the devastating impact of the global financial crisis in 2007. It is well known that banks' solvency is susceptible to credit risk shocks as a consequence of poor loan quality. Therefore, monitoring the interaction between the health of financial institutions and macroeconomic stability becomes a necessity given the interlinkages of financial systems in the SEE region. The experience with the business cycle in the developed economies shows that non-performing loans rise as the recession progresses while they peak after the end of the recession. In this respect, the non-performing loans in the SEE region are expected to reach very high levels by 2010–2011, given that the global crisis caught most of the respective economies overheating with unprecedented credit expansion.[1]

The key motivation of this paper is to improve our understanding of the deterministic factors propelling the Romanian banks' nonperforming loans while exploring potential contagion effects from the Greek debt crisis. This is particularly

[1] Authors' estimates based on SEE Central Banks reports suggest that the average annual credit growth over the period 2005–2007 reached 49 % in Romania and 41 % in Bulgaria.

E. Nikolaidou (✉)
Business Administration and Economics, CITY College – International Faculty of the University of Sheffield, Thessaloniki, Greece
e-mail: enikolaidou@city.academic.gr

S.D. Vogiazas (✉)
South East European Research Centre, Research Centre of the University of Sheffield and CITY College, Thessaloniki, Greece
e-mail: svogiazas@seerc.org

A. Karasavvoglou and P. Polychronidou (eds.), *Balkan and Eastern European Countries in the Midst of the Global Economic Crisis*, Contributions to Economics,
DOI 10.1007/978-3-7908-2873-3_7,

important given that the Romanian financial system is dominated by foreign-owned commercial banks while among them, the Greek banks' subsidiaries have a substantial presence. More specific, the Greek banks' subsidiaries hold 30.7 % of aggregate foreign capital while they account for the second largest market share in the Romanian banking system (NBR 2011). Recent work by Vogiazas and Nikolaidou (2011a, b) on the determinants of credit risk in Romania employing uni-variate and multi-variate OLS regressions indicated that macroeconomic variables, specifically the construction and investment expenditure, the inflation and the unemployment rate, and the country's external debt to GDP and M2 together with Greek-specific variables influence the credit risk of the Romanian banking system.

This study extends the authors' previous work by employing the ARDL approach to cointegration to examine the relationship between the ex-post credit risk as reflected on the loss loan provisions to total loans ratio (LLP) for the Romanian banking system and a set of macroeconomic and Romanian bank-specific variables. This approach allows us to investigate both the long-run and the short-run determinants of credit risk and has only recently been employed in the relevant literature. To capture the potential effect of the significant Greek presence in the Romanian banking system and to examine a potential transmission channel from the Greek crisis, relevant proxies are introduced. In this direction, we utilize monthly time series data that span from December 2001 to November 2010, thus, covering both the booming period and the downturn following the financial crisis as well as the ensuing manifestation of the Greek financial distress.

The paper is organized as follows. Section 2 presents the literature on the determinants of loan portfolio quality while Sect. 3 provides the data and the methodological framework followed by the empirical findings in Sect. 4. Finally, Sect. 5 concludes the paper.

2 Literature Review

The aim of this section is to review the empirical findings on the relation between macroeconomic variables and credit risk. Many studies investigate the factors that induce financial crises by examining potential links between bank-related variables and macroeconomic indicators. Gavin and Hausmann (1996) argue that excessive credit growth is a primary factor that triggers banking crises as usually it goes hand in hand with a decline in credit standards. The authors' findings indicate that, among other variables, the interest rates, the anticipated inflation, the credit growth and the monetary and exchange rate regime constraint borrowers' loan servicing capacity. Demirgüc-Kunt and Detragiache (1998) propose that banks face insolvency due to declining asset values when bank borrowers cannot service their debt as a result of adverse shocks to the economy. Similarly to Gavin and Hausmann (1996), their findings suggest that inflation and the real interest rates are positively associated with a banking crisis, whilst the GDP has an inverse relationship. Hardy and Pazarbasioglu (1998) explore the macroeconomic and financial conditions which are indicative of banking distress. Their results indicate that the likelihood of banking distress increases with the declining economic growth. Further, capital inflows and credit expansion to private sector, associated with rising consumption and real interest rates, typically precede banking crises.

Recently, the macro stress-testing[2] approach in assessing a financial sector's vulnerabilities, received considerable attention by central banks and regulatory bodies. These studies examine the potential links between non-performing loans and macroeconomic factors. Initially, the process involves estimating the sensitivity of banks' balance sheets to adverse changes in macro fundamentals based on historical data. At a later stage, the estimated coefficients can be used to simulate the impact on the financial system of possible stress scenarios. The relevant literature focuses primarily on credit risk, which by large, represents the most significant risk faced by banking systems worldwide.

Studies analysing the macroeconomic determinants of banks' loan losses or non-performing loans (NPLs) include Pesola (2001) for the Nordic countries, Kalirai and Scheicher (2002) for Austria, and Delgado and Saurina (2004) for Spain. Typically, these studies find that loan loss provisions are negatively related to GDP growth and positively related to interest rates. For instance, Kalirai and Scheicher (2002) estimate a time series model of aggregate loan loss provisions as a function of an extensive set of macroeconomic variables. Results indicate that increasing short-term rates, declining stock markets and industrial production have an adverse impact on Austrian banks' loss loan provisions.

Several recent studies employ the VAR modelling approach as proposed by Sims (1980) to investigate the macro-fundamentals' transmission mechanism in various countries.[3] These models include an array of macroeconomic factors, usually ranging from 2 to 5, depending on the country's macroeconomic conditions. In this regard, variables such as economic growth, unemployment, interest rates, equity prices and corporate bond spreads contribute to default risk (Foglia 2008). Recently, market-based indicators were introduced in the credit risk models.[4]

Blaschke et al. (2001) propose the VAR methodology to investigate the impact of inflation, interest rates, output and other variables to NPLs of the banking sector. Gambera (2000) employs bivariate VAR models to investigate the influence of macroeconomic variables on a substantial sample of US banks' loan delinquencies. The significant predictors of bank asset quality are the unemployment rate, farming income, housing permits, state annual product and bankruptcy fillings. Similarly,

---

[2] The term refers to a range of techniques used to assess the vulnerability of a financial system to 'exceptional but plausible' macroeconomic shocks.

[3] These models are used in the studies conducted at the Central Banks of the UK, Japan, Spain, the Netherlands, and at the European Central Bank.

[4] Introducing market variables such as interest rates, foreign exchange rates, and equity and real estate price indices into credit risk models is a way of explicitly integrating the analysis of market and credit risks.

Hoggarth et al. (2005) study for the UK applied the VAR methodology between loan write-offs and the output gap, retail and house price inflation, nominal short-term interest rate and the real exchange rate.

Baboucek and Jancar (2005) apply an unrestricted VAR[5] model to investigate the effects of macroeconomic shocks on the loan quality of the Czech banking sector. Authors find robust relationships between asset quality and a number of macroeconomic variables based on impulse response functions' analysis. Both the unemployment and the inflation rate were found to have negative influence on the NPLs, thus, confirming theory and related studies. However, other macroeconomic variables, such as the loan stock, real exchange rate and M1 failed to concur with economic theory as innovations in all variables except M1 appear to improve the loan quality.

Several papers (Boss 2002; Virolainen 2004) analyse the impact of macro fundamentals on the credit quality of banks' debtors. Virolainen (2004) estimates a macroeconomic credit risk model for the Finnish corporate sector over the period 1986–2003. The SUR model results suggest a significant relationship between corporate sector default rates and key macroeconomic factors including GDP, interest rates and corporate indebtedness. As in most studies, the estimated model is employed to analyse corporate credit risks conditional on current macroeconomic conditions. The findings are in line with previous studies using observed bankruptcies for default rate measures. Boss (2002) estimates a macroeconomic credit risk model for the aggregated corporate default rate for the Austrian banking sector. Findings suggest that industrial production, inflation, the stock index, the nominal short-term interest rate, and the oil price are the most important determinants of corporate default rates. Following Virolainen (2004) methodology, Trenca and Benyovszki (2008) estimate a macroeconomic credit risk model for the Romanian corporate sector over the period 2002–2008. Results suggest a significant relationship between industry-specific default rates and macroeconomic factors such as GDP growth rate, consumer price index, real interest rate charged on loans, the exchange rate and industry-specific indebtedness.

A leading role in the development of stress tests has been performed by the IMF, in cooperation with the World Bank. The IMF conducted for the first time in Greece a financial sector assessment program (Kalfaoglou 2006) in 2005. Similar to Boss (2002), Kalfaoglou (2006) emphasises that credit risk remains the key risk in the Greek banking sector. Despite the satisfactory stress tests' results, the author indicates that the cross-border operations increase banks' vulnerability to external shocks which, in turn, require more intensive risk management. The IMF's (2010)

[5] The VAR model is based on transmission that includes the following nine endogenous variables: the real effective exchange rate, exports, monetary aggregate M2, imports, aggregate bank loans to clients, the unemployment rate, the consumer price index, the domestic real 3-month interest rate and the share of non-performing loans in aggregate bank loans to clients.

Romanian stress tests[6] conclude that the financial system is particularly vulnerable to the effects of a slowing or reversal of capital inflows and the associated downward pressure on the exchange rate.

Surprisingly, the cointegration analysis received limited only attention in the relevant literature. Although several methods are available for conducting cointegration tests with the most commonly used methods being the Engle-Granger test and the maximum likelihood based Johansen test, it is the Autoregressive Distributed Lag approach to cointegration (ARDL) that has become increasingly popular in recent years. The latter approach re-examined by Pesaran and Shin (1999) presents flexibility as well as other favourable aspects[7] that cannot be found in other cointegration techniques. In the credit risk determinants literature, co-integration analyses are generally limited with the ARDL approach being almost non-existent, though it is extensively used in other economic fields such as the finance-growth nexus. This can be attributed solely to the fact that the ARDL approach is relatively new as is the case with the literature on credit risk and the macro economy. Among the limited studies that apply cointegration techniques to study the short-term and long-term relationship between nonperforming loans and a set of macroeconomic variables such as GDP, unemployment, and interest rates, we can identify Delgado and Saurina (2004) and Zeman and Jurca (2008) that employ a vector error correction model to assess the impact of a slowdown in real GDP, interest rates and exchange rate on the NPLs of the Slovak banking system. The Johansen cointegration test on the employed variables indicates the existence of one cointegrating equation (Zeman and Jurca 2008). Turning to the studies that employ the ARDL approach to cointegration, Abedola et al (2011) investigate the determinants of nonperforming loan in Malaysia, an islamic banking system while Greenidge and Grosvenor (2009) employ the ARDL framework for forecasting purposes in Barbados. In a rather small sample Abedola et al (2011) indicate a significant long run impact of interest rates on NPLs. On the other hand, Greenidge and Grosvenor (2009) conclude that the multivariate ARDL model slightly outperforms the univariate time series models, with the main limitations of the study being the unavailability of a large data set due to no standard treatment of non-performing loans in the Barbados banking system.

The abovementioned studies, in general, corroborate theoretical postulates with respect to the macroeconomic factors on loan portfolio quality and, consequently, on banking sector stability. The following section presents the data used and the methodological framework employed.

---

[6] The Romanian stress tests were based on data up to the end-June 2008 (IMF 2010). Thus, the exercise takes no account of developments in macro-financial variables and balance sheets since then. Furthermore, it does not explicitly assess the impact of the sharp slowing of lending, either as a result of tightening credit standards or in response to reduced funding from foreign parent banks.

[7] As long as the ARDL model is free of residual correlation, endogeneity is less of a problem. Pesaran and Shin (1999) demonstrated that the appropriate lags in the ARDL model correct for both serial correlation and endogeneity problems.

3 Data and Methodology

3.1 Data

It becomes evident from the literature reviewed that credit risk is sensitive to macroeconomic, financial and bank-specific factors. Similarly, Vogiazas and Nikolaidou (2011a, b) indicate that macroeconomic variables, specifically the construction and investment expenditure, the inflation and the unemployment rate and the country's external debt to GDP and M2 influence the credit risk of the Romanian banking system. Furthermore, the authors introduce in their studies Greek crisis-specific variables given the significant presence of Greek banks in the Romanian banking industry. Findings indicate that the previously mentioned macroeconomic variables jointly with the Greek banks' credit risk, proxied by the loss loan provisions to total loans ratio and the spread differential between the Greek and the German sovereign debt are significant in explaining the Romanian asset quality. Following the authors' previous work, this paper employs the provisioning approach in measuring credit risk.[8] Figure 1 presents the plot of LLP which has clearly an upward trend and as such reflects the declining asset quality of the Romanian banking system especially after the beginning of the global financial crisis.

The macroeconomic variables used in this study are the unemployment rate and M2 that indicates the intermediate money comprising of M1 and the highly liquid deposits and proxies economic activity. Increasing unemployment is considered to have a significantly adverse effect on loan portfolio quality (Quagliariello 2004; Baboucek and Jancar 2005; Vogiazas and Nikolaidou 2011a, b). Among the Romanian aggregated bank-specific indicators we use the credit growth given the dynamic and highly competitive Romanian banking sector. Thus, it requires a proactive approach from institutions desiring to maintain a prominent position in terms of market share. Inevitably, this proactive-ness translates to credit expansion that in turn plays a vital role in private sector led growth. SEE central banks statistics indicate that the average annual credit growth rate over the period 2005–2007 reached 49.3 % in Romania, considerably higher than any other country in the region. Thus, the growth rate of credit is expected to interact with the LLP ratio providing support to the hypothesis that 'lending booms often end in tears'. Alternatively, it poses the question whether the quality of loans granted during the booming period prior to the financial crisis was accurately evaluated by the banking system (Louzis et al 2010). As already mentioned a substantial part of the Romanian banking system's assets is owned by Greek banks. In this regard, we include in this study an indicator related to

[8] Credit risk is defined as the ratio of loss and doubtful loans to total loans (LLP). See Vogiazas and Nikolaidou (2011b) justification for selecting this proxy.

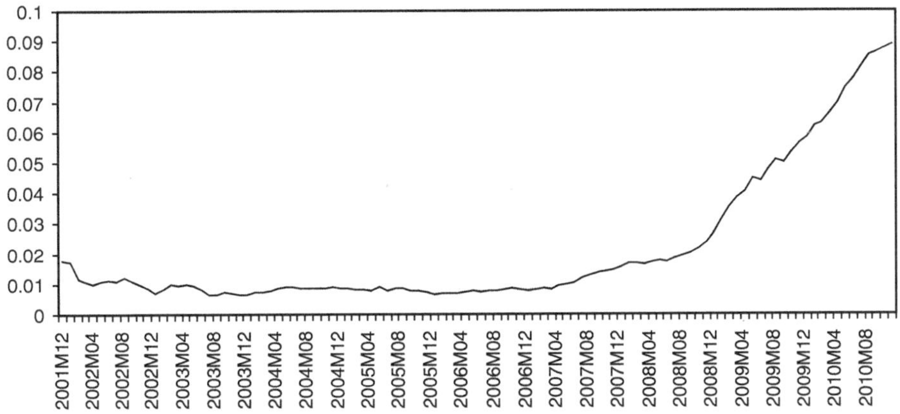

Fig. 1 Credit risk in the Romanian Banking System (Source: NBR & Authors' calculations)

the Greek banking system aiming to explore whether its dynamics[9] matter for the Romanian non-performing loans.

To sum up, we use monthly data over the period December 2001 to November 2010 on money supply (M2), unemployment (UN), total loans of the Romanian banking system (LOANS), Greek banks' loan loss provisions (LPG) and Romanian banks' loan loss provisions (LLP) as a proxy for the credit risk. The time period chosen is based on the following issues:

- To ensure that the dataset covers the booming period as well as the downturn after the global financial crisis. The SEE region imported the crisis at the end of 2008 through a sudden shrinkage of capital inflows, thus with a lag compared to more developed economies.
- The Romanian authorities initiated the first privatizations in the banking system by 1999 (Vogiazas and Nikolaidou 2011b). The expansion of foreign (and among them the Greek) banks in the Romanian banking system took place around 2001 concurrently with the introduction of the euro and the sharp decline in interest margins in the foreign banks' homeland.

Data for the selected time-series come from the National Bank of Romania, the European Central Bank and the Bank of Greece (for further details, see Table A.1 in the Appendix).

The proposed equation of the determinants of credit risk to be estimated within the ARDL framework over the period December 2001–November 2010 is:

$$\mathbf{LLP = f(LLP_{-t}, LLPG, LM2, LLOAN, UN)} \quad (1)$$

[9] Alternatively, as banking crises have historically been contagious, we aim to investigate whether the Greek banking crisis has affected the neighbouring countries.

where:

LLP is the loan loss provisions as a share of total loans of Romanian banks;
LLP_{-t} is the lagged value of LLP;
LLPG is the loan loss provisions as a share of total loans of Greek banks;
LM2 is the log of Romania's M2;
LLOAN is the log of total loans of Romanian banks;
UN is the Romanian unemployment rate.

Theoretically, we would expect a positive impact on LLPs from LLOAN as a credit expansion may imply deterioration in the loan quality, a negative impact from M2 as it proxies economic activity (so, the higher the economic activity, the lower the credit risk), a positive impact from unemployment (though with a relatively high time lag) and a positive impact from the Greek banks' loan loss provisions given the significant presence of Greek banks in Romania.

3.2 Methodology

In this paper we employ the ARDL approach to cointegration (see Pesaran and Pesaran 1997; Pesaran and Smith 1998 and Pesaran and Shin 1999) as it offers various advantages over the most commonly employed methods for cointegration (the residual based Engle and Granger (1987) test and the maximum likelihood based Johansen (1991, 1995) and Johansen and Juselius (1990) tests). Furthermore, this approach has not yet been fully employed in the relevant literature as already indicated at Sect. 2, although it has become very popular in other areas of economics in recent years.

A key advantage associated with the ARDL modelling approach is that it can be applied to variables that have different order of integration (which is the case in the particular study – see the order of integration of the variables on Table A.2 in the Appendix). In this respect, there is no need to test the integration properties of the series a priori when employing this approach. Furthermore, the ARDL model allows a large number of lags to be considered in order to capture the data generating process in a general to specific framework while it allows a dynamic error correction model (ECM) to be derived which integrates the short-run dynamics with the long-run equilibrium without losing long-run information (see Masih and Hamdan 2008; Mallick and Agarwal 2007; Shrestha and Chowdhury 2005).

Given that the variables used in this study have different orders of integration (mix of I(0), I(1) and I(2)), and the fact that this approach has not been fully employed in previous studies that investigate the determinants of credit risk, it seems that it is the most appropriate method to be used here.

The ARDL approach to cointegration estimates $(p+1)^k$ number of regressions to get the optimal lag length for each variable, where p is the maximum number of lags to be used while k is the number of variables in the equation. In this study, we use monthly data and as such we choose 12 lags as the maximum lag (see Pesaran and Pesaran 1997). The optimal lag-length of each variable in the model is based on either the Schwartz-Bayesian selection criterion or the Akaike selection criterion.

The ARDL framework for (1) is the following:

$$\Delta LLP_t = \delta_0 + \sum_{i=1}^{p} \varepsilon_i \Delta LLP_{t-1} + \sum_{i=1}^{p} \varphi_i \Delta LLPG_{t-i} + \sum_{i=1}^{p} \phi_i \Delta LM2_{t-i} + \sum_{i=1}^{p} \kappa_i \Delta LLOAN_{t-i} + \sum_{i=1}^{p} \gamma_i \Delta UN_{t-i} + \lambda_1 LLP_{t-1} + \lambda_2 LLPG_{t-1} + \lambda_3 LM2_{t-1} + \lambda_4 LLOAN_{t-1} + \lambda_5 UN_{t-1} + u_{1t} \quad (2)$$

In the above equation, the terms with the summation signs represent the error correction dynamics while the second part (the terms with λ_s) corresponds to the long-run relationship. The null hypothesis in the above equation is: $\lambda_1 = \lambda_2 = \lambda_3 = \lambda_4 = \lambda_5 = 0$ which indicates the non-existence of a long-run relationship.

4 Empirical Findings

Given the maximum number of lags set (12) and the number of variables used (5), the total number of regressions estimated within the ARDL framework is $(12+1)^5 = 371{,}293$. In view of the significant computational burden, we reduced the number of variables included in the lag selection process. Specifically, after various specification trials and following the empirical literature findings[10] we set the lag-length of unemployment at 10. We select the Schwarz-based model which is $(1, 1, 0, 0)$ as it has lower prediction error in comparison to the Akaike-based model.

Table A.3 in the Appendix provides the key regression statistics and the diagnostic test statistics of the ARDL model which are all very satisfactory apart from heteroskedasticity (which is normal to detect given that the variables are of mixed orders of integration). To deal with this we provide the adjusted estimates based on White's adjusted standard errors (see Table A.4 in the Appendix).

[10] Related literature suggests that unemployment has an impact on non-performing loans after almost a year. See Jakubic and Hermanek (2008), Baboucek and Jancar (2005).

Table 1 Estimated long run coefficients using the ARDL approach (Dependent variable is LLP)

Regressor	Coefficient	t-ratio
LLPG	2.8581	(20.67)
LM2	−0.0142	(4.22)
LLOAN	0.0118	(4.83)
C	0.0109	(3.19)
UN(−10)	.9861E-4	(2.52)

Table 2 Error correction representation for the selected ARDL model (Dependent variable is dLLP)

Regressor	Coefficient	t-ratio
dLLPG	2.0972	(12.09)
dLM2	−0.0042	(3.56)
dLLOAN	0.0035	(3.97)
dC	0.0033	(2.75)
dUN(−10)	.2935E-4	(2.66)
ecm(−1)	−0.2977	(5.05)
$R^2 = 0.84$	DW-statistic = 2.0602	

The long-run estimates of the ARDL on Table 1 below, indicate that all variables are statistically significant (at the 1 % level) and have the expected sign. Specifically, the Greek crisis (proxied by Greek banks loan-loss provisions) seems to have a high positive influence in the long run on Romanian defaults while unemployment has a significant positive impact on non-performing loans with a 10 month lag. Furthermore, Romanian credit expansion has a positive impact on non-performing loans in the long run which may suggest that Romanian banks expand loans at the expense of their quality. This finding supports Gavin and Hausmann (1996) who argue that excessive credit growth is a primary factor that triggers banking crises as usually it goes hand in hand with a decline in credit standards. Finally, M2 that proxies economic activity has the expected negative effect on defaults. Our findings support the evidence provided by Quagliariello 2004; Baboucek and Jancar 2005; Vogiazas and Nikolaidou 2011a, b among others.

The short-run dynamics of the model are given on Table 2. Again all variables are statistically significant and have the expected sign. As in the long-run, the Greek crisis appears to have a very influential role on Romania's non-performing loans also in the short-run. A change in economic activity has a statistically significant negative effect on the change in non-performing loans while the change in loans granted and in unemployment has a statistically significant positive effect (with unemployment having a very small coefficient, though). The ECM is highly significant and with the expected negative sign pointing to the existence of a long-run relationship between the variables. Also, the size of the ECM's coefficient (−0.30) suggests a relatively quick adjustment process. Almost 30 % of the disequilibria of the previous month's shock adjust back to the long run equilibrium in the current month.

5 Conclusions

Internationally, the number of empirical studies trying to link macroeconomic factors and the asset quality of the banking sector has been growing rapidly in recent years. Addressing the high level of nonperforming loans remains a major challenge as important post-crisis challenges remain.

In this study we used the ARDL approach to cointegration to investigate the deterministic factors of non-performing loans in the Romanian financial system; a system dominated by foreign-owned commercial banks. The use of this approach seems to be the most appropriate given the different levels of integration of variables and the fact that it offers various advantages over the Engle-Granger and the Johansen's ML approach to cointegration. The novelty of the paper lies in the fact that it introduces proxies for the Greek crisis. Apart from the standard hypotheses investigated in the empirical literature, the study is motivated by the hypothesis that the Greek crisis matters for the neighbourhood. Empirical evidence suggests that macroeconomic variables, specifically the unemployment rate and M2 jointly with bank-specific variables (credit growth) and the Greek-specific variable (Greek loan loss provisions) influence the credit risk of the Romanian banking system both in the short and the long-run. Based on these findings, the hypothesis that Romanian credit risk is responsive to the country's macro fundaments and bank-specific factors is confirmed. Furthermore, there is strong evidence that supports the hypothesis of linking Greek-specific indicators to the quality of the Romanian loan portfolio. The Romanian non performing loans seem to be adversely affected by risks arising from the Greek twin crises.

Our findings have several implications in terms of policy and regulation. Specifically, the macroeconomic significant variables identified may serve as leading indicators of credit risk deterioration. As most SEE economies rely heavily on the financial sector in terms of growth prospects, regulators should ensure financial stability by remaining vigilant on the neighbourhood countries' macroeconomic prospects and the potential contagion risk arising from the Greek banks' subsidiaries in Romania.

This study proxied credit risk by loan loss provisions. Given the increasing research interest on macroeconomic credit risk modelling, there is a need for further empirical investigations using alternative proxies (such as non-performing loans) and methodological approaches (such as VECM). This way, we can validate the consistency and robustness of the results. Furthermore, and as more data series become available, it would be interesting to re-examine the issue using sample period sub-sets.

Appendix

Table A.1 The dataset

Indicators	Definition – interpretation	Source
Credit risk indicator		
Loss loan provisions/ total loans (R)	Doubtful and loss loans provisions to total loans granted by credit institutions, excluding off-balance-sheet items	National Bank of Romania & Authors' calculations
Macroeconomic indicators		
Unemployment	Registered unemployment rate (%)	National Bank of Romania and European Central Bank
M2	Intermediate money. Comprises M1 plus highly liquid deposits	National Bank of Romania
Credit	Total loans granted by Romanian credit institutions	National Bank of Romania
Greek crisis indicators		
Loss loan provisions/ total loans (GR)	Loss loans provisions to total loans granted by Greek credit institutions	Bank of Greece and Authors' calculations

Table A.2 Unit root tests

	ADF test statistic (constant)	p-value	ADF test statistic (constant and trend)	p-value	Transformation
Loss loan provisions/total loans (R)	−2.898[a]	0.049	−3.775	0.021	First differences
Unemployment	−6.024	0.000	−4.600	0.001	None
M2	−12.393	0.000	−12.590	0.000	First differences logs
Credit	−4.246	0.000	−4.480	0.002	First differences logs
Loss loan provisions/total loans (GR)	−5.093	0.000	−5.237	0.000	Second differences

[a]5 % significance level

Table A.3 ARDL(1,1,0,0) selected based on Schwarz Bayesian Criterion (Dependent variable is LLP)

Regressor	Coefficient	t-ratio	
LLP(−1)	0.7023	(11.91)	
LLPG	2.0972	(12.09)	
LLPG(−1)	−1.2464	(4.70)	
LM2	−0.0042	(3.59)	
LLOAN	0.0035	(3.97)	
C	0.0033	(2.75)	
UN(−10)	.2935E-4	(2.66)	
$R^2 = 0.99856$			
S.E. of regression = .5625E-3	F-stat. F(6, 79) 9113.9[.000]		
Mean of dependent variable = 0.016	S.D. of dependent variable .014278		
Residual sum of squares = .2500E-4	Equation log-likelihood 525.1700		
Akaike Info. criterion = 518.1700	Schwarz Bayesian criterion 509.5798		
DW-statistic = 2.0602	Durbin's h-statistic = −.33315[.739]		
	Diagnostic tests		
Test statistics	LM version		F version
Serial correlation	$X^2(12) = 18.1513$ [.111]		F(12, 67) = 1.4937 [.149]
Functional form	X^2 (1) = .27172 [.602]		F(1, 78) = .24722 [.620]
Normality	X^2 (2) = 18.9182 [.000]		Not applicable
Heteroscedasticity	$X^2(1) = 22.5167$ [.000]		F(1, 84) = 29.7936 [.000]

Table A.4 ARDL(1,1,0,0,10) selected based on Schwarz Bayesian criterion (Based on white's heteroscedasticity adjusted S.E.'s. Dependent variable is LLP)

Regressor	Coefficient	t-ratio
LLP(−1)	0.7023	(8.22)
LLPG	2.0972	(6.97)
LLPG(−1)	−1.2464	(3.03)
LM2	−0.0042	(3.13)
LLOAN	0.0035	(3.21)
C	0.0033	(2.83)
UN(−10)	.2935E-4	(1.50)

References

Abedola SS, Wan Yusoff WS, Dalahan J (2011) An ARDL approach to the determinants of nonperforming loans in Islamic banking system in Malaysia. Kuwait Chap Arabian J Bus Manag Rev 1(1):20–30

Baboucek I, Jancar M (2005) Effects of macroeconomic shock to the quality of the aggregate loan portfolio. Czech National Bank, working paper series, no. 1, pp 1–62

Blaschke W, Jones M, Majnoni G, Peria SM (2001) Stress testing of financial systems: an overview of issues, methodologies, and FSAP experiences. IMF working paper, no. 188, pp 2–56
Boss M (2002) A macroeconomic credit risk model for stress testing the Austrian credit portfolio. OeNB, financial stability report, no. 4, pp 64–82
Delgado J, Saurina J (2004) Credit risk and loan loss provisions. An analysis with macroeconomic variables. Banco de Espana working paper, no. 12, p.11–41
Demirgüc-Kunt A, Detragiache E (1998) The determinants of banking crises in developing and developed countries. IMF Staff Pap 45:81–109
Engle R, Granger C (1987) Co-integration and error correction: representation, estimation and testing. Econometrica 35:251–276
Foglia A (2008) Stress testing credit risk: a survey of authorities' approaches. Bank of Italy working paper, no. 37, p.1–24
Gambera M (2000) Simple forecasts of bank loan in the business cycle. Emerg Issues Ser 3:1–27
Gavin M, Hausmann R (1996) The roots of banking crises: the macroeconomic context. Inter-American bank working paper, no. 318, pp 1–20
Greenidge K, Grosvenor T (2009) Forecasting non-performing loans in Barbados. Bank of Barbados working paper p.1–34
Hardy D, Pazarbasioglu C (1998) Leading indicators of banking crisis: was Asia different? IMF working papers, no. 91, pp 1–32
Hoggarth G, Logan A, Zicchino L (2005) Macro stress tests of UK Banks. BIS papers, no. 22, pp 392–408
IMF (2010) Romania: financial sector stability assessment. Country report no. 10/47, pp 1–66
Jakubic P, Hermanek J (2008) Stress testing of the Czech banking sector. Institute of Economic Studies. Charles University in Prague working paper, 2, p.1–19
Johansen S (1991) Estimation and hypothesis testing of cointegration vectors in Gaussian vector autoregressive models. Econometrica 59:1551–1580
Johansen S (1995) Likelihood-based inference in cointegrated vector autoregressive models. Oxford University Press, Oxford
Johansen S, Juselius K (1990) Maximum likelihood estimation and inference on cointegration – with applications to the demand for money. Oxf Bull Econ Stat 52:169–210
Kalfaoglou F (2006) Stress testing of the Greek banking system. Bank Greece Econ Bull 27:43–62
Kalirai H, Scheicher M (2002) Macroeconomic stress testing: preliminary evidence for Austria. OeNB, financial stability report, no. 3, pp 58–74
Louzis D, Vouldis A, Metaxas V (2010) Macroeconomic and bank-specific determinants of non-performing loans in Greece: a comparative study of mortgage, business and consumer loan portfolios. Bank of Greece working paper, no. 110, pp 1–41
Mallick H, Agarwal S (2007) Impact of real interest rates on real output growth in India: a long-run analysis in a liberalized financial regime. Singapore Econ Rev 52(2):215–231
Masih M, Hamdan B (2008) The impact of monetary policy on deposit and lending rates in industrial and developing countries: an application of ARDL approach. J Int Finance Econ 8(3):114–122
NBR (2011) Financial stability report 2010, pp 1–116
Pesaran MH, Pesaran B (1997) Working with Microfit 4.0: interactive econometric analysis. Oxford University Press, Oxford
Pesaran MH, Smith RP (1998) Structural analysis of cointegrating VARs. J Econ Surv 12:471–505
Pesaran MH, Shin Y (1999) An autoregressive distributed lag modelling approach to cointegration analysis. In: Strom S, Holly A, Diamond P (eds) Econometrics and economic theory in the 20th century: the Ragner Frisch Centennial Symposium. Cambridge University Press, Cambridge
Pesola J (2001) The role of macroeconomic shocks in banking crises. Bank of Finland discussion paper, no. 6, 1–64
Quagliariello M (2004) Banks' performance over the business cycle: a panel analysis on Italian intermediaries. University of York, Discussion papers in economics, 17, p.1–56.

Shrestha MB, Chowdhury K (2005) ARDL modelling approach to testing the financial liberalisation hypothesis, University of Wollongong working paper, pp 5–15
Sims C (1980) Macroeconomics and reality. Econometrica 48:1–48
Trenca I, Benyovszki A (2008) Credit risk, a macroeconomic model application for Romania. Finance Challenges Future 7:118–126
Virolainen K (2004) Macro stress testing with a macroeconomic credit risk model for Finland. Bank of Finland discussion papers, no. 18, p. 1–48
Vogiazas S, Nikolaidou E (2011a) Investigating the deterministic factors of non-performing loans: evidence from the Romanian banking system. Paper presented at the 3rd international conference on the economies of Balkan and Eastern Europe countries in the changed world, EBEEC, Pitesti, 5–8 May
Vogiazas S, Nikolaidou E (2011b) Investigating the determinants of non-performing loans in the Romanian banking system: an empirical study with reference to the Greek crisis. Econ Res Int J, Article ID 214689. doi:10.1155/2011/214689
Zeman J, Jurca P (2008) Macro stress testing of the Slovak banking sector. National bank of Slovakia working paper, pp. 1–26

Part III
Regional Policy, Rural Development and Information Society

Competitiveness and Cohesion in the European Union: A Dilemma?

Stilianos Alexiadis, Christos Ladias, and Sotirios Milionis

1 Introduction

The Lisbon strategy, and its successor 'Europe 2020', aims to make Europe the most competitive and dynamic knowledge-based economy in the world capable of sustainable growth (promoting a more resource efficient, greener and more competitive economy) with more and better jobs and greater social and territorial cohesion (inclusive growth). Nevertheless, it might be argued that this is in sharp contrast to another aim of the EU, that of regional cohesion. This paper attempts to approach this issue empirically using a model that attributes the process of regional growth to the degree of technology adoption. The rest of the paper is laid out as follows: Sect. 2 summarizes what we can learn from an overview of the issue of regional cohesion in Europe. These considerations are introduced in the ambit of a single model in Sect. 3. This model is submitted to the usual econometric tests yielding the main findings in Sect. 4. Section 5 concludes the paper.

The findings, interpretations and conclusions are entirely those of the authors and do not necessarily represent the official position, policies or views of the Ministry of Rural Development and Foods and/or the Greek Government.

S. Alexiadis (✉)
Department of Agricultural Policy and Documentation, Division of Agricultural Statistics, Ministry of Rural Development and Foods, Athens, Greece
e-mail: salexiadis7@aim.com

C. Ladias
Department of Regional Economic Development, University of Central Greece, Levadia, Greece

S. Milionis
Hellenic Tourist Properties SA, Athens, Greece

A. Karasavvoglou and P. Polychronidou (eds.), *Balkan and Eastern European Countries in the Midst of the Global Economic Crisis*, Contributions to Economics,
DOI 10.1007/978-3-7908-2873-3_8,

2 Regional Cohesion in the European Union

'Economic and social cohesion', is mentioned in the Preamble of the Treaty of Rome and has become one of the major goals of the EU. This is formulated in the Single European Act (title XIV, currently title XVII, Articles 2 and 4). According to Article 158 of the Rome Treaty 'reducing disparities between the levels of development of the various regions and the backwardness of the least favoured regions or islands, including rural areas' is one of the primary objectives of EU development policies. This objective can be justified on the ground that 'imbalances do not just imply a poorer quality of life for the most disadvantaged regions and the lack of life-chances open to their citizens, but indicate an under-utilisation of human potential and the failure to take advantage of economic opportunities which benefit the Union as a whole' (European Commission 1996, p. 13).

Regional cohesion is seen as vital to the success of several other key policy objectives, such as the single market, monetary union, and EU competitiveness (European Commission 2004). The strongest argument for regional policies lies in the long-run persistence and even widening of regional disparities. Market forces and social trends are increasing the geographical concentration of activities. Differences in output, labour productivity and income across the regions of the EU are far more extreme than in similar economies such as the US or Japan. The richest regions on the EU are eight times richer than the poorest regions. The primary dimension of income disparities remains East–west, with a weaker North–south dynamic and core-periphery at both EU and national levels. As a result, the EU has implemented a range of development policies and projects (and continues to do so) to achieve regional convergence, such as the Mediterranean Integrated Programs, the direction of funds towards less-advanced areas of Europe from sources, such as the European Regional Development Fund (ERDF), the European Social Fund (ESF) – the two 'Structural Funds' – and the 'Cohesion Fund'. Cohesion policy aims to promote a more balanced territorial development; a policy broader than the 'conventional' regional policy, which is specifically linked to the ERDF. The Structural Funds cover a wide range of areas – technological Research and Development (R&D), the information society, support for business, infrastructure development (transport, telecoms, healthcare and education), energy, risk prevention, the environment, employment, tourism, culture, etc. There are many potential recipients, such as business (especially SMEs),[1] associations, public bodies and individuals. It is up to each individual country to divide the funds between the EU's 'Convergence Objective' and regions covered by the 'Competitive and Employment Objective'. Countries then use the funds to finance thematic programmes covering the whole country (for instance on environment, transport, etc.) or programmes channelling funds to particular regions.

[1] Recent empirical research has produced clear evidence that new and small firms can be a key contributor to job creation but this contribution varies spatially.

The current economic crisis has revealed structural weaknesses in several European regions, irrespective of their level of economic and social or sectoral development. Some sectors are more vulnerable to crisis than others. For instance, regions with a high share of export-oriented activities, such as tourism, face the challenge of decreasing demand and job-losses. Consequently, the degree of vulnerability of the EU regions is unevenly distributed across Europe. This puts the issue of regional cohesion in Europe in a fresh premise. The enlargement of the EU to 25 Member States, and later to 27, together with the intensification of cooperation between the EU and Norway and Switzerland, presents an unprecedented challenge for the competitiveness and internal cohesion of the Union. As a result, regional policy in the EU has to tackle with an 'inconsistent triangle' (Mancha-Novarro and Garrido-Yserte 2008): budget restrictions, the aspirations of the new member-states as the main beneficiaries of the European regional policy and the vindication of the four cohesion countries (Ireland, Spain, Portugal and Greece) of maintaining their financial resources.

Given this context, the next section attempts to construct an appropriate framework to examine empirically the possible contradiction between the aim of regional cohesion and overall competitiveness.

3 Regional Cohesion and Technology Adoption

A useful starting point is the neoclassical theory, since the assumptions of this theory actually carry implications for the regional convergence/divergence debate. In the neoclassical model, a factor that promotes, and accelerates, regional convergence is the process of technology diffusion; a sort of 'entropic trend' towards spatial homogeneity (Camagni and Capello 2010). A central tenant of this model is that all regions are able to absorb technology to the same degree, so that the higher the technological gap the higher the effect on growth, ceteris paribus. However, it may be argued that large gaps do not necessarily promote convergence in this way. The argument runs as follows. Technology adoption is not a simple and automatic process. Instead, it requires that lagging regions should have the appropriate *infrastructure* to adopt the technological innovations; an argument commonly attributed to Abramovitz (1986). It is quite possible that a significant technological gap is associated with unfavourable conditions for the adoption of new technological innovations.[2]

The starting point of the model in this paper is the idea that, in order to make sense of these recent empirical results, we must depart from the standard neoclassical framework and think in terms of a broader model that allows for convergence mechanisms other than diminishing returns. Assume that the ability of a region to implement technological innovations (ξ) is *endogenously* determined, as a decreasing

[2] Innovation is an iterative process, building upon the results of R&D activities and in turn informing and being informed by new research and innovations in product and processes.

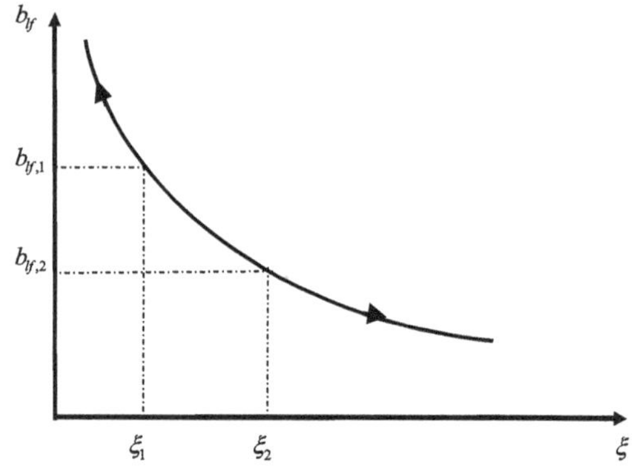

Fig. 1 Regional divergence

function of the 'technological proximity', expressed in terms of the *initial* technological gap, which we subsequently denote as $b_{lfi,0}$. Thus, $\xi_i = f(b_{lfi,0})$, with $f' < 0$, or in a non-linear specification: $\xi_i = \rho b_{lfi,0}^{-\pi}$ with $\rho, \pi > 0$. According to this specification, the rate of adoption is not constant but varies across regions, according to the size of the gap.[3] For a given value of ρ, a high technological gap implies a low capacity to absorb technology. The parameter ρ can be interpreted as a constant underlying rate of diffusion, which would apply to all regions if there were no infrastructure/resource constraints upon technological adoption. However, the existence of such constraints causes the actual rate to diverge from ρ, depending on the value of π, which determines the extent to which the existing gap impacts on the rate of diffusion. Alternatively, the higher the technological gap, the slower the rate of technological adoption (ξ_i). To add an extra injection of realism we assume that the growth rate of output per-worker (y_i) is an increasing function of ξ_i: $g_{y_i} = h(\xi_i)$ with $h' > 0$, then $g_{y_i} = h(f(b_{lfi,0}))$, with $h' \cdot f' < 0$. Consider a two-region's economy ($i = 1,\ 2$) with $b_{lf1,0} - b_{lf2,0} > 0$, and $\xi_1 - \xi_2 < 0$, implying that $g_{y_1} - g_{y_2} < 0$. If $(\Delta\xi_{1,2})_t \to \infty$, then $(\Delta b_{lf1,2})_t \to \infty$, as $t \to \infty$ the two regions move towards different directions (Fig. 1). Regions with relatively large technology gaps may fall progressively behind. In this example catch-up is feasible only if ξ increases from ξ_1 to ξ_1', or more generally $\frac{\partial \xi_i}{\partial t} > 0$, as shown in Fig. 2. One further point is worth noticing in Fig. 2. If $(\Delta\xi_{1,2})_t \to 0$, then $(\Delta b_{lf1,2})_t \to 0$, and region 1 converges with region 2.

According to the model outlined in this section, regional policy[4] should enhance investment in low-income regions in order to increase their adoptive abilities. However, a high technological gap might indicate that they lack the necessary conditions to allow for an effective adoption of technology. Investment in regions

[3] A more detailed elaboration of this model can be found in Alexiadis (2010).

[4] Regional policy can take several forms, e.g. transfer payments, public investment, provision of incentives to encourage private investment, etc.

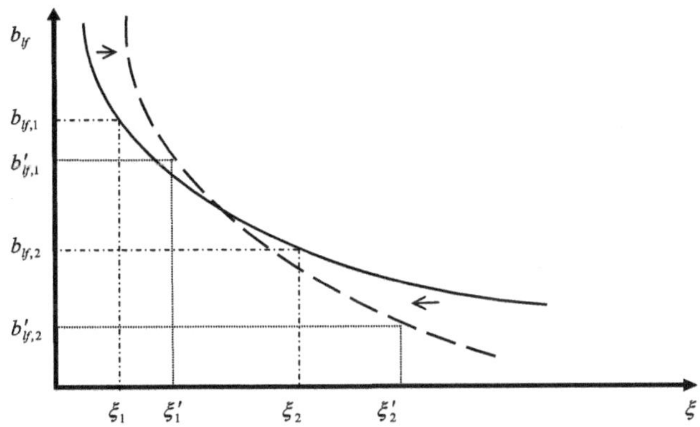

Fig. 2 Catch-up

with high adaptive abilities will increase their growth rates and the growth of the economy as a whole. Regions with low adaptive ability will, however, experience a fall in their growth rates, widening the gap between low and high productivity regions. A dilemma between competitiveness and regional convergence seems to be inevitable. Nevertheless, it is possible to identify cases in which the two aims can be achieved simultaneously. Transfer payments, for example, in poor regions and investment in advanced regions will increase both regional convergence and overall competitiveness. Which specific measure will be applied depends on the available resources, budget constraints, the weight that policy-makers attach to regional cohesion, the 'tolerable' level and time length of regional inequalities.

The econometric analysis contained in this paper draws upon such tools as empirical literature on regional convergence and makes extensive use of two alternative tests for convergence, namely *absolute* and *conditional* convergence:

$$g_i = a + b_1 y_{i,0} + \varepsilon_i \tag{1}$$

$$g_i = a + b_1 y_{i,0} + b_{\mathbf{X_i}} \mathbf{X_i} + \varepsilon_i \tag{2}$$

where $g_i = (y_{i,T} - y_{i,0})$ is the growth rate and ε_i is the error-term. The rate of convergence is calculated as $\beta = -[\ln(b_1 + 1)]/T$, where T is the number of years in the period. Absolute convergence is signalised by $b_1 < 0$. Conditional convergence is based upon the argument that different regional characteristics, such as technological conditions, will lead to different steady-states. A test for conditional convergence, therefore, is more suitable to accommodate the empirical analysis.

Technical change originates either from within the region, namely indigenous innovation (IC_i), or technological spillovers from adopting innovations created elsewhere, i.e. adoption of technology (ADP_i). In the former case, technical change may be approximated in several ways.[5] Nevertheless, in this paper technical change is approximated in terms of the 'Human Resources in Science and Technology' (HRST), i.e. persons who have completed a tertiary education in a field of science or technology and/or are employed in science and technology. The second source of technical growth is approximated as the percentage of total employment in technologically dynamic sectors (ADP_i), which indicates a capacity for technology adoption, since these are taken to apply high technology. Therefore, a 'technologically-conditioned' model of regional cohesion can be structured as follows:

$$g_i = a + b_1 y_{i,0} + b_2 IC_{i,0} + b_3 ADP_{i,0} + \varepsilon_i \tag{3}$$

The time dimension of variables describing technology[6] refers to the initial time. From an econometric point of view, this helps to avoid the problem of endogeneity. Moreover, Pigliaru (2003) claims that models which include measures of technology require data on total factor productivity. In the absence of such data, econometric estimation requires that the technological variables ought to be included in initial values. Broadly speaking, it is anticipated that $b_2 > 0$, since high levels of innovation are normally associated with high levels of growth and vice versa. However, it is not automatically the case that this condition promotes convergence. If poor regions have a low level of $IC_{i,0}$, then no significant impacts on growth are anticipated and, hence, it may be difficult to converge with advanced regions. The latter case is more likely. The $ADP_{i,0}$ variable reflects two distinct features, namely the initial level of 'technological adoption' and the degree to which existing conditions in a region allow further adoption of technology. A low level of $ADP_{i,0}$ combined with a high rate of growth may indicate, ceteris paribus, that less advanced regions are able to adopt technology, which is transformed into high growth rates and subsequently to catch-up with the advanced regions. Conversely, a low value for $ADP_{i,0}$ may indicate that although there is significant potential for technology adoption, infrastructure conditions are not appropriate to technology adoption and, therefore, there are no significant impacts on growth. If the latter effect dominates then convergence between technologically lagging and advanced regions is severely constrained.

---

[5] Just as an example, Pigliaru (2003) uses the 'propensity to innovate', which can be measured in terms of the number of patents per-capita in each region. Empirical applications can be found in Alexiadis (2010b), Alexiadis and Korres (2010).

[6] These two variables are in accordance with the notion of 'smart growth', as formulated in the strategy 'Europe 2020', i.e. strengthening knowledge and innovation as drivers of future growth. The structural funds are the most important financial instruments for supporting the renewed Lisbon strategy and in some countries were able to increase their GDP by almost 4 %. This strategy is monitored by a set of indicators, covering the domain of employment, innovation, research, economic reforms, social cohesion, overall economic and environmental background. In 2004, the European Commission suggested a 'short list' of 14 structural indicators, allowing for a "concise presentation and a better assessment of achievement over time vis-à-vis the Lisbon agenda". These indicators include for example, gross domestic product per-capita and per-worker, employment rate, gross domestic expenditure on R&D, long-run unemployment rate, etc. Of these indicators only the 'dispersion of employment rates' has, by definition, an explicit spatial dimension.

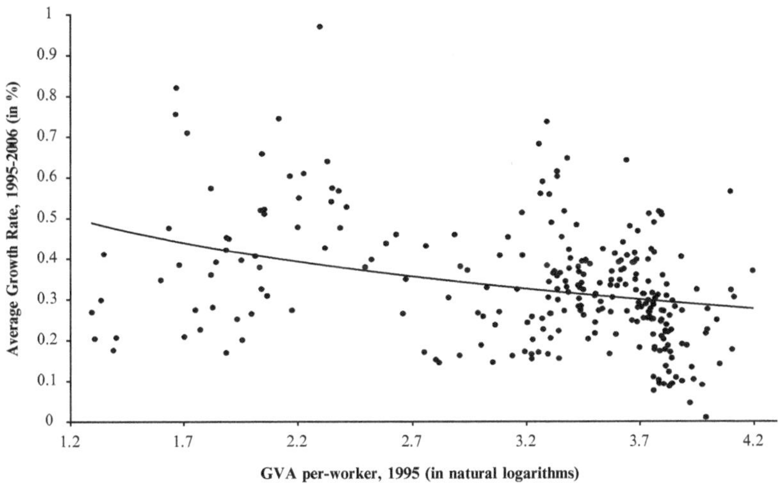

Fig. 3 Absolute convergence

4 Econometric Estimation and Discussion

In this paper we exploit data on Gross Value Added (GVA) per-worker since this measure is a major component of differences in the economic performance of regions and a direct outcome of the various factors that determine regional competitiveness (Martin 2001). The European Statistical Office (EUROSTAT) is the main source for data used in this paper. Regional GDP data and all the structural data stem from this source. The regional groupings used in this paper are those delineated by EUROSTAT and refer to 267 NUTS-2 regions.[7]

The dynamics of regional growth for Europe between 1995 and 2006 are summarised in Fig. 3, which shows a scatterplot of the average annual growth rate against the initial level of GVA per-worker. Even a cursory analysis of the EU-27 data suggests that the inverse relationship between growth rate and initial level of labour productivity is not so obvious. A closer examination of Fig. 3, however, suggests that the convergence property is restricted to a group of regions exceeding a certain level of initial labour productivity in 1995 (about 3 in natural logarithms). Regions above this threshold could be described as exhibiting β-convergence. On average this group has experienced a rate of growth over the period of 0.71 % per annum while the regions with initial GVA per-worker below the threshold have grown at a

[7] Each EU country has a different way of dividing its territory into administrative units. For the purposes of managing programmes and comparing statistics, the EU devised the NUTS system – dividing each country into statistical units (NUTS regions). The NUTS (Nomenclature des Unités Territorial les Statistiques) regions are not the same with the so-called 'Euro-regions', which are associations without a precise legal status, dating back to the period after World War II when local politicians in border regions tried to promote common interests on both sides of the borders.

Table 1 Regional convergence, GVA per-worker, EU regions: 1995–2006

N = 267 NUTS-2 regions, ordinary least squares	Equation (1)	Equation (3)
a	0.5714[a]	0.6144[a]
b_1	−0.0747[a]	−0.0825[a]
b_2		0.0014
b_3		0.0203[b]
Implied β	0.0065[a]	0.0071[a]
LIK	147.552	153.832
AIC	−291.104	−299.664
SBC	−283.929	−285.315

AIC, *SBC* and *LIK* denote the *Akaike*, the *Schwartz-Bayesian* information criteria and Log-Likelihood, respectively
[a]indicates statistical significance at 95 % level of confidence
[b]90 % level

rate of 1.68 %. The latter group corresponds to almost one quarter of the total NUTS-2 regions of the EU27 while its composition refers mainly to regions from the New Member-States with fewer regions from the 'old' Member-States, located in Greece and Portugal; two member-states characterized by low productivity, relative to the EU-27 average.

The presence or absence of regional convergence, however, cannot be confirmed by visual inspection alone. Therefore, the models of absolute and conditional convergence are estimated econometrically (Table 1).

Estimation of (1) suggests that the regions of the EU converge at a low rate (0.65 % per-annum). This cross-section test provides some, albeit, very limited evidence that the NUTS2 regions of EU-27 are in the process of absolute convergence with low productivity regions growing faster than high productivity areas. Nevertheless, given the extremely slow convergence rate estimated,[8] it would take a very long time for all regions to reach a common level of productivity.

A positive coefficient is estimated for the variable describing technology creation, which does not necessarily promote convergence as such, since regions with relatively high initial level of innovation, normally regions with high levels of productivity, exhibit relatively higher rates of growth. A positive value for the $ADP_{i,0}$ variable is also estimated. This suggests that, on average, regions with low values of $ADP_{i,0}$ at the start of the period grow slower than regions with high values, ceteris paribus. If technologically backward regions were successful in adopting technology, which subsequently is transformed into faster growth, then the estimated coefficient b_3 would be negative. While lagging regions may not be

[8] This slow process of regional convergence can, possibly, be explained by the low degree of labour mobility that characterises the European regions, due to linguistic and cultural barriers. As Boldrin and Canova (2001, p. 243) state 'while capital is moving around Europe, labour is definitely not'. Obstfeld and Peri (1998) report that labour mobility in Germany, Italy and the UK over the period 1970–1995 was only about one-third of the US level.

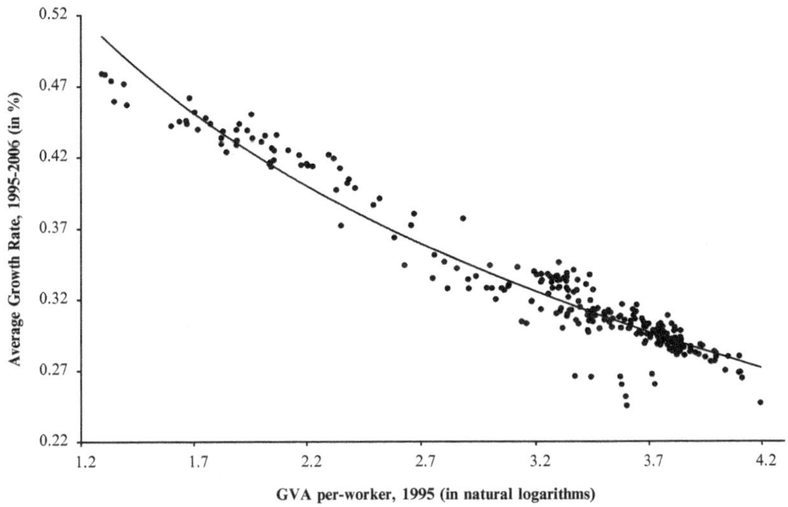

Fig. 4 Conditional convergence

innovative deserts, the evidence suggests that these regions do have specific problems. In particular, the condition $b_3 > 0$ indicates that infrastructure conditions in lagging regions are inhibiting this process of technology adoption. Technology adoption, although it might be the best 'vehicle' for lagging regions, nevertheless, this is a process which might be difficult, especially during the early stages of development when conditions are least supportive. Normally, conditional convergence implies a slower rate of convergence. Nevertheless introducing the technological variable increases the estimated rate of convergence (0.71 %).

Figure 4 partial out the logs of $IC_{i,0}$ and $ADP_{i,0}$ from both the productivity level and average growth rate variables. Clearly, there is a trend for relatively 'poor' regions (i.e. those with an initial level of productivity less than 3, as indicated by Fig. 3) to exhibit faster rates of growth. Comparing Figs. 3 and 4, it might be argued that *if* the EU regions did not vary in their initial level of technology creation and adoption, there would be a strong tendency for low-productivity regions to grow faster than high-productivity ones.

The superiority of the model described by (3) is supported by both the criteria for model selection applied here, namely the *Akaike* (AIC) and the *Schwartz-Bayesian* (SBC) information criteria. As a rule of thumb, the best fitting model is the one that yields the minimum values for the AIC or the SBC criterion. As shown in Table 1, both the AIC and SBC are minimised for (3) and, consequently this specification is to be preferred. Furthermore, the value of the Log-likelihood (LIK), which increases with the introduction of the technological variables, lends clear support to a perspective that emphasises the importance of technology adoption in the process of regional cohesion.

The empirical analysis is extended further by estimating a model that incorporates the possibility of 'club-convergence'. Although, there are several intuitive approaches for identifying convergence-clubs (e.g. Fisher and Stirböck 2006) nevertheless, the empirical analysis is based upon application of Baumol and

Table 2 Club-convergence

n = 267 NUTS-2 regions, OLS	Equation (4)
a	−0.1226
b_1	0.4486[a]
b_2	−0.0922[a]
b_3	−0.0124
b_4	0.0439[a]
Implied y^*	2.43[a]

[a]indicates statistical significance at 95 % level of confidence
[b]90 % level

Wolff's (1988) specification[9]: $g_i = a + b_1 y_{i,0} + b_2 y_{i,0}^2 + \varepsilon_i$. A pattern of club-convergence is established if $b_1 > 0$ and $b_2 < 0$. Members of a convergence-club are identified as those regions which exhibit an inverse relation between the growth rate and initial level of GVA per-worker and exceed a threshold value of initial GVA per-worker, calculated as: $y^* = -b_1/2b_2$. From a policy point of view, the impact of the technological variables is of particular importance. Thus, introducing these variables in a club-convergence context yields the following regression equation:

$$\mathbf{g_i} = a + b_1 y_{i,0} + b_2 y_{i,0}^2 + b_3 \ln IC_{i,0} + b_4 \ln ADP_{i,0} + \varepsilon_i \qquad (4)$$

The results in Table 2 illustrate several points. The coefficients b_1 and b_2 have the appropriate signs suggesting the existence of two groups across the EU-27 regions; one which includes regions with $y_{i,0} - y^* > 0$ and another including regions with $y_{i,0} - y^* < 0$. The former group corresponds to the convergence-club while the latter constitutes a diverging-club. Turning to the impact of the other explanatory variables, only the $ADP_{i,0}$ variable yields a statistically significant coefficient at the 95 % level. The $IC_{i,0}$ variable indicates a negative relationship with growth for the overall period, which can be interpreted as a source of convergence. The condition $b_4 > 0$, however, suggests a substantial barrier to the diffusion of technology across the regions of the EU-27. In the long-run, regions with high technological gaps at the start of the period grow slower than regions with low gaps, ceteris paribus.

Bearing in mind that a high initial technological gap may also signify inappropriate conditions for technology adoption, then a large gap may not promote convergence. Since $b_4 > 0$, this suggests that for technologically poor regions this problem exists. Alternatively, $b_4 > 0$ indicates that regions with high technological gaps do not have the potential to adopt technology. The empirical findings reported in this section enhance the argument put forward by Fisher and Stirböck (2006) that "technology does not instantaneously flow across regions and countries in Europe" (pp. 710–711). In the lagging and geographically remote regions of the EU, the

[9] Alexiadis (2010a) applies this method in the case of the Greek regions.

Fig. 5 Converging and diverging clubs

adoption process is not immediate and these regions generally access innovations at a later stage. If this time-lag remains, then regional disparities in the EU and the centre-periphery pattern will take a persisting character. Figure 5 shows the spatial distribution of the convergence-club member regions. The convergence club includes, almost exclusively, regions from the 'old' and 'advanced' members-states of the European Union (EU-15). Such an outcome is in accordance with the view put forward by Dunford and Smith (2000), which highlight a significant '*development divide*' between the EU-15 and the East Central Europe (Table 3).

Table 3 Regional convergence and technology, diverging group

n = 49 NUTS-2 regions, OLS	Equation (3)
a	−0.1583
b_1	0.2863[a]
b_2	−0.0062[b]
b_3	0.0486[a]
Implied β	−0.0210[a]

[a]Indicates statistical significance at 95 % level of confidence
[b]90 % level

Conditioning upon levels of technology indicates a diverging tendency for the regions *excluded* from the convergence-club. The estimated value of β is negative and implies a rate of divergence about 2.1 % per-annum. Attention should be drawn to the fact that the estimated value of the adoptive parameter is positive, indicating that regions with a low (high) level of $ADP_{i,0}$ grow at a relatively lower (higher) rate. While $b_2 < 0$ is consistent with the catch-up hypothesis, nevertheless the condition $b_3 > 0$ indicates an opposite effect.

In this light, regional policy should first identify which regions belong in a diverging group and then to determine which regions in this group are characterised by relative high adoptive levels.[10] Improving conditions in these regions will therefore increase their growth rates, enabling them, in a subsequent period, to join the initial convergence-club. This will cause positive effects to the degree of competitiveness of the EU-27 as a whole, improving also the *long-run* process of regional convergence. In this context, a critical question arises: which particular conditions should be the target of regional policy? Accordingly, it may be adequate, but with much caution, to associate the prevailing conditions in the diverging group with a series of structural elements that characterize the regions in this group.

Although it is beyond the scope of this paper to go into detail, nevertheless it is worth mentioning that the list of these elements includes the usual suspects such R&D and conditions related to the structure of the regional economy. In 2005, the R&D intensity[11] measured in terms of R&D expenditure as a percentage of GDP in

[10] These regions have more possibilities to innovate if they are connected to central regions; a view put forward by Rodríguez-Pose and Crescenzi (2008).

[11] A target set is the EU as whole to reach R&D intensity above 3 % βυ 2010, corresponding to the new world-wide division of labour and globalisation. This target is set by the Barcelona Council in 2002 and maintained in the EUROPE 2020 strategy. Only 10 % of the EU regions were able to reach this target. In 2007, only 19 out of 287 NUTS-2 regions corresponding to only (6.6 %) were able to meet the target of 3 %. In particular, three regions in Finland (Pohjois-Suomi, Länsi-Suomi and Etelä-Suomi), four in Sweden (Stockholm, Östra Mellansverige, Västsverige and Sydsverige), seven in Germany (Dresden, Oberbayern, Darmstadt, Karlsruhe, Unterfranken, Stuttgart and Berlin), two in France (Île-de-France and Midi-Pyrénées), two in Austria (Wien and Steiermark) and one in the Netherlands (Noord-Brabant). In some of these regions, capital-cities are located (e.g. Paris, Vienna, Berlin, Stockholm and Helsinki).

the diverging group was less than 0.5 %.[12] Only in two regions the R&D intensity is about 1 % (Mazowieckie in Poland and Bucuresti-Ilfov, the capital-region of Romania[13]). The patent applications to the European Patent Office (EPO) in this group, is less than 5 patents per million inhabitants. In 2006, the HRST indicator was less than 35 %. An exemption is the region of Bucuresti-Ilfov with a percentage above 40 %.[14] An average share of high-tech sectors in total employment was less than 4 % in the diverging group, contrary to the central regions (above 5 %). A similar share can be found in regions Közép-Dunántúl, Közép-Magyarország Nyugat-Dunántúl (in Hungry) and in Bratislavský-Kraj (in Slovakia). The three Hungarian regions are located in close geographical proximity while the regions Bratislavský Kraj and Nyugat-Dunántúl are close to Austria. Agriculture is of importance to the diverging regions and contributes about 3–6 % in their GDP and in several cases over 6 % (mainly in Romania and Bulgaria). The percentage of rural population in these regions is in the range between 20 % and over 50 %. Furthermore, the diverging group exhibits a low degree of business concentration (an exception is Bucuresti-Ilfov) due demographic decline[15] and the rural nature of those regions.[16] These regions are characterized by high unemployment,[17] a large proportion of the labour force employed in declining industrial sectors and a relatively small proportion of young people, reflecting migration to other areas as well as low fertility rates. Low population density[18] and a shrinking labour force

[12] Overall, there is a tendency for R&D expenditure to be higher in urban parts of Europe. R&D spending in Europe is below 2 %, compared to 2.6 % in the US and 3.4 % in Japan, mainly due to low levels of private investment. It would take more than 50 years for Europe to reach the US level of innovation performance.

[13] Over the periods 1998–2000 and 2005–2007, GDP per-capita in these regions was above 75 % of the EU average; a threshold, which is a key criterion for being eligible to support from the Structural Funds. In the remaining regions GDP per-capita is still below the threshold.

[14] The best educated labour force is located in the urbanised regions of. There is a tendency for the best educated labour force to concentrate in or around capital cities; a pattern obvious in Northern Europe and particularly in countries with a low overall proportion of HRST.

[15] Only few EU-27 NUTS-2 regions (e.g. Ireland, Malta and Cyprus) appear to be in a relatively favourable position. An inspection, however, at the NUTS-3 level might reveal a different picture.

[16] Nevertheless, a rural character of a region is not always a disadvantage. Several rural regions, for example, attract retirees, which provide a source of income and future growth.

[17] In 2008, regions with the highest unemployment rates (above 10 %) are mainly located in Southern Spain, Southern Italy, Greece, Eastern part of Germany, Poland, Hungary and Slovakia. The lowest levels can be found in the United Kingdom, Belgium, and the Netherlands as well as in capital city-regions of Eastern Europe.

[18] Population density is defined as the ratio of the population of a territory to its size (inhabitants per km^2). A ratio between 60 and 120 is estimated for the diverging group. In EU-27, the capital city-regions are among the most densely populated, located in central areas of Europe especially around Brussels. In this context, some remarks by Krugman (1991) are highly pertinent: 'It has often been noted that night-time satellite photos of Europe reveal little of political boundaries but clearly suggest a *centre-periphery pattern* whose hub is somewhere in or near Belgium.' (p. 484) [Emphasis added]

intensify income disparities in the diverging group. This puts them in a difficult position to finance essential public goods and services (e.g. health care, housing, transportation, ICT infrastructure) in a sustainable manner in order to avoid increasing social polarisation and poverty and, as a result, the operation of favourable externalities, which will put them in a path of fast growth, is constrained.

In terms of implications for public policy, especially regional policy, this paper raises a number of pertinent issues. 'Spatial development is increasingly understood as a complex, multi-dimensional phenomenon and the illusion about the existence of simple, short-cut strategies progressively abandoned' (Camagni and Capello 2010, p. 12). An important point to grasp from a policy perspective is the impact of technology adoption in the process of regional growth and convergence. The regions in the diverging group lag in terms of headline indicators such as output per-capita and employment levels, as well as knowledge-based indicators such as innovation, patenting and proportion of knowledge-intensive firms. The econometric results, if taken into account by policy makers, require that regional policies should promote high-technology activities and R&D including universities, scientific and research institutions. The list of policy measures, which is not exhaustive, also includes cluster support, modernizes the framework of copyright and trademarks, improves access of SMEs to Intellectual Property Protection, speeds up setting of interoperable standards, and improves access to capital by reducing transaction costs of doing business; identifies bottlenecks and develops strong industrial and knowledge base; encourages knowledge partnerships and strengthens links between business, research, innovation and education. Improvements in education also help employability and progress in increasing the employment rate and thus help poverty to be reduced. A greater capacity for R&D as well as innovation across all sectors, combined with increased efficiency, will foster job creation and improve competitiveness. Reform of regional R&D and innovation systems reinforce cooperation between universities, research and business, implement joint programming and enhance cross-border cooperation; a factor that increases the need for policy coordination. Adjust school curricula towards creativity, innovation and entrepreneurship. Support internationalisation of SMEs, technologies and production methods that reduce natural resource use and increase investment in the EU's existing natural assets. Of particular importance is the transition of manufacturing sectors to greater energy and resource efficiency. Research in cleaner, low carbon technologies will not only help the environment by contributing to fighting climate change, but also will create new business and employment opportunities. Finally, an important question for policy makers is how this situation changes with time. Alternatively, which is the appropriate *timing* for policy intervention? The answer depends very much on the time horizon and the chosen spatial unit given that policy effects differ from region to region.

Nevertheless, developing answers to policy issues requires a good deal of further work. More empirical research with better specified counter-factuals is necessary to evaluate the efficiency of regional policies and programs and the contexts in which they are likely to succeed.

5 Conclusion

In this paper an attempt was made to develop a model of regional cohesion and competitiveness. Taken as a whole, we think that the empirical results are important for the ongoing debate about the dilemma between regional convergence and overall competitiveness. More than ever, policy makers in the EU need independent and encompassing studies like this which can provide critical new information about regional convergence. As in any modelling situation, we cannot know for certain whether a lack of correspondence between our theoretical presuppositions and the available empirical evidence is the result of falsify of our target theory or the approximations and omissions that we employed in specifying the empirical model. Such a study is, by its very nature, limited; it simplifies a complex reality and focuses on a single regional level. It cannot substitute for a detailed analysis of specific regional contexts, not take into consideration the capacity of regions to respond. Regional convergence is a complex phenomenon, based upon a number of factors, which shape, to a considerable extent, the regional policies. There is a need to rethink regional policy along the lines of the implementation of more innovative and region-specific development strategies. Hence, new analytical tools are needed. The relatively fragmented nature of the spatial patterns of mobility and persistence suggests that broad administrative regions are a poor basis for the implementation of policy. Problems of persistence at the lower level end of the distribution and downward mobility are widely spread across the European regions. The regional-geographical dimension is increasingly important for European policy-making by identifying and mobilising territorial capital in each region, by explicitly recognising it as a significant unit in policy-making. Consequently, policy may need to be targeted towards specific localities rather than broad areas such as those, for example, covered by the current regional grouping of the EU. A classification of areas based on the notions of 'converging' and 'diverging' clubs, identified in this paper, may provide a useful framework for policy development at the regional level.

References

Abramovitz M (1986) Catching up forging ahead and falling behind. J Econ Hist 46:385–406

Alexiadis S (2010a) Interregional differences in adoptive abilities: an alternative framework. Reg Sci Inquire 1(2):41–52

Alexiadis S (2010b) Regional convergence clubs and dynamic externalities. Italian J Reg Sci 9(1):41–64

Alexiadis S (2010c) The Nexus between regional growth and technology adoption: a case for club-convergence? Theor Pract Res Econ Fields 1(1):4–11

Alexiadis S, Korres G (2010) Adoption of technology and regional convergence in Europe. Eur Spat Res Policy 17(2):95–105

Baumol W, Wolff E (1988) Productivity growth, convergence and welfare: a reply. Am Econ Rev 78(5):1155–1159

Boldrin M, Canova F (2001) Inequality and convergence in Europe's regions: reconsidering European regional policies. Econ Policy 16:207–253

Camagni R, Capello R (2010) Macroeconomic and territorial policies for regional competitiveness: an EU perspective. Reg Sci Policy Pract 2(1):1–19

Dunford M, Smith A (2000) Catching-up or falling behind? Economic performance and regional trajectories in the New Europe. Econ Geogr 76(2):169–195

European Commission (1996) First report on economic and social cohesion. Office for Official Publications of the European Communities, Luxemburg

European Commission (2004) Third report on social cohesion. Official Publication Office, Luxembourg

Fischer M, Stirböck C (2006) Pan-European regional income growth and club-convergence. Ann Reg Sci 40:693–721

Krugman P (1991) Increasing returns and economic geography. J Polit Econ 99:483–499

Martin R (2001) EMU versus the regions? Regional convergence and divergence in Euroland. J Econ Geogr 1(1):51–80

Mancha-Novarro T, Garrido-Yserte R (2008) Regional policy in the European Union: the cohesion-competitiveness dilemma. Reg Sci Policy Pract 1(1):47–66

Obstfeld M, Peri G (1998) Regional non-adjustment and fiscal policy. Econ Policy 26:205–247

Pigliaru F (2003) Detecting technological catch-up in economic convergence. Metroeconomica 54:161–178

Rodríguez-Pose A, Crescenzi R (2008) Research and development, spillovers, innovation systems and the genesis of regional growth in Europe. Reg Stud 42:51–67

Local Cooperation: A Dynamic Force for Endogenous Rural Development

Fotios Chatzitheodoridis, Anastasios Michailidis, Georgios Theodosiou, and Efstratios Loizou

1 Introduction

Globally, regional development through endogenous forces constitutes a very important rural policy aim especially under the recent global economic context (Theodosiou et al. 2010a). In particular, under the ongoing financial crisis in Greece the endogenous socio-economic development of rural areas focusing on local population or local resources seems to be one-way developmental opportunity. According to Ray, (1999) such practices have been gaining significant acceptance as the most effective way for robust and sustainable rural development. Although the theory of endogenous rural development has been explored by many researchers (Lowe et al. 1998), this paper extends the socio-economic analysis pointing out that any developmental activity must focus not only on localities and their resources but on the interface between the local and extra-local sectors as well.

F. Chatzitheodoridis (✉) • E. Loizou
Department of Agricultural Products Marketing and Quality Control, Terma Kontopoulou, Technological Educational Institute of Western Macedonia, 53100 Florina, Greece
e-mail: fchatzitheo@gmail.com; lstratos@auth.gr

A. Michailidis
School of Agriculture, Department of Agricultural Economics, Aristotle University of Thessaloniki, 54124 Thessaloniki, Greece
e-mail: tassosm@auth.gr

G. Theodosiou
Department of Business Administration, Technological Educational Institute of Larissa, 41110 Larissa, Greece

Technological Educational Institution of Western Macedonia, Kozani, Greece
e-mail: geortheo@yahoo.gr

A. Karasavvoglou and P. Polychronidou (eds.), *Balkan and Eastern European Countries in the Midst of the Global Economic Crisis*, Contributions to Economics, DOI 10.1007/978-3-7908-2873-3_9, © Springer-Verlag Berlin Heidelberg 2013

The dairy industry in Greece has strong positive development prospects as the average monthly expenditure of households for dairy food is about 20% of their total average monthly expenditure and it is continuously increasing (NSSG 2005; Galatoulas 2009). Moreover, with the price rigidity of these products, factors such as consumer preferences and dietary issues crucially affect the need for more healthy and quality products and as a result increase the demand of high added value products (ICAP 2007). According to the same source, the export activity of Greek milk industries is limited mainly to yoghurt products or to "*feta cheese*" which are intended to the European Union.

The production structure of the domestic market of milk and dairy products is characterized by an intense duality. On the one hand there is a relatively large number of enterprises (small or medium), which are designed to meet the local demands and on the other hand there is a small number of big industries which are productively updated and have an excellent distribution network. Moreover, the puzzle of the dairy products market is completed by several food importing enterprises which, inter alia, import and sell milk and dairy products. Additionally, the Association of Greek Livestock (AGL), which has been founded by more than 50 agricultural or livestock cooperatives, edge into the Greek market in order to suspend the constant reduction of milk price that is mainly formed by the big dairy industries. The main aim of AGL is to strengthen the cooperative enterprises of the dairy market by investing to new cooperative dairy plans. More specifically, the adoption of a single cooperative label of fresh milk and dairy products as a barrier to the promotion of long-life milk included among others to the core of the developmental actions of the AGL. In addition, the promotion of dairy and milk cooperative products through a network of a well known super market enterprise, in which the Pan-Hellenic Confederation of Unions of Agricultural Cooperatives is a member, is also a spearhead. According to the data given by the Hellenic Organization of Milk and Meat (ELOGAK 2009), during 2009, there was a positive outcome for the main cooperative dairy and milk industries, since they absorbed the milk production, by increasing their sales and recording profits. The positive economic results of cooperative dairy enterprises, along with the ensuring of the farmers' income, especially in this period of crisis, motivate the cooperative organizations to explore the possibilities in investing to the dairy production sector (Theodosiou et al. 2009, 2010b).

The relatively positive perspectives of the sector due to the increasing trend in the demand for dairy and milk products will be accompanied not only by an increasing competition among big dairy products industries but also by a greater presence of the cooperative dairy industries. The disposal of raw material, in this case of milk, by the producers is the main factor that affects the viability of dairy industries and especially of the cooperatives (Tsourgiannis et al. 2008).

Population, natural resources, technology and local institutions are the basic structural elements that determine an area's development. These four elements, in the light of systems theory, facilitate the analysis of complexity that lays in the area's structure and dynamics, whereas the development is determined by the respective equilibrium established among them, which is a dynamic situation (Chatzitheodoridis 1998).

Historically, agricultural cooperatives have led a successful course which was connected to the life and activities of people in rural areas. On being economic and social organizations they usually have a strategic role in local development (Sdrali and Apostolopoulos 2006; Madane 2002). The recession of agricultural cooperatives' dynamics, mainly due to the declinc of the primary sector and the intense competition that were established by the new globalised market development pattern, was followed by their recovery. The recovery of the agricultural cooperatives was based onto their adjustment, either to new generation cooperatives or to specialized cooperatives upon certain products (Pischke and Rouse 2004). Moreover, the changes that occurred since the 1880s in the rural areas of developed countries and the applied policies oriented the cooperatives to other sectors such as tourism, culture, energy and other activities that are usually connected to the special and particular characteristics and resources of their own regions (Johdal 2003; Karafolas 2007). This shift primarily enhanced the cooperatives' economic character and subsequently their role in the regional development process (Brennan and Luloff 2005).

In Greece, despite the fact that cooperatives were the basis of the rural economy, during the recent decades they have demonstrated a generalized image of degradation and decline. This negative effect mainly derives from the limited presence (or even absence) of "leaders" in the Greek rural regions, the development of "customer relations" between cooperatives' administrations and their members, resulting by this way in a limited use of qualified manpower, partisanship and state intervention, poor management of resources (human and non-human), absence of partnership culture and inability to update their practices on time so that they would be able to face up with the constant national and to update their practices on time so that they would be able to face up with the constant national and international competition (Patronis and Mavreas 2004; Kamenidis 2008).

Nowadays, the Greek economic reality affects significantly the questioning about the possibilities, the role and the future perspectives of the cooperatives. In parallel, there are efforts that aim to the revival of the cooperatives through the activation of actors and local societies as well as through efforts to modernize the current legislation. At present, several cooperatives are connected to the processing and trading of branded Greek, mainly agricultural products boosting by this way the local employment and income in their region, with significant export activities and a strong presence in the Greek market (Vakoufaris et al. 2007; Rigas et al. 2008). Some of them are gradually changing to "new generation hybrid cooperatives" through organizational and financial restructuring while at the same time they undertake business initiatives and carry out important investing plans (Sergaki and Semos 2006). The cooperative entrepreneurship can significantly contribute to the confrontation of economic and development problems that many rural regions have at present (Sdrali and Apostolopoulos 2006; Benos et al. 2007).

The main aim of the present study is to examine the willingness of the local society to accept and support a local factor such as an investment proposal of the local union of agricultural cooperatives, by revealing the foremost reasons thereof. More specifically, this paper investigates the level of the Western Macedonia residents' adherence and support of a cooperative investment proposal by the Union of

Agricultural Cooperatives of Amyndeo (UACA), which refers to the construction and operation of a dairy product plant, mainly through the intention of consuming their own products.

2 The Region Under Study and Methodology

Western Macedonia (WM) is a mountainous region that accounts 7.20% of Greece's total territory (Fig. 1). Its population is 301,539 representing the 2.75% of the total population. This region sustains mainly livestock and agricultural activities and in its prefectures there is great production of milk which represents approximately 7% of the total milk production in Greece. In 2008, at Florinas' prefecture, farms produced 25,071 tons of cow milk (64% of its total production). 81.00% of the total number of veal farmers (733) in the region is located in Florina. Kozanis' prefecture farmers produced 4,169 tons of goat milk out of a total of 9,232 that stands for the 45% in county's level, as well as the greatest quantity of sheep milk, 11,652 tons (41%) (Theodosiou et al. 2009).

During the years 2004–2005, the average expenditure for fresh full fat milk and cheese was higher in the Western Macedonia region compared to the rest of the country (13.11 € and 11.33 € for milk, 25.73 € and 24.24 € for cheese, respectively), (NSSG 2005). Mostly large national dairies operate in the particular region, while recently smaller local dairy and cheese industries have started some activity. Also, small cooperative dairy enterprises in neighboring prefectures have expanded their distribution network realizing the gap in the regional market.

UACA was founded in 1946 and consists of 27 primary cooperatives, counting more than 2,100 members. Besides strengthening, expansion and coordination of the primary cooperatives – members and the producers' groups, the aim of this Union is the promotion and support of all the agricultural products of the region. UACA having modernized its operation and ensured traditional production processes (wine production) adopts a "dynamic" strategy with the purpose to further promote the local raw material production and to enhance the agricultural income and the productive base of the region. An investment proposal for establishing a modern dairy industry is examined that will use the local raw material production to benefit both the producers and the consumers by creating a trustworthy network of collecting and distributing its dairy products (Theodosiou et al. 2010a). The present research was conducted to record the possible adherence of the prefecture's consumers towards the dairy and milk products as well as the level of their support to the planned investment.

In order to investigate the aims of this research qualitative and quantitative survey was conducted in the region. The qualitative survey was carried out during September and October 2009. Fifty consumers were divided into five Focus Groups, each one consisting of ten persons. Based on their answers on the qualitative survey, the closed type questionnaire which was used for the quantitative survey was formed.

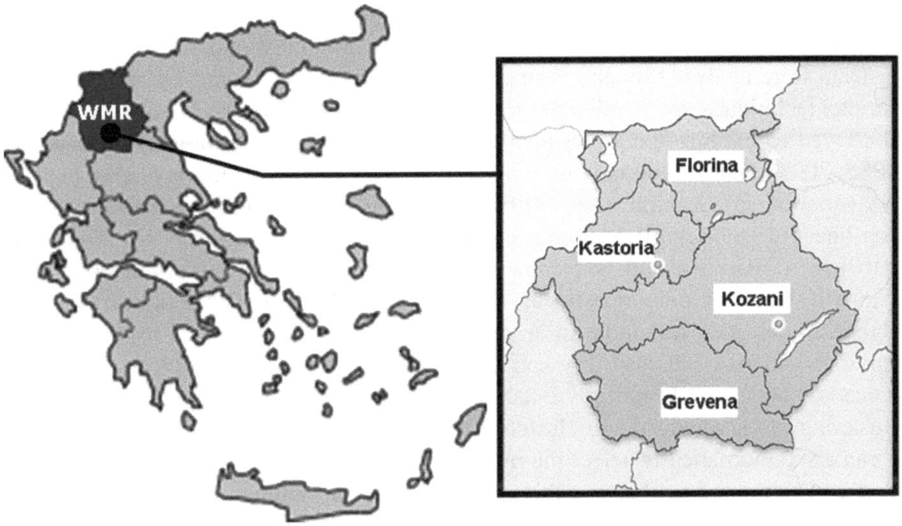

Fig. 1 West Macedonian Region, Greece

The final questionnaire was divided in five units in total and in fact it consisted of two autonomous questionnaires which were completed simultaneously. The first questionnaire consisted of two units and referred in general to the consumers' adherence towards dairy products while the second questionnaire consisted of three units and referred to consuming trends towards the new products of UACA. The interviews were based on the same questionnaire, which was completed by phone interviews, consisted of 24 Open Type Questions and of 69 variables in total.

The survey was conducted from 2 to 5 of November 2009 in the geographical boundaries of WM, as they are determined by the telephone numbers index. The survey was conducted through telephone with the use of a formulated questionnaire among 500 residents of the prefecture over 18 years old. The choice of samples was conducted by the method of multistage sampling. In its primary level the planning of sampling included the analogical representation of the four counties of the prefecture, and in its second level the respective representation of urban and rural areas of each county, so that a generalization for the whole population of the survey region could be achieved. The technique of proportional analogical sampling was used (multistage sampling) as well as an attempt to analogically approach the population on a basis of region, gender and age. By this way a total sample of 500 consumers was collected. However, after the collection of the sample it was observed that the analogical distribution was not sufficient since a small number of questionnaires did not meet the primary conditions of proportionality. This was due to the difficulty in identifying the consumers from Grevena and Kastoria's counties since the telephone number prefix is the same for both counties. Therefore, there was a separate identification of each questionnaire and a value from 0.44 to 2.10 was contributed to them. Only two questionnaires were permanently excluded by the sampling to which the minimum load value 0.1 (almost zero) was attributed for statistical reasons. The average load value of the 500 questionnaires was 1.

Data were analysed by employing both summary statistics and non-linear multivariate techniques. In particular, a two-step cluster analysis (TSCA) was first employed to explore the strata of local factor's (UACA) adoption (Siardos 2002; SPSS 2007) and a binomial logit model (BLM) was then employed to explain the variation in adoption rates. Although several researchers have also employed non-linear methodologies (Tserkezos and Thanou 2008; Thanou and Tserkezos 2010) the TSCA method is completely different and offers important potentials. The TSCA is not only non-linear in nature but also a scalable cluster analysis algorithm designed to handle in an optimal way: (a) large datasets, (b) categorical variables and (c) attributes. Although it requires only one dataset, it follows a two-step procedure: (a) pre-clustering of the cases into many small sub-clusters and (b) clustering of the obtained sub-clusters into the desired number of clusters. However, it can also automatically select the number of clusters. Furthermore, a BLM regression was estimated so that possible relations between willingness to adopt endogenous development and a set of selected socioeconomic predictors could be found out. The specific version of the applied BLM can be seen as a special case of a general utility maximisation model (Jimenez and Salas-Velasco 2000).

3 Results

Up to the synthetic results of the descriptive statistical analysis the identity of the sample agrees with the census data of 2001. However, it is understandable that certain deviations are acceptable up to the level that they do not affect the effort of generalization to the entire population of the survey region. For this purpose loads were put in each one of the questionnaires and thus it was equated with the census data of 2001. Hence, according to summary statistics (Fig. 2), the most representative respondents of the sample are: over 65 years old (23.8%), married (71.8%), retired (26.1%), living in a household with two adult members (53.9%) with no adolescent members (66.2%), of a higher educational level (university or technical college graduates) (39.4%), of low income (44.4%), living permanently in Kozani's county (51.5%), in urban areas (93.0%). Moreover, using statistical frequencies the whole sample is segmented into three general representative groups of respondents with similar occupation: (a) cattle breeders (4.8%), (b) entrepreneurs or farmers (44.0%) and (c) rest rural residents (51.2%).

It should be noted that a significant percentage of the respondents (45.20%) are willing to buy milk products from the UACA, while an also significant percentage (40.60%) are willing to replace the dairy products they used to buy with the respective UACA ones (Fig. 3). The most important reason for purchasing these products is the fact that in this way not only the income of the farmers of the entire WM region is enhanced, but also of other professionals.

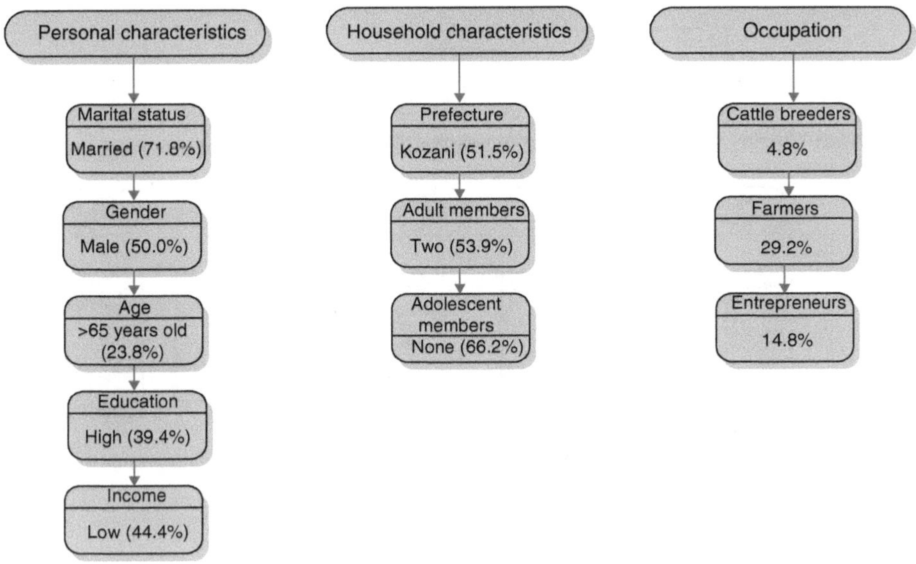

Fig. 2 Description of the representative respondent (mean participant)

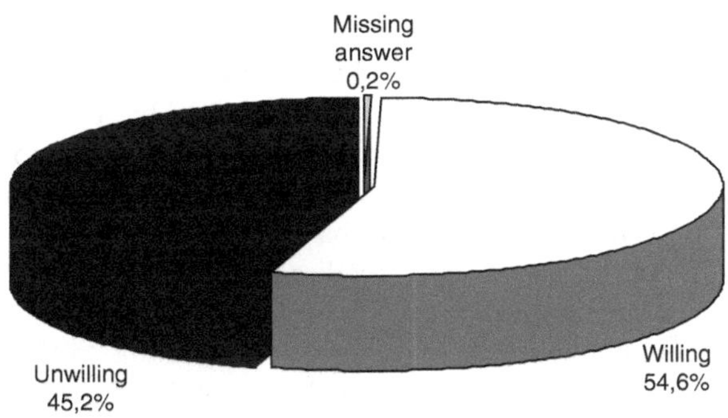

Fig. 3 Willingness to adopt UAC Amyntaio

Afterwards, the rural residents of the sample were asked how much more money they are willing to pay in order to buy dairy products from the UACA. The question was presented in the form of percentage scale clusters and five general categories: (a) no, (b) up to 10%, (c) 10–20%, (d) 20–50% and (d) more than 50%. It should be noted that a percentage of 75% are willing to pay more money than usual and what is more, some consumers (10.81%) are willing to pay more than 50% over the price of conventional dairy products. Similarly, in the next question the rural residents of the sample were asked to declare how much more quantities they would be willing to purchase by consuming dairy products from the UACA. The question was also presented in the form of percentage scale clusters and five general categories as above. In contrast to the previous question, the majority of the interviewed

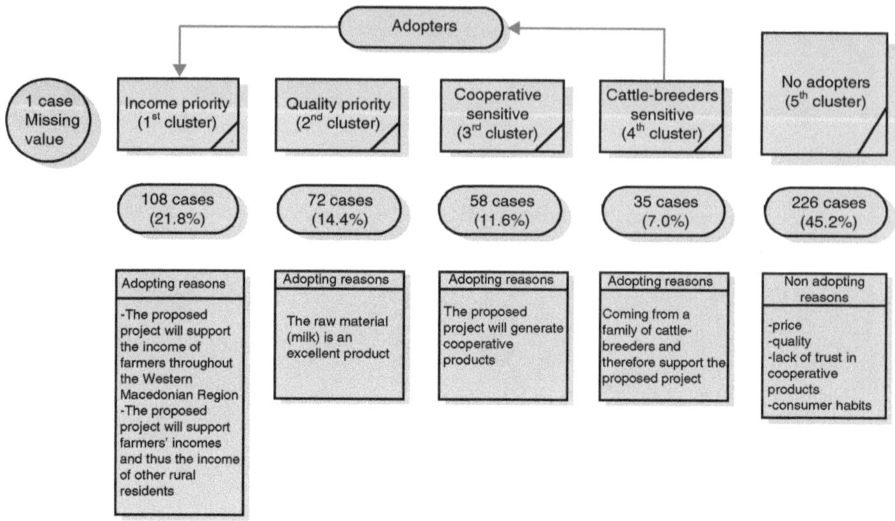

Fig. 4 TSCA modeling

(57.21%) are not willing to consume more quantities than usual. However, an important percentage (11.71%) is willing to consume more than 150% of the normal amounts of dairy products. The most important reason for this reluctance or non-intention of buying is the fact that the consumers trust the company they have chosen choice so far and they are pleased by it.

Using clustering methodologies it was possible to categorise the rural residents based on their attitudes towards a suite of adopting reasons (statements). In particular, employing a TSCA analysis, based upon the agreement level of the several attributive items of Fig. 4 (1 = strongly disagree, 2 = disagree, 3 = neither agree nor disagree, 4 = agree and 5 = strongly disagree), the respondents were classified in some discernible clusters in order to explore the different levels of their adopting behaviour. SPSS V.17 for Windows (SPSS 2007) was employed for the multivariate statistical analysis of the whole dataset. The TSCA method extracted automatically the optimal solution of five clusters. According to Fig. 4, the majority of the respondents (226 or 45.2%) were included in the fifth cluster (no adopters), 108 of them (21.8%) in the first cluster (income priority), 72 of them (14.4%) in the second cluster (quality priority), 58 of them (11.6%) in the third cluster (cooperative sensitive) and finally 35 of them (7.0%) in the first cluster (cattle breeders sensitive).

Then, the empirical econometric model was employed to relate factors that influence patterns of the UACA adoption by rural residents. This was achieved by using MINITAB for Windows, release 14.1.3 (MINITAB 2006). Actually, the UACA adoption was treated as a separate decision process and analyzed using a discrete choice model that related the use probability to the socioeconomic factors of Table 1. In particular, a BLM identifies the importance of determinants of UACA adoption by sample strata. More specifically, the dependant variable "adoption",

Table 1 *UACA* model variables and description

Variable	Description
Employment status	1 = employed, 0 = unemployed
Family status	1 = married, 2 = otherwise
Gender	1 = male, 0 – female
Distance	Distance between respondent residence and the UACA (in km)
Income	Annual income
Education	Years of general education
Persons	Number of persons residing in the households
Young residents	Number of residents aged under 18 years
Age	Respondents' age

Table 2 *UACA* model estimates

Model	Variable	Coefficient	t-ratio
Cattle-breeders model	*Constant*	–0.11	–0.77
	Age	0.31	1.11
	Distance	0.54	1.32
	Income	**1.48**	**2.97**
	Persons	0.17	0.81
	Observations	*24 (4.8 %)*	
Rural enterprise and farm model	*Constant*	–0.32	–1.02
	Gender	**1.14**	**2.17**
	Education	0.11	0.56
	Employment status	0.17	0.62
	Age	**1.93**	**3.41**
	Observations	*220 (44.0 %)*	
Rural household model	*Constant*	–0.74	–1.27
	Education	**1.52**	**2.74**
	Employment status	**1.13**	**2.46**
	Young residents	**1.16**	**2.53**
	Income	0.46	1.03
	Observations	*256 (51.2 %)*	

splits the sample in two subgroups: (a) UACA adopters (=1: always, oftentimes or sometimes) and (b) UACA non-adopters (=0: rarely or never). The selection of the nine independent explanatory variables of Table 1 was based on prior analysis of local factor's adoption while it is adapted to the research area particularities (Theodosiou et al. 2010a).

In order to explore some different drivers of UACA adoption among rural residents the sample has been stratified in three general groups of respondents based on their occupation: (a) cattle breeders, (b) entrepreneurs or farmers and (c) other cases. About one third (4.8%) of the respondents are cattle breeders, while 44.0% of them manage small enterprises including farms and the rest 51.2% are employees or occupied in several other vocations. The importance of this sample stratification is clearly demonstrated by the model results as the drivers for UACA adoption are significant different for these strata (Table 2).

More specifically, the "*cattle breeders' model*" suggests that UACA adoption is driven only by "income" variables. In particular, the high coefficient of "income" variable indicates that the construction and operation of the UACA is expected to function as a driver of income increase especially for the cattle breeders of the region. On the other hand, in the "*rural enterprise and farm model*", the significant drivers are "age" and "gender", a fact which most likely demonstrates the deferent levels of UACA adoption between younger and older rural residents and between males and females. Finally, the explanation of UACA adoption in the rural household model is more complex and related to "education", "employment status" and "young residents" variables. The importance of the presence of a resident under 18 years old implies the increased value of UACA for the young population while "education" indicates that UACA is most likely to be adopted by well educated rural residents and "employment status" demonstrates the different levels of UACA adoption between employed and unemployed rural residents.

4 Conclusions

The strengthening of development progress, through investment and support measures towards local production, is a necessity for the country. Moreover, when these actions aim at the local communities, by investing local capitals and using local resources and raw materials, they point out decentralized institutions and forces, which may be activated under adverse economic and social conditions. Several cooperatives that are engaged in processing and marketing of brands have managed to achieve positive financial results and contribute to the local development and economy. The dairy product sector seems to have positive perspectives, a fact that is proved by the profitability of many cooperative dairy industries. The cooperatives in an effort to gain from the opportunities the dairy sector provides, and also to face the distortions that are created by the dominant market position of the big dairy industries (reduction of the price paid to the producer, cartels, sale networks etc.) are led to investments in order to found new milk and dairy enterprises as well as achieve the modernization of the existing ones.

Results clearly demonstrate the importance of sample stratification, as the drivers for UACA adoption are entirely different among these strata. Thus, the input of new policy measures, in order to encourage or take advantage of the adoption of local factors, should be specifically targeted towards these segments of the rural population, taking into account the specificities of each group. UACA is willing to found a dairy industry of milk and dairy products aiming at the profitable use of the milk production in WM region and at providing the local farmers with a steady income. Despite the fact that the success of such an investment proposal depends upon many and different factors, the results of this survey indicate the confidence of the local communities in the local initiative.

The present study has several implications, both theoretical and practical, since its empirical results support the basic argument that local factors cover significant needs of rural residents and therefore cause significant changes in remote and marginalized areas. Concluding, we believe that a more detailed analysis of local factor's adoption sheds light on the structural changes in social and human behavior, especially in rural areas, but also on the principles and mechanisms that enable these changes. Such results will advance the conceptual framework in the social sciences and economics and may result in new approaches to rural development policy.

References

Benos Th, Kalogeros N, Vertices FJHM (2007) Influence of organizational characteristics of cooperatives to market-oriented brands, and performance: the case of Greek agricultural cooperatives. In: Papageorgiou K (ed) Cooperative reflections 2006–2007. Stamoulis Editions, Athens (in Greek)

Brennan MA, Luloff AE (2005) A cooperative approach to rural development in Ireland: cultural artifacts and the Irish diaspora as an example. J Int Agri Ext Educ 12(1):15–25

Chatzitheodoridis F (1998) Multiactivity and special quality products in to the frame of Islands integrated development: the case of Lemnos Island. Ph.D. thesis, University of Aegean, Mytilini (in Greek)

ELOGAG – Hellenic Organization of Milk and Meat (2009) Analytical trade tables 2009. ELOGAG, Athens (in Greek)

Galatoulas I (2009) The market of fresh pasteurized milk in Greece: factors affecting the demand, trends and prospects of the sector. Master thesis, Harokopion University, Athens (in Greek)

ICAP (2007) Dairy products: sectoral study. ICAP Group, Athens

Jimenez JDD, Salas-Velasco M (2000) Modelling educational choices. A binomial logit model applied to the demand for higher education. High Educ 40:293–311

Jodahl T (2003) Consumer co-operatives in Norway. Rev Int Co-op 96(1):9–16

Kamenidis C (2008) Cooperatives. Principles–financial–political–development– organization-legislation. Kyriakidis Editions, Thessaloniki (in Greek)

Karafolas S (2007) Wine roads in Greece: a cooperation for the development of local tourism in rural areas. J Rural Coop 35(1):71–90

Lowe P, Ray C, Ward N, Wood D, Woodward R (1998) Participation in rural development: a review of European experience. Research report, Centre for Rural Economy, University of Newcastle

Madane M (2002) Co-operative rejuvenation through self-help groups and other alternatives. Rev Int Co-op 95(1):104–114

MINITAB (2006) MINITAB for windows release 14.1.3, MINITAB Inc, Coventry, United Kingdom.

NSSG – National Statistical Service of Greece (2005) Household budget survey 2004–05. NSSG, Athens

von Pischke JD, Rouse J (2004) New strategies for mobilizing capital in agricultural cooperatives. F.A.O, Rome

Patronis V, Mavreas K (2004) Agricultural cooperative organizations in Greece throughout the 20th century: a critical overview. J Rural Coop 32(1):51–62

Ray C (1999) Endogenous development in the era of reflexive modernity. J Rural Stud 15(3):257–267

Rigas N, Papantoniou S, Kantas D, Rigas G (2008) An empirical research on biological products in Greece. In: Proceedings of the 2nd conference on animal production, Larissa, June 30–July 2

Sergaki P, Semos A (2006) The Greek Unions of agricultural cooperatives as efficient enterprises. Agr Econ Rev 7(2):15–27

Sdrali D, Apostolopoulos KD (2006) The contribution of the agricultural cooperatives in local development – the case of cooperative Binding Kozani Crocus Producers. In: Papageorgiou K (ed) Cooperative reflections 2004–2005. Stamoulis Editions, Athens (in Greek)
Siardos G (2002) Methods of multivariate statistical analysis. Part two. Investigation of dependence between variations, 3rd edn. Stamoulis Editions, Athens (in Greek)
SPSS – Statistical Package for Social Sciences (2007) SPSS 17.0 for windows. User's guide. SPSS, Chicago
Thanou E, Tserkezos D (2010) Non-linear diachronic effects between stock returns and mutual fund flows: additional empirical evidence from the Athens stock exchange. J Financ Decis Making 6(1):33–46
Theodosiou G, Loizou E, Chatzitheodoridis F, Michailidis A (2009) Market research for the establishment of a milk factory in Western Macedonia Region. Technological Educational Institution of Western Macedonia, Florina (in Greek)
Theodosiou G, Michailidis A, Loizou E, Chatzitheodoridis F, Sergaki P (2010a) Endogenous rural development: evidence from a typical Greek region. Econ Rural Dev 6(2):17–23
Theodosiou G, Michailidis A, Loizou E, Chatzitheodoridis F (2010b) Rural areas development through endogenous potentials. In: Proceedings of the 118th seminar of E.A.A.E., Rural development: governance, policy design and delivery, E.A.A.E, Ljubljana, pp 931–938
Tserkezos D, Thanou E (2008) Portfolio management: an investigation of the implications of measurement errors in stock prices on the creation, management and evaluation of stock portfolios, using stochastic simulations. Int J Financ Econ Economet 1(2):13–26
Tsourgiannis L, Eddison J, Warren M (2008) Factors affecting the marketing channel choice of sheep and goat farmers in the region of East Macedonia in Greece regarding the distribution of their milk production. Small Ruminant Res 79(1):87–97
Vakoufaris H, Spilanis I, Kizos T (2007) Collective action in the Greek agrifood sector: evidence from the North Aegean region. Brit Food J 109(10):777–791

Exploring Consumers' Purchasing Behaviour Regarding Organic Wine in a Convergence E.U. Region: The Case of East Macedonia and Thrace, Greece

Lambros Tsourgiannis, Anastasios Karasavvoglou, and Michael Nikolaidis

1 Introduction

In many cases, studies that examine consumers' acceptance of value added or differentiated products focus on niche marketing. A large number of studies on branding, product differentiation, labelling issues and consumer behaviour is mentioned in marketing and business literature.

According to Booth and Shepherd (1988), cultural and economical factors, consumer's personality and attitudes, as well as values and emotions have an impact on consumers' decision making process regarding food selection Years later, Steenkamp (1996) argued that biological, psychological and socio-demographical consumer characteristics, marketing of the product, economic and cultural environment affect consumers' purchasing decisions. Kotler (1994) as well identified that cultural, social, individual and psychological factors influence consumers' buying behaviour.

As far as the consumers' buying behaviour within the E.U. countries is concerned, it is also affected by food quality characteristics, the fact that consumers highly appreciate the importance of healthy diet, price, governmental actions, cultural factors, distribution channels and finally the prevalence of the supermarket chains (Murray et al. 1996; Allen 1997; Davies et al. 2000; OECD 2000; Tsourgiannis 2008). Furthermore, religious prohibitions, cultural beliefs and counterculture attitudes together with the social characteristics of the consumers (i.e. size of the

L. Tsourgiannis (✉)
Region of East Macedonia and Thrace, Regional Unit of Xanthi and Research Fellow in the Department of Accountancy, School of Business and Economy, Region of East Macedonia and Thrace,
Xanthi, Greece
e-mail: ltsourgiannis@gmail.com

A. Karasavvoglou • M. Nikolaidis
Accountancy Department, School of Business and Economy, Kavala Institute of Technology, Kavala, Greece

A. Karasavvoglou and P. Polychronidou (eds.), *Balkan and Eastern European Countries in the Midst of the Global Economic Crisis*, Contributions to Economics,
DOI 10.1007/978-3-7908-2873-3_10,

family and the role of the head of the family) have a significant impact on Greek consumers' purchasing decisions towards food products (Michalopoulos and Demoussis 2001; Sdrali and Apostolopoulos 2002; Lazaridis 2003).

The food crises that arose during the previous decade such as the BSE crisis, foot and mouth outbreak, as well as the dioxin scandals increased the demand for organic products substantially (Siderer et al. 2005). European consumers have partially lost their confidence towards conventional farming practices as they had to face such crises and their results (Remaud et al. 2008). Loureiro (2003) argues that as far as the wine market is concerned, environmental quality perceptions determine consumers' preferences substantially.

The term "organic" generally refers to those farming practises that use organic manure and exclude synthetic fertilisers, pesticides, chemicals or growth promoters of any type (Gil et al. 2000). "Organic wine", therefore, is solely made from grapes which are both organically farmed and processed in accordance with the standards of organic winemaking practices. The maximum level of sulphur dioxide in organic wines is half the level found in other wines (Iland and Gago 2002). In the E.U. organic agricultural products and foodstuffs are defined by Council Regulation EEC 2092/91 as it has been amended up to date. This regulation with its amendments has established a specific framework within the E.U. as regards organic farming; it has also defined the requirements for agricultural products and foodstuffs in association with the production methods used in organic farming as well as the development of the market of organic food. In particular, Regulations E.C. 834/2007 and E.C, 889/2008 refer to the certification of organic wines. Furthermore, the European Commission launched its Organic Farming Campaign in 2008 aiming to inform consumers about the importance and benefits of organic farming and food production (E.U. 2011). The campaign focuses on increasing consumers' awareness and recognition of organic products.

Studies on consumers and organic food products occupy a large part in literature. Due to the fact that the cost for purchasing organic food products is generally bigger than the cost for the conventional ones, numerous empirical studies have focused on determining the maximum price premium consumers are willing to pay for organic products and the factors explaining this premium. With the help of a survey in retail chains in Athens in 2003, Krystallis and Chryssohoidis (2005) examined the factors that make Greek consumers willing to spend money on organic food. They identified that consumers are willing to pay (WTP) a premium price for organic food but the type and magnitude of factors that affect it differ according to the organic food category. Such factors are: food quality and security, trust in the certification and for some products brand name. Organoleptic characteristics, prices and consumers' socio-demographic profiles do not constitute determinants of WTP for organic products. Botonaki et al. (2006) examined consumers' attitude and behaviour towards organic products and products produced under the system of integrated management (SIM); they also compared the socio-economic characteristics and attitudes that affect consumers' WTP, a premium for those two different certification systems in Greece. They found that the WTP for organic products is higher among consumers who attach importance to health, consume organic fruits and vegetables and are aware of food and nutrition issues. Brugarolas et al. (2005) tried to determine the premium price that consumers are willing to pay for organic wine in Spain. They identified that the average premium price that people are willing to pay is between 16.29 % and 16.92 %. What is more, their study revealed three different types of consumers. The first is characterized by a healthy life style and environmental concern. The second type of consumers consists of people who are least worried about environmental issues but they are concerned about health and diet ones. Consumers of the third type do not show any of the given life styles. WTP according to Brugarolas et al. (2005) is higher for consumers concerned about environmental issues.

In our days consumption habits are ever changing and people take ethical, environmental and health factors into serious consideration when they are to choose food products (Torjusen et al. 2001; Smith and Marsden 2004). Many empirical studies have examined the factors determining the attitude towards organic food, and have profiled as well as differentiated the organic consumer from the non organic one. Thompson and Kidwell (1998) found that families with children were more likely to buy organic food. Nimon and Beghin (1999) identified a significant and robust premium for organic cotton fibres embodied in apparel goods, although they did not find any evidence of a premium associated with environment friendly dyes. On the other hand, other studies have suggested that consumers with higher income are more likely to buy organic products (Kiesel and Villas-Boas 2007; Tsakiridou et al. 2006). The income of organic consumers in Italy ranges from medium to high according to Crescimanno et al. (2002); however, other studies identified that income does not really affect consumers to purchase organic food products (Adamsen et al. 2007). Young consumers are unlikely to consume organic products according to Gil et al. (2000) and Tsakiridou et al. (2006). On the other hand, Reichs et al. (1997) argued that the factor "age" significant affect consumers and young consumers in particular to purchase organic food products. Furthermore, Krystallis et al. (2006) found that post graduate and graduates are more likely to buy organic products than people who have not attained a university education or high school level of learning. Household size, the existence of young children within the family affects consumers to purchase organic food (Tsakiridou et al. 2006; Chryssohoidis and Krystallis 2005). Regarding the socio-demographic profile of the consumers of organic food according to Fotopoulos and Krystallis (2003), they mainly are female. Small difference identified between males and females regarding their WTP a premium price (Davis et al. 1995). Baourakis (2004) identified four groups of consumers and potential consumers of organic products according to their attitudes and beliefs. These groups were named as followed: (a) environmental militants, (b) traditional, (c) dietary, and (d) "youthful" organic consumers. Eves et al. (2004) grouped consumers under the titles "deeply rooted", "pioneers", "pragmatists" and "nostalgias" whilst Chryssohoidis and Krystallis (2005) identified four groups of Greek consumers, the health conscious consumers, the explorers, the independents and the organic loyal consumers. Regarding the wine consumption, Fotopoulos et al. (2003) compared buyers versus non buyers of organic wines in Greece and developed their socio-demographic profiles. They argued that organic buyers more often purchase food at specialty shops, are more concerned about their health and diet and use more media than the non organic consumers. Hutchins and Greenhalgh (1997) identified that consumers mainly buy organic food products due to health reasons and the fact that they consider them more nutritious for kids. On the other hand, the main reasons consumers do not purchase organic food products are their high price and low availability in the market.

These groups are mainly descriptive and change enormously depending on the study area and its unique environment (Remaud et al. 2008). Although some studies took place concerning the examination of the purchasing behaviour of organic food products in Greece and worldwide there is no study that aimed to identify the motives that affect the consumers' buying behaviour towards organic wine. As most of the knowledge about the consumers attitudes regarding organic wine is derived from international studies or from some studies that have been conducted in Greece 4–5 years ago, the examination of the factors that affect buying behaviour of Greek consumers towards organic wine in a Convergence Region (which is a quite poor region) during the period of economic depression in Greece is very important because different cultural, economical, social and demographical characteristics affect consumers buying behaviour in a different way (Davies and Worrall 1998; Kupiec and Revell 1998; Michalopoulos and Demoussis 2001; Kotler 1994). Hence, this study examines which of the factors presented in the literature review affect the attitudes of the consumers to buy organic wine in the Region of East Macedonia and Thrace (REMTH) in Greece because it consists of an elected regional authority and has been designated by the E.U. as Convergence Region which means that the per capita income in this Region is below the 75 % of the average per capita income within E.U. Besides, the examined area is situated in North East part of Greece, is quite isolated for the main urban centres as well as is a border region. Therefore the development of niche market for local products (such as the certified organic products) will diversify, add value and protect the local production from the imported rival food products. According to ESYE (2009) vineyards consists an area of 1,548 ha within the REMTH comprising the 2 % of the area is cultivated for vineyards in the whole country. Organic vineyards consist of about 183 ha according to Hellenic Ministry of Agricultural Development and Food (2011) comprising about the 4.6 % the total vineyards exist in the region. Considering the fact that organic vineyards comprise the 2 % of the total area used for vineyards in Greece, it can be assumed that organic vineyards are an important issue for the economy of the examined study area. Furthermore, the agricultural sector is an important pillar of the local economy as the 38 % of the population in the Prefecture of Drama – Kavala – Xanthi is rural according the National Statistical Service in Greece (ESYE 2009). In this study the authors decided to explore the consumers' attitudes towards organic wine because these issues are quite important for the local economy and the Region of East Macedonia and Thrace is very actively involved in them. Moreover these issues and generally the Green Economy as well as the development of a market for niche products comprise important elements of the National Economic Policy of Greece within the near future.

As many of the characteristics of the examined study area may be similar to the characteristics of other E.U. regions the issues this study addresses can be interesting for researchers and policy makers of such regions; in particular in areas where the development of organic products as niche market products can be an important element for the improvement of the competitiveness of the products are produced within their area and therefore for the increase of their GDP.

2 Methods

2.1 The Conceptual Model

A conceptual model was developed to place key concepts outlined in the literature into an identifiable framework (Fig. 1). In particular it tries to investigate the relationships between the factors that affect the consumers' attitudes towards the purchase of organic food and more particular of organic wine and the development of key strategic dimensions that may influence consumers to adopt a specific buying behaviour. Furthermore it will examine the association between the consumers' attitudes towards the marketing outlet they prefer in order to buy organic wine, their opinion about the organic products, their willingness to pay more for certified organic food, their personal characteristics and the adoption of particular consumption behaviour.

Operationalising the conceptual model (Oppenheim 2000) gave rise to the following research hypotheses:

H1: Consumers in the Region of East Macedonia and Thrace can be classified into groups according to the factors that affect their purchasing behaviour towards organic wine.
H2: Consumers' opinion about the organic food products is significant related to particular purchasing behaviour.
H3: Consumers' preferences regarding the utilisation of a particular marketing outlet in order to buy organic wine are significant related to particular purchasing behaviour.
H4: Consumers' willingness to pay more for organic food and organic wine are significant related to particular purchasing behaviour.
H5: Consumers' personal characteristics are significant related to particular purchasing behaviour.

2.2 Survey Procedure

The researchers undertook a survey to a sample of consumers in order to gather data necessary to identify the factors that affect consumers buying behaviour in the

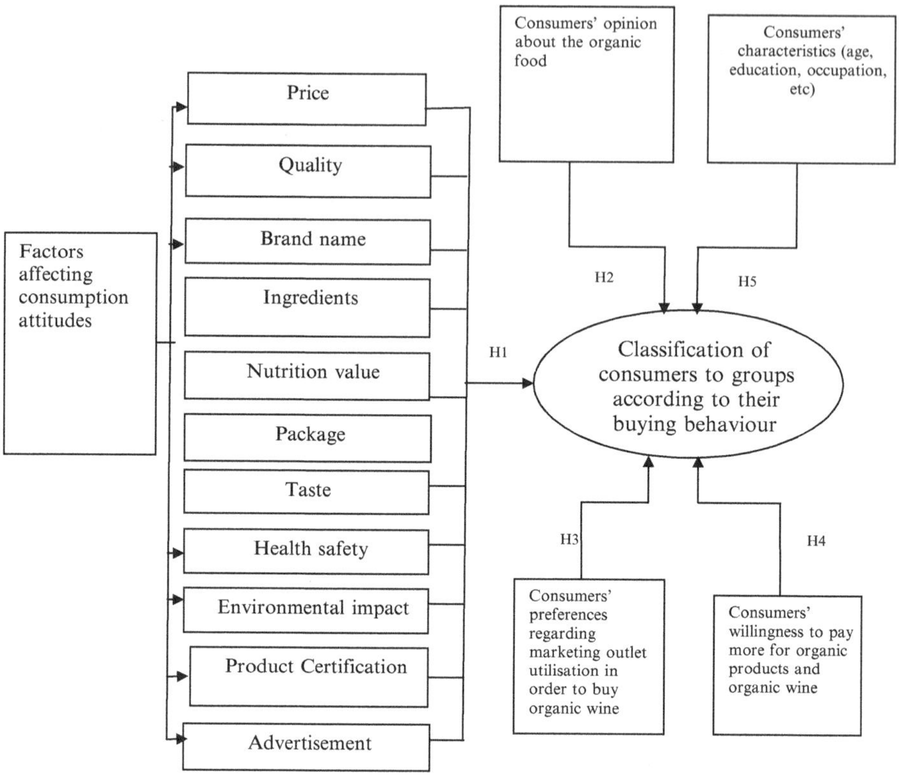

Fig. 1 The conceptual model

Region of East Macedonia and Thrace towards organic wine. Hence, the research focuses on a sample of Greek consumers, purchasers of organic food products. Information were gathered through an interview survey as the consumers in the Region of East Macedonia and Thrace are familiar with this kind of research and their educational level is suitable for the use of this kind of survey method (Moser 1958; Errington 1985; Barnett 1991; Oppenheim 2000). Moreover this is a widely used method for examining consumers buying behaviour by many researchers (Kamenidou et al. 2002; Fotopoulos and Krystallis 2002; Arvanitoyiannis and Krystallis 2005; Psomas et al. 2005; Tzavaras et al. 2005). Additionally, the cost of conducting large postal or telephone survey to develop a typology was considered prohibitive. Furthermore, as many consumers do not have an internet access, the electronic survey method was not suitable for surveying a representative to a general population sample.

An effort was made to reach consumers at the same time and place where actual purchase decisions are made hoping to better elicit consumers' true preferences about the products. Data were collected in locations frequented by consumers such

Table 1 Description of the sample

Regional division	Number of consumers >20 years old (census data)[a]	Proportion of each Prefecture to the total population	Sample	Proportion of the sample in each Prefecture to the total sample
Drama	79,460	17 %	87	17 %
Kavala	111,196	24 %	122	24 %
Evros	115,837	25 %	127	25 %
Xanthi	74,691	16 %	82	16 %
Rhodopi	85,437	18 %	93	18 %
Region EMTh	466,621	100 %	511	100 %

[a]Compiled data from ESYE (2010)

as supermarkets, groceries, wine cellars. Interviews took place throughout the day to reduce time of shopping related bias (Chryssohoidis and Krystallis 2005). Hence, one quarter (25 %) of the interviews were conducted between 9:00 and 15:00 during the week (Monday–Friday), one quarter between 15:00 and 21:00 during the week and 50 % during Saturday (9:00–19:00). All the respondents were aged above 20.

In this survey, a systematic stratified sampling method was chosen to form the sample due to the fact that the authors wished to generalize their findings beyond the sample of consumers covered by the survey. As Errington (1985) argued the only way in which this can be achieved is to ensure that the units for survey are selected at random from the larger population about which generalization are to be made. Therefore, consumers were selected randomly, with the criterion that the interviewer was to solicit every sixth customer who came into the survey area (McCluskey et al. 2003). The sample that was selected consists of 511 consumers over 20 years old that would be reasonably representative of some larger population about which useful generalization could be made. The size of the sample is detailed in Table 1 and is considered reasonable regarding the total population of the area as this size of samples were mostly used by other researchers in Greece regarding consumer behaviour towards food purchases. In particular Tzavaras et al. (2005) used a sample of 238 consumers in the area of Thessaloniki in order to explore consumers' behaviour towards rice. Furthermore, Vlachos and Fotoloulos (2005) interviewed 170 consumers in the area of Halkida in order to explore the consumers' attitudes towards GM food whilst Lykouropoulou and Lazaridis (2005) used a productive sample of 342 questionnaires in order to identify the factors that affect consumers willingness to pay for organic meat.

In order to establish the representatives of the surveyed sample, demographic information from the questionnaire is compared with census information of the population of the REMTH following the methodology that Errington (1985), Tsourgiannis et al. (2006, 2008), Tsourgiannis (2008) and Chen (2007) used in their studies. The characteristics of the selected sample with those of total population are compared in Table 2. As Table indicates all the characteristics of the sample do not differ from those of the total population based on Census data and therefore can be assumed that the sample is representative of the total population.

Table 2 Evaluation of the sample

Characteristics of the total population

Age groups	Total population[a]	Proportion of each age group to total population (%)	Not married[a]	Proportion of each age group of not married to total population (%)	Married[a]	Proportion of each age group of married to total population (%)	Male[a]	Proportion of each age group of male to total population (%)	Female[a]	Proportion of each age group of female to total population (%)
20–29	89,097	19	59,306	13	29,791	6	48,736	10	40,361	9
30–44	124,619	27	24,984	5	99,635	21	62,126	13	62,493	13
45–64	144,909	31	20,962	4	123,947	27	70,175	15	74,734	16
65+	107,996	23	37,501	8	70,495	15	48,222	10	59,774	13
Total	466,621	100	142,753	31	323,868	69	229,259	49	237,362	51

Characteristics of the sample population

Age groups	Sample population	Proportion of each age group to total population (%)	Not married	Proportion of each age group of not married to total sample population (%)	Married	Proportion of each age group of married to total sample population (%)	Male	Proportion of each age group of male to total sample population (%)	Female	Proportion of each age group of female to total sample population (%)
20–29	97	19	71	14	26	5	47	9	51	10
30–44	138	27	31	6	112	22	77	15	68	13
45–64	158	31	25	5	143	28	78	16	82	16
65+	118	23	31	6	72	14	47	9	61	12
Total	511	100	158	31	353	69	249	49	262	51

[a]Compiled data from ESYE (2010)

2.3 Questionnaire Design

Factors that affect the consumers' behaviour towards organic food products were identified by the researchers after searching the literature. Furthermore they designed a questionnaire in order to meet the research objectives and pre-tested it in academics, food marketing experts and consumers. In the next stage the questionnaire was piloted in January of 2010 to 100 consumers of the Region of EMTh. The pilot survey indicated that no modification needed to the questionnaire and therefore the main survey was conducted in April and May of 2010 as mentioned above.

The questionnaires were designed in four parts

Part 1 – This part consists of three questions regarding consumers' knowledge about organic food and purchases of organic food products.

Part 2 – This part consists of ten attitudinal statements on a 5 point Likert scale relating to their buying behaviour. These questions covered areas such as price, quality, health protection, locality, taste, certification, advertisement.

Part 3 –This part consists of six questions related to consumers' opinion regarding organic products, consumers willingness to pay more for an organic wine and food product and their attitudes towards the preference of a particular marketing outlet.

Part 4 –This part consists of seven questions regarding consumers' personal information including age, education, marital status, number of children, occupation, income.

2.4 Statistical Methodology

Multivariate analysis techniques were used to the 511 consumers that buy organic wine to reveal the key information contained in the responses, and these analyses were applied in three stages. First, principal component analysis (PCA) was used to identify the variables that accounted for the maximum amount of variance within the data in terms of the smallest number of uncorrelated variables (components).[1]

In this study, PCA reduced the five key attitude variables, which relate to various aspects of consumers behaviour towards organic wine, to a smaller set of underlying factors (or consumption dimensions).[2] These factor scores were then subjected to cluster analysis to group consumers with similar patterns of scores into similar

[1] The anti-image correlation matrix was used as well as Bartlett's test of sphericity and measure of sampling adequacy (MSA) in order to check the appropriateness of the data for subsequent factor analysis. The variables that had a high proportion of large absolute values of anti –image correlations as well as MSA less than 0.5 were removed before analysis.

[2] An orthogonal rotation (varimax method) was conducted and the standard criteria of eigenvalue = 1, scree test and percentage of variance were used in order to determine the factors in the first rotation (Hair et al. 1998). Different trial rotations followed where factor interpretability was compared.

clusters based on their buying behaviour.[3],[4] Quadratic discriminant analysis was performed to assess how accurately the identified key consumption dimensions that were derived from the factor analysis could predict and discriminate cluster membership.

Statistical tests based on the outcomes of the multivariate statistical techniques presented above (factor, cluster and discriminant analysis) were used to test five hypotheses presented in previous section.

3 Results

3.1 *Consumers' Buying Behaviour and Attitudes Towards Organic Wine*

Principal components and factor analyses (through a varimax rotation) were conducted, and the latent root criterion (eigenvalue =1), the scree plot test and the percentage of variance were used to determine the number of factors. The latent root criterion (eigenvalue =1), the scree plot test (Fig. 2) suggested that there were two factors in the first rotation which explained the 66.46 % of the total variance (Table 3).[5]

The factor loading scores of the five variables onto the two factors are presented in Table 4. The cut-off point for interpretation of loading scores was 0.782 according to Hair et al. (1998) and Tabachnick and Fiddell (1989) suggestions.

In the next stage, hierarchical and non-hierarchical clustering methods were used to develop a typology of the buying behaviour of the consumers in the Region of East Macedonia and Thrace (Harrigan 1985; Helsen and Green 1991; Hair et al. 1998; Siardos 1999). Cluster analysis was conducted on the 511 observations, as there were no outliers.

It identified three groups of consumers that were named according to their buying behaviour patterns towards organic wine (Table 5). These are: (a) those who are influenced by prestige and curiosity, (b) the opportunists (those who are not influenced by any factor) and (c) those who are orientated to buy healthy products.

In particular, the consumers who are influenced by prestige and curiosity comprise 19 % of the sample. These consumers are influenced in their buying decisions

[3] In this study, both hierarchical and non-hierarchical methods were used according to the recommendations of Hair et al. (1998) and Punj and Stewart (1983) in order to develop a typology of the consumers' buying behaviour.

[4] A non-parametric Kruskal–Wallis one way ANOVA was conducted to validate the cluster solutions by examining if variables not used in cluster analysis differ significantly among the identified clusters.

[5] Several different trial rotations were conducted to compare factor interpretability as suggested by Tabachnick and Fiddell 1989 and Hair et al. 1998.

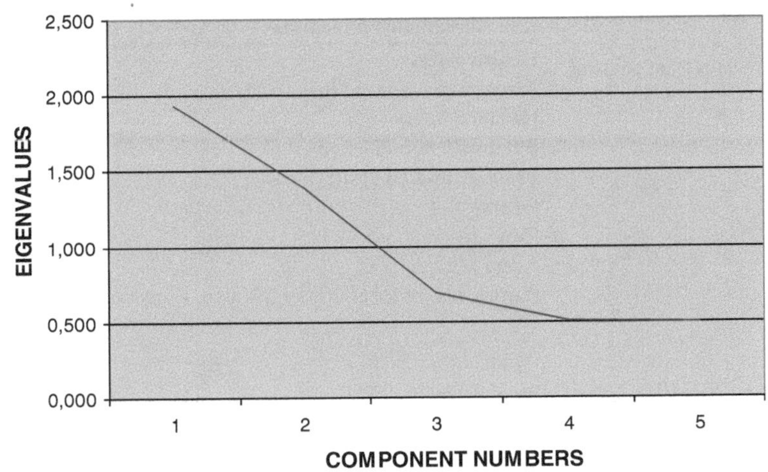

Fig. 2 Scree plot test

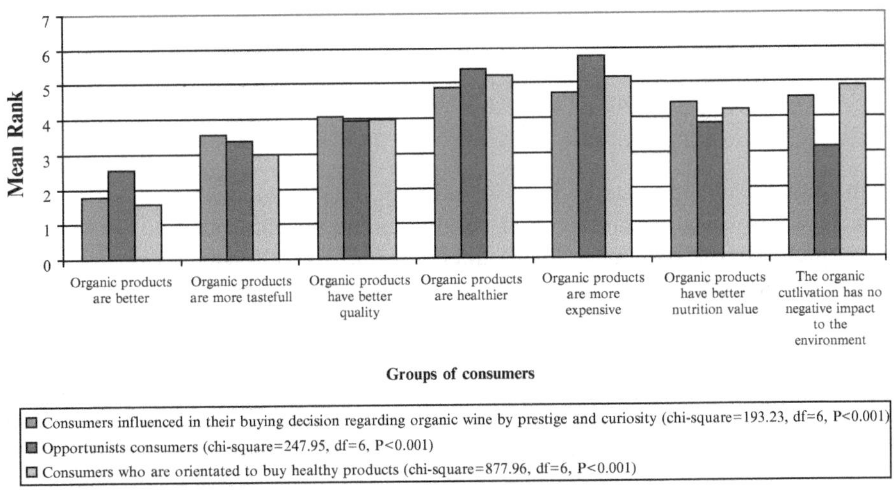

Fig. 3 Consumers' opinion about organic products

Table 3 Results of principal components analysis of consumption preference variables

Components	Eigenvalues	% of variance	Cumulative variance (%)	Communalities
1	**1.929**	**38.577**	**38.577**	**0.611**
2	**1.394**	**27.884**	**66.460**	**0.651**
3	0.671	13.423	79.883	0.664
4	0.507	10.136	90.019	0.694
5	0.499	9.981	100.00	0.7025

Table 4 Key consumption dimensions derived from principal component analysis

Key consumption dimensions	Factor loading
Health safety	
Absence of chemical ingredients	0.807
Nutrition value	0.807
Environment protection	0.782
Prestige and curiosity	
Prestige	0.837
Curiosity	0.833

KMO MSA = 0.613
Bartlett test of sphericity = 398,016, P <0.001

Table 5 Characteristics of the two consumers' groups

	Groups of consumers			
Key consumption dimensions	Consumers influenced by prestige and curiosity	Opportunists consumers	Consumers orientated to buy healthy products	P
Health safety	0.379	−1.614	0.437	0.0001
	0.709	*0.586*	*0.499*	
Prestige and curiosity	1.568	−0.118	−0.460	0.0001
	0.816	*0.714*	*0.526*	
Number of consumers (n = 511)	98	106	307	

NB: Means are reported in standard text and standard deviations in italics

by the prestige the purchase and consumption of organic wine will provide to them as well as by curiosity. On the other hand, they are not interested in the nutrition value, protection of the environment and consuming healthy products.

The opportunists comprise the 21 % of the sample and are the consumers who act opportunistically. They buy organic wine but they are not influenced either by health and environment protection or by their curiosity or prestige.

On the other hand, consumers who are orientated to buy healthy products consist of the 60 % of the sample. These consumers are interested in buying products with no chemical additives. Furthermore, the environmental consequences of the product as well as the nutrition value of the product are also some factors that affect consumers buying behaviour.

Furthermore these three groups of consumers were validated using Kruskal–Wallis non-parametric one-way ANOVA with five (5) consumption variables describing the way they buy organic wine and were not used in factor analysis; as this test is more robust in cases of ordinal data (Kinnear and Gray 2000).

As Table 6 illustrates the three identified consumers groups found to good validity as the examined variables are significant associated with consumers' buying behaviour towards organic wine. In particular the consumers influenced in their buying decision regarding organic wine by prestige and curiosity, are also significantly affected in their food purchases in general by the fact that is a local

Table 6 Miscellaneous characteristics of the two consumers groups according to Kruskal–Wallis test

	Groups of consumers			
Key consumption dimensions	Consumers influenced by prestige and curiosity	Opportunists consumers	Consumers orientated to buy healthy products	P
Quality of the product	267.70[a] *4.000*	167.70[b] *3.500*	282.80[c] *4.000*	0.0001
Taste	277.20[a] *4.000*	151.20[b] *3.000*	285.40[c] *4.000*	0.0001
Origin/topicality of the product	329.70[a] *3.000*	191.80[b] *2.000*	254.60[c] *3.000*	0.0001
Advertisement	318.50[a] *3.000*	235.20[b] *2.000*	243.20[c] *2.000*	0.0001
Health safety issues	242.80[a] *5.000*	183.90[b] *4.000*	285.10[c] *5.000*	0.0001
Number of Consumers (n = 511)	98	106	307	

NB: Within rows, average ranks with different superscript differ significantly at $P < 0.05$ according to Q non-parametric test (Eddison 2000). Average ranks are reported in standard text and medians in *italics*

product and its advertisement. The consumers who are orientated to buy healthy products are influenced in their purchase decision by products' quality, taste and the fact that they want to protect their health. On the other hand, the opportunists consumers are not interested in any particular of the examined factors to their buying behaviour towards organic wine.

Moreover discriminant analysis was conducted to evaluate the prediction of group membership by the predictors derived from the factor analysis. Initially the normality of the key strategic dimensions was checked. The Box's M test statistic (Box M = 57,736 approx F = 9.549, df = 825,221.3, P <0.001) indicated that the variance–covariance matrices were violated.

Thus, the Bartlett Box F statistic and the Levene's Test were conducted additionally using Minitab to asses the homogeneity of variance for each depended variable (Siardos 2000). The summary of the cross validation classification derived by the quadratic discriminant analysis is shown in Table 7.

Thus, the two consumption dimensions could accurately predict and discriminate consumers' group membership.

Therefore, the hypothesis **H1:** Consumers in the Region of East Macedonia and Thrace can be classified into groups according to the factors that affect their purchasing behaviour towards organic wine may be accepted.

In the next stage, bivariate statistical analysis was performed to in order to identify consumers' attitudes towards organic products. In particular the non parametric Friedman one way Anova Test was performed to the three groups of

Table 7 Summary of classification with cross-validation

Actual classification	Predicted classification: Consumers influenced by prestige and curiosity	Opportunists consumers	Consumers orientated to buy healthy products
Consumers influenced by prestige and curiosity	98	0	5
Opportunists consumers	0	106	5
Consumers orientated to buy healthy products	0	0	297
Total N	98	106	307
N correct	98	106	297
Proportion of correct classification	100 %	100 %	96.7 %
N = 511	**N correct = 501**	**Proportion correct = 0.980**	

consumers that buy organic products in order to examine their opinion about these products. The results of the test indicated that the consumers who are influenced in their buying decision by prestige and curiosity and those who are orientated to buy healthy products consider organic products healthier, more expensive in comparison with the conventional and that the way they are produced has no negative impact to the environment (Fig. 3). On the other hand, the "opportunists" mainly believe that organic products are more expensive, healthier and with better quality.

Thus hypothesis, ***H2:*** *Consumers' opinion about the organic food products is significant related to particular purchasing behaviour* may be accepted.

Moreover the one sample chi-square analysis employed to identify consumers' preferences regarding marketing outlet utilisation, the organic food they usually buy except organic wine as well as their willingness to pay more for certified organic products in general and for wine in particular. The statistical analysis indicated that all the three groups have similar profile (Table 8). Most of the consumers of each group are familiar with the definition of "organic wine", have bought organic wine at least once, they usually buy organic fruits except wine mainly from shops that sell organic products and are willing to pay 5 % more for buying organic wine. On the other hand, most of the consumers who are influenced by prestige and curiosity, and the opportunists are willing to pay 5 % more for purchasing organic products while those who are orientated to buy healthy products would like to pay 25 % more for organic products. More over they "opportunists" and the consumers who are orientated to buy healthy products would purchase organic food even their only difference with the conventional was the fact that their cultivation is more friendly to the environment.

Hence the hypotheses ***H3:*** *Consumers' preferences regarding the utilisation of a particular marketing outlet in order to buy organic wine are significant related to particular purchasing behaviour* and ***H4:*** *Consumers' willingness to pay more for organic food and organic wine are significant related to particular purchasing behaviour* maybe accepted.

Table 8 Consumers' attitudes regarding organic food and wine

Consumers attitudes		Consumers influenced by prestige and curiosity			Opportunists consumers			Consumers orientated to buy healthy products		
		x^2	% consumers	Standardized residuals	x^2	% consumers	Standardized residuals	x^2	% consumers	Standardized residuals
Familial with the definition of organic wine	NO	$x^2 = 44.449$df = 1 $P < 0.001$	16.6 %	-4.71^{a}	$x^2 = 33.962$, df = 1 $P < 0.001$	21.7 %	-4.62^{a}	$x^2 = 208.498$, df = 1 $P < 0.001$	8.8 %	-10.21^{a}
	YES		83.7 %	4.71^{a}		*78.3 %*	4.62^{a}		91.2 %	10.21^{a}
Purchases of organic wine	NO	$x^2 = 25.510$, df = 1 $P < 0.001$	24.5 %	-3.57^{a}	$x^2 = 13.623$, df = 1 $P < 0.001$	32.1 %	-2.61^{c}	$x^2 = 161.984$, df = 1 $P < 0.001$	13.7 %	-9.00^{a}
	YES		75.5 %	3.57^{a}		67.9 %	2.61^{c}		86.3 %	9.00^{a}
Organic product preferences except wine	Pasta	$x^2 = 23.429$, df = 6 $P < 0.001$	12.5 %	n.s.	$x^2 = 24.226$, df = 6 $P < 0.001$	10.4 %	n.s.	$x^2 = 86.528$, df = 6 $P < 0.001$	10.7 %	n.s.
	Cereals		5.1 %	-2.41^{c}		5.7 %	-2.35^{c}		6.5 %	-3.60^{a}
	Fruits		26.5 %	3.21^{b}		27.4 %	3.56^{b}		29.0 %	6.82^{a}
	Olive oil		21.4 %	n.s.		11.3 %	n.s.		13.0 %	n.s.
	Vegetables		14.3 %	n.s.		19.8 %	n.s.		22.1 %	3.65^{a}
	Dairy products		7.1 %	n.s.		9.4 %	n.s.		9.1 %	-2.39^{b}
	Other		13.3 %	n.s.		16.0 %	n.s.		9.4 %	-2.24^{c}
Marketing outlet utilisation	Open market	$x^2 = 82.735$, df = 3 $P < 0.001$	11.2 %	-2.73^{b}	$x^2 = 34.755$, df = 3 $P < 0.001$	27.4 %	n.s.	$x^2 = 246.807$, df = 3 $P < 0.001$	7.2 %	-6.25^{a}
	Shops with organic products		64.3 %	7.78^{a}		47.2 %	4.57^{a}		61.2 %	12.69^{a}
	Supermarkets		17.3 %	n.s.		16.0 %	n.s.		26.1 %	n.s.
	Shops with food for healthy nutrition		7.1 %	-3.54^{a}		9.4 %	-3.21^{b}		5.5 %	-6.82^{a}

(continued)

Table 8 (continued)

Consumers attitudes		Consumers influenced by prestige and curiosity: x^2	% consumers	Standardized residuals	Opportunists consumers: x^2	% consumers	Standardized residuals	Consumers orientated to buy healthy products: x^2	% consumers	Standardized residuals
Willingness to pay premium for organic products	5 %	$x^2 = 44.776$,	28.6 %	2.89^{b}	$x^2 = 97.434$,	42.5 %	6.50^{a}	$x^2 = 132.446$,	25.4 %	3.75^{a}
	10 %	df = 5	25.5 %	2.14^{b}	df = 5	34.0 %	4.36^{a}	df = 5	14.7 %	n.s.
	15 %	$P < 0.001$	13.3 %	n.s.	$P < 0.001$	12.3 %	n.s.	$P < 0.001$	26.7 %	4.31^{a}
	25 %		27.6 %	2.64^{b}		9.4 %	n.s.^{b}		28.0 %	4.87^{a}
	Other		5.1 %	-2.80^{b}		1.9 %	-3.73^{aq}		5.2 %	-4.92^{a}
	No more		0.0 %	-4.04^{z}		0.0 %	-4.20^{a}		0.0 %	-7.15^{a}
Willingness to pay premium for organic wine	5 %	$x^2 = 66.939$,	40.8 %	5.86^{a}	$x^2 = 146.453$,	49.1 %	8.17^{a}	$x^2 = 306.153$,	49.2 %	13.96^{a}
	10 %	df = 5	27.6 %	2.64^{b}	df = 5	38.7 %	5.55^{a}	df = 5	25.7 %	3.89^{a}
	15 %	$P < 0.001$	14.3 %	n.s.	$P < 0.001$	7.5 %	-2.30^{c}	$P < 0.001$	13.4	n.s.
	25 %		12.2 %	n.s.		0.9 %	-3.97^{a}		6.2 %	-4.50^{a}
	Other		5.1 %	-2.80^{b}		2.8 %	-3.49^{a}		5.5 %	-4.78^{a}
	No more		0.0 %	-4.04^{z}		0.9 %	-3.97^{a}		0.0 %	-7.15^{a}
Preference of organicproducts only because their cultivation is more friendly to the environment	NO	$x^2 = 4.939$	38.8 %	n.s.	$x^2 = 21.736$	27.4 %	-3.30^{a}	$x^2 = 74.270$	25.4 %	-6.09^{a}
	YES	df = 1, $P < 0.001$	61.2 %	n.s.	df = 1, $P < 0.001$	72.6 %	3.30	df = 1, $P < 0.001$	74.6 %	6.09^{a}

$^{a}P < 00.001$
$^{b}P < 0.01$
$^{c}P < 0.05$
n.s. $P > 0.05$

3.2 *Profiling Each Consumer Group According to Consumers' Characteristics*

A one-sample chi-square test was performed for each consumer group in order to develop the profile of the consumers who have a particular buying behaviour towards organic wine regarding their personal characteristics.

The profiles of the three consumers groups regarding their personal characteristics are illustrated in Table 9.

As Table 9 illustrates consumers who **are influenced by prestige and curiosity and the opportunists** have similar profiles as most of them held a university degree and do not have children. On the other hand most of the consumers **who are orientated to buy healthy products** have finished the high school, are married, have two children and are mainly women. Furthermore, most of the opportunists and those who are orientated to buy healthy products are free licensed whilst the majority or the consumers who **are influenced by prestige and curiosity** are either civil servants or private employees. Most of the consumers of each of the three identified groups are between 30 and 44 years old.

Therefore the hypothesis ***H5****: Consumers' personal characteristics are significant related to particular purchasing behaviour* may be accepted.

4 Discussion: Conclusion

A number of limitations can be identified in this survey with the most important being the followings:

(a) Some answers in the questionnaire may not represent the true beliefs and attitudes of consumers due to the fact that they are asked in the place and at the time they make their shopping and their time to answer the questionnaire is some times limited. Of course this limitation exists in most of consumers preferences surveys.
(b) The samples in such surveys can not be quite large due to financial constrains.
(c) The adopted statistical methodology even it explore the factors that affect consumers' buying behaviour and create a taxonomy of consumers with similar buying behaviour (which is the purpose of the current study) useful for marketing analysis and strategy development can not measure the demand of a product or determine the importance of the characteristics of a product that affect consumers' behaviour. These measurements can be made with the use of other statistical techniques such as conjoint analysis and contingent valuation.

Nevertheless, the value of the current study is incontestable. It is the first study (to the knowledge of the authors) that explores Greek consumers' attitudes towards organic wine in a Convergence Region in a period during the recent economic crisis.

Table 9 Profile of each consumer group regarding consumers' personal characteristics

Consumers characteristics		Consumers influenced by prestige and curiosity			Opportunists consumers			Consumers orientated to buy healthy products		
		x^2	% consumers	Standardized residuals	x^2	% consumers	Standardized residuals	x^2	% consumers	Standardized residuals
Sex	Female	n.s.			n.s.			$x^2 = 34.557$ df = 1 P < 0.001	66.8 %	4.16[a]
	Male								33.2 %	−4.16[a]
Age	20–29	$x^2 = 39.6.33$, df = 3 P < 0.001	23.5 %	n.s.	$x^2 = 47.434$df = 3 P < 0.001	27.4 %	n.s.	$x^2 = 98.746$ df = 3 P < 0.001	18.2 %	−2.37[c]
	30–44		48.0 %	4.55[a]		50.0 %	5.15[a]		45.6 %	7.22[a]
	45–64		25.5 %	n.s.		18.9 %	n.s.		29.0 %	n.s.
	65+		3.1 %	−4.34[a]		*3.8 %*	*−4.37[a]*		7.2 %	−6.25[a]
Education	Primary School	$x^2 = 28.939$, df = 4 P < 0.001	11.2 %	n.s.	$x^2 = 31.816$, df = 4 P < 0.001	13.2 %	n.s.	$x^2 = 152.114$, df = 4 P < 0.001	10.4 %	−3.75[a]
	Secondary School		13.3 %	n.s.		12.3 %	n.s.		11.7 %	−3.24[a]
	High School		27.6 %	n.s.		30.2 %	2.80[a]		38.8 %	7.35[a]
	TEI/University Degree		37.8 %	3.93[a]		34.9 %	3.93[a]		35.5 %	6.07[a]
	Postgraduate Degree		10.2 %	−2.17[c]		9.4 %	−2.17[c]		4.6 %	−6.05[a]
Marital Status	Not married	$x^2 = 4.082$ df = 1 P < 0.001	39.8 %	n.s.	n.s.			$x^2 = 57.619$ df = 1 P < 0.001	28.3 %	−5.37[a]
	Married		60.2 %	n.s.					71.7 %	5.37[a]

Number of Children	1 child	$x^2 = 12.857$	14.3 %	-2.12^{a}	$x^2 = 39.358$ df = 3	12.3 %	-2.62^{b}	$x^2 = 55.827$	18.6 %	-2.25^{c}
	2 children	df = 3	26.5 %	n.s.	$P < 0.001$	29.2 %	n.s.	df = 3	40.1 %	5.28^{a}
	3 children	$P < 0.001$	20.4 %	n.s.		10.4 %	-3.01^{b}	$P < 0.001$	12.1 %	-4.54^{a}
	No children		38.8	2.73^{b}		*48.1 %*	*4.76^{a}*		29.3 %	n.s.
Occupation	Private employee	$x^2 = 23.143$,	24.5 %	2.67^{b}	$x^2 = 48.082$,	27.4 %	2.70^{b}	$x^2 = 61.537$,	20.8 %	3.04^{a}
	Public servant	df = 6	24.5 %	2.67^{b}	df = 6	14.2 %	n.s.	df = 6	21.5 %	3.34^{a}
	Free licence	$P < 0.001$	15.3 %	n.s.	$P < 0.01$	31.1 %	3.65^{a}	$P < 0.001$	22.5 %	3.80^{a}
	Retiree		6.1 %	-2.14^{c}		4.7 %	-3.01^{b}		10.1 %	n.s.
	Students		9.2 %	n.s.		12.3 %	n.s.		7.5 %	-3.15^{b}
	Unemployed		9.2 %	n.s.		4.7 %	-3.01^{b}		8.5 %	-2.70^{b}
	Other		11.2 %	n.s.		5.7 %	$-2.78^{.b}$		9.1 %	-2.39^{c}

[a]P <0.001
[b]P <0.01
[c]P <0.05
n.s. P >0.05

This study indicated that there was a significant association between the adoption of a buying behaviour and the factors that influence them to choose organic wine.

It also found that the two identified consumers' groups which prefer to buy organic wine wittingly have similar opinion about the organic food products as they consider them healthier, more expensive but with no negative impact on the environment in comparison with the conventional products. "Opportunists" on the other hand consider the organic food products more expensive, healthier and with better quality than the conventional. Moreover all the three groups have similar attitudes as most of them are familiar with the definition of organic food, prefer the special shops that sell organic products as a marketing outlet, usually buy organic fruits except the organic wines and are willing to pay a premium price of 5 % more for organic wine. With the exception of the consumers who are orientated to buy healthy products and are willing to pay a premium of 25 % for organic food, the other two groups of consumers are willing to pay a premium of 5 %. This finding is in accordance with the finding of Botonaki et al. (2006).

This study indicated that the existence of a family mainly affect the people who are orientated to buy healthy products to purchase organic wine. On the other hand, consumers who are influenced by prestige and curiosity and the opportunists do not have children. Educational level is also related with consumers buying patterns regarding organic wine. In particular, consumers who are influenced by curiosity and prestige as well as the opportunists consumers held a university degree whilst the consumers who are orientated to buy healthy products have finished the high school. Occupation is another characteristic that is significant related with a particular purchasing behaviour towards organic wine. Most of the opportunists and those who are orientated to buy healthy products are free licensed while the majority of the consumers who are influenced in their purchases by prestige and curiosity are either civil servants or private employees. This study also indicated that most of the consumers who buy organic wine are relatively young and in particular between 30 and 44 years old. All these findings are in accordance with the results of other studies including Thompson and Kidwell (1998), Reichs et al. (1997), Tsakiridou et al. (2006), Chryssohoidis and Krystallis (2005), Fotopoulos et al. (2003) and Hutchins and Greenhalgh (1997).

The major finding of this study is that identified that factors including prestige, lack of chemical additives, environment protections, nutrition value, product quality, the fact that the product is local, advertisement, taste, and health safety influence Greek consumers to buy organic wine. Hence this study support the results of the other studies identified in the literature review (Baourakis 2004; Eves et al. 2004; Chryssohoidis and Krystallis 2005).

According to the results of this study the local producers in the Region of EMTH should focus on the adoption of organic wine in order to add value to their products and differentiate them from the products produced in other areas or imported from other countries and launched in very low prices by supermarkets and other retailers. Furthermore, they should structure their marketing and promotion mix and focus on the factors and consumers characteristics presented above. In particular they should target to consumers who are interested in product's taste, nutrition value, quality; to those who are influenced by psychological factors such as prestige and curiosity as well as to the consumers who are interested in health safety and environment protection. They should certify and label their products as organic and differentiate them according to this quality certification. Moreover a systematic promotion of the organic food products should be undertaken by all the involved stakeholders within the value chain of the products in order to motivate consumers to prefer such products. This systematic promotion should include advertisement, price incentives and campaigns organised by the local authorities and consumers organisations and hence they will also comply with E.U. promotion campaign for organic food. They will also contribute to the Green Economy and the development of niche market products such as the local certified and organic food.

References

Adamsen JM, Lyons K, Winzar H (2007) An agenda to construct an improved understanding of Australian organic consumers. In: Proceedings from ANZMAC conference: 3Rs – reputation, responsibility and relevance, Dunedin, New Zealand

Allen D (1997) Planned beef production and marketing. BSP Professional Books, Oxford

Arvanitoyiannis I, Krystallis A (2005) Consumers' beliefs, attitudes and intentions towards GM foods, from the "perceived safety vs. benefits" point of view. Appl Biotechnol Food Sci Policy 40:343–360

Baourakis G (ed) (2004) Marketing trends for organic food in the twenty first century, Series on computers and operations research, vol 3. World scientific, Singapure

Barnett V (1991) Sample survey, principles and methods. Edward Arnold, Kent, pp 1–173

Booth DA, Shepherd R (1988) Sensory influences on food acceptance: the neglected approach to nutrition promotion in British nutrition. Found Nutr Bull 13:39–54

Botonaki A, Polymeros K, Tsakiridou E, Mattas K (2006) The role of food quality certification on consumers' food choices. Br Food J 108(2):77–90

Brugarolas M, Martinez-Carrasco L, Martinez Poveda A, Rico M (2005) Determination of the surplus that consumers are willing to pay for an organic wine. Span J Agric Res 3(1):43–51

Chen M (2007) Consumers attitudes and purchase intentions in relation to organic foods in Taiwan: moderating effects of food-related personality traits. Food Qual Prefer 18:1008–1021

Chryssohoidis G, Krystallis A (2005) Organic consumers' personal values research: testing and validating the list of values (LOV) scale and implementing a value-based segmentation task. Food Qual Prefer 16:585–599

Crescimanno M, Ficani GB, Guccione G (2002) The production and marketing of organic wine in Sicily. Br Food J 104:274–286

Davies B, Worall S (1998) Basket analysis: profiling British costumers. Br Food J 100:102–109

Davies D, Eddison JSC, Kirk J (2000) Does farm business marketing behaviour effect livestock channel utilisation. Agricultural Economic Society Conference, Manchester, 14–17 April 2000, pp 1–22

Davis A, Titterington AJ, Cochrane C (1995) Who buys organic food? A profile of purchasers of organic food in Northern Ireland. Br Food J 97(10):17–23

E.U. (2011). http: eu./rapid/pressReleases Action.do?reference=IP/08/1209. accessed 10 April 2011

Eddison J (2000) Quantitative investigations in the biosciences using Minitab. CRC Press/ Chapman and Hall, Boca Raton

Errington A (1985) Delegation on farms: an examination of organisation structure and managerial control on farms in the vale of the white horse. Ph.D. thesis, University of Reading

ESYE (2009) Agricultural statistics of Greece – year 2005. National Statistic Service of Greece, Peraus

ESYE (2010). http://www.statistics.gr/portal/page/portal/ESYE/PAGE-themes?p_param=A1604&r_param=SAP06&y_param=2001_00&mytabs=0. accessed 22 November 2010

Eves A, Lumbers M, Morgan J (2004) Factors affecting consumption of organic food. In: Baourakis G (ed) Marketing trends for organic food in the twenty first century. World scientific, Chania, Greece, pp 231–245

Fotopoulos C, Krystallis A (2002) Historical evolution of consumer's behaviour and qualitative marketing studies. Stamulis Edition, Athens

Fotopoulos C, Krystallis A (2003) The Greek consumer of organic products. A national Greek marketing research with the use of cluster analysis, discriminant analysis and conjoint analysis. Stamulis Edition, Athens

Fotopoulos C, Krystallis A, Ness M (2003) Wine produced by organic grapes in Greece: using means-end chains analysis to reveal organic buyers' purchasing motives in comparison to the non-buyers. Food Qual Prefer 14(7):549–566

Gill JM, Garcia A, Sanchez M (2000) Market segmentation and willingness to pay for organic products in Spain. Int Food Agribus Manag Rev 3:207–226

Hair JF, Anderson RE, Tatham RL, Black WC (1998) Multivariate data analysis. Prentice Hall, Englewood Cliffs

Harrigan KR (1985) An application of clustering for strategic group analysis. Strateg Manag J 6:55–73

Hellenic Ministry of Agricultural Development and Food (2011). http://www.minagric.gr/greek/data/ΦYTIKH %20ΠAPAΓΩΓH %202005 %20.xls. accessed 6 February 2011

Helsen K, Green PE (1991) A computational study of replicated clustering with an application to market segmentation. Decis Sci 22:1124–1141

Hutchins RK, Greenhalg LA (1997) Organic confusion: sustaining competitive advantage. Br Food J 99(9):336–338

Iland P, and Gago P (2002) Australlian Wine. Styles and tastes. Patrick Iland Wine promotions, Adelaide

Kamenidou E, Michaelidis A, Arabatzis G, Mattas K (2002) Information, notification and attitures of consumers for organic bread in Munich market. In: Proceedings of the 7th Greek national conference of agricultural economy, Ministry of Agricultural Development and Food, Athens

Kiesel K, Villas-Boas SB (2007) Got organic milk? Consumer valuations of milk labels after implementation of the USDA organic seal. J Agric Food Ind Organ 5:1–38

Kinnear P, Gray C (2000) SPSS for windows made simple, release 10. Physochology Press, Hove

Kotler P (1994) Marketing management – analysis, planning, implementation, and control. Prentice Hall, Englewood Clifts, pp 1–801

Krystallis A, Chryssohoidis G (2005) Consumers willingness to pay (WTP) for organic food: factors that affect it and variation per organic product type. Br Food J 107(5):320–343

Krystallis A, Fotopoulos C, Zotos Y (2006) Organic consumers' profile and their WTP for selected organic food products in Greece. Journal of International Consumer Marketing, 19(1):81–109

Kupiec B, Revell B (1998) Speciality and artisanal cheeses today: the product and the consumer. Br Food J 100:236–243

Lazaridis P (2003) Household meat demand in Greece: a demand system approach using microdata. Agribusiness 19:43–59

Loureiro ML (2003) Rethinking new wines: implications of local and environmentally friendly labels. Food Policy 28:547–560

Lykoropoulou E, Lazaridis P (2005) Determined factors about willingness to pay for organic meat. In: Proceedings of the 8th Greek national conference of agricultural economy, Agrotypos, Thessaloniki

McCluskey J, Grimsrud K, Ouchi H, Wahl T (2003) Consumer response to genetically modified food products in Japan. Agric Res Econ Rev 32(2):222–231

Michalopoulos VG, Demoussis MP (2001) Greek household consumption of food away from home: a microeconometric approach. Eur Rev Agric Econ 28:421–432

Moser CA (1958) Survey methods in social investigation. Heinemann, London, pp 1–268
Murray K, Cullinane S, Eddison J, Kirk J (1996) Agriculture in the far south west. Seale Hayne Faculty of Agriculture, Food, and Land Use. University of Plymouth, Newton Abbot, pp 1–102
Nimon W, Beghin J (1999) Are eco-labels valuable? Evidence from the apparel industry. Am Agric Econ 81:801–811
OECD (2000) OECD agricultural outlook 2000–2005. OECD, Paris, France pp 29–93
Oppenheim AN (2000) Questionnaire design, interviewing and attitude measurement. Continuum, New York
Psomas E, Krystallis A, Arvanitogiannis I (2005) The Greek meat consumer: exploring the meaning of quality and tracing of the existence of different types of consumers according to it. In: Proceedings of the 8th Greek national conference of agricultural economy, Thessaloniki
Punj G, Stewart D (1983) Cluster analysis in marketing research: review and suggestions for application. J Agric Econ 20:134–48
Reichs M, Splett P, Fishman A (1997) Shelf labeling of organic foods: effects on customer perceptions and sales working paper 97–03. The Retail Food Industry Center, Univeristy of Minnesota, Minneapolis
Remaud H, Mueller S, Chvyl P, Lockshin L (2008) Do Australian wine consumers value organic wine? In: 4th international conference of the academy of wine business research, Sienna
Sdrali D, Apostolopoulos K (2002) The role of the economic and demographic characteristics of the household in Greek rural area on food expenditures: the case of Prefecture of Fthiotida. In: Proceedings of the 7th Greek national conference of agricultural economy, Ministry of Agricultural Development and Food, Athens
Siardos G (1999) Methods of multivariate statistical analysis. Examination of the association between variables, part 1. Ziti Publications, Thessaloniki
Siardos G (2000) Methods of multivariate statistical analysis. Examination of the association between variables, part 2. Thessaloniki, Ziti publications, 639
Siderer Y, Maquet A, Anklam E (2005) Need for research to support consumer confidence in the growing organic food market. Trends Food Sci Technol 16:332–343
Smith E, Marsden T (2004) Exploring the "limits to growth" in UK organics: beyond the statistical image. J Rural Stud 20(3):345–357
Steenkamp JE (1996) Dynamics in consumer behaviour with respect to agricultural and food products. In: Wierenga B, VanTilburg A, Grunert K, Steenkamp J, Webel M (eds) Agricultural marketing and consumer behaviour in a changing world. Kluwer, London
Tabachnick BG, Fidell LS (1989) Using multivariate statistics. Harper Collins, New York
Thompson GD, Kidwell J (1998) Explaining the choice of organic produce: cosmetic defects, prices, and consumer preferences. Am J Agric Econ 80:277–87
Torjusen H, Lieblien G, Wandel M, Francis CA (2001) Food system orientation and quality perception among consumers and producers of organic food in Hedmark County, Norway. Food Qual Prefer 12:207–219
Tsakiridou E, Mattas K, Tzimitra-Kalogianni I (2006) The influence of consumer characteristics and attitudes on the demand for organic olive oil. J Int Food Agribus Mark 18(3–4):23–31
Tsourgiannis L (2008) The marketing strategies of livestock enterprises in objective one regions: a comparitive study between Greece and United Kingdom. Ph.D. thesis, University of Plymouth
Tsourgiannis L, Eddison J, Warren M, Errington A (2006) Profiles of sheep and goat farmers' marketing strategy in the region of East Macedonia and Thrace in Greece. J Farm Manage 12:443–463
Tsourgiannis L, Eddison J, Warren M (2008) Factors affecting the marketing channel choice of sheep and goat farmers in the region of East Macedonia in Greece regarding the distribution of their milk production. Small Ruminant Res 79:87–97
Tzavaras M, Tzimitra-Kalogianni E, Tsakiridou E, Mattas K (2005) Exploring consumer behaviour regarding rice. In: Proceedings of the 8th Greek national conference of agricultural economy, Thessaloniki
Vlachos A, Fotopoulos C (2005) Exploring the degree of knowledge and the attitudes of consumers of Halkida towards genetic modified (GM) food. In: Proceedings of the 8th Greek national conference of agricultural economy, Thessaloniki

Information Society: Statistical Profiles and Development Stages

Kateryna Kononova

1 Introduction

Prof. Y. Hayashi is considered to be the first to have used the term "Information Society". According to Hayashi, Information Society was defined as the society where the process of computerization gave people an access to reliable information, rescued them from routine work, and provided a high level of automation. Production also changes – its product becomes more informational – the role of innovation, design and marketing is increasing in its value. The production of information items (rather than material ones) is becoming the basis of the economic growth (Masuda 1983). In the 1970s this concept became popular in the US and Europe and developed into a universal ideology.

The US sociologist D. Bell, the author of the Post-Industrial Society concept, has presented a version of convergence of Post-Industrial and Information Society (Bell 1980, 1973). According to Bell's studies, Information Society is a new name for Post-Industrial Society, emphasizing not its position (in the sequence of the social development stages after the Industrial Society), but a basis for determining its social structure, i.e. information.

Many interpretations of the Information Society have been suggested since the late 1960s (Clark 1957; Machlup 1962; Drucker 1969; Porat 1977; Lyotard 1984; Castells 2000; Webster 2002; Barney 2003). With all variety of accents, whether technological, economic or social processes, the Information Society is considered in the framework of the basic concepts as having at least the following characteristics. First of all, it has a high level of computer, information and telecommunication technologies, with a powerful information infrastructure. Therefore, it exhibits increasing information access for a wider range of people. Finally, almost all IS concepts are based on the idea that information and

K. Kononova (✉)
V. N. Karazin Kharkiv National University, Svobody sq., 4, 61077 Kharkiv, Ukraine
e-mail: kateryna.kononova@gmail.com

A. Karasavvoglou and P. Polychronidou (eds.), *Balkan and Eastern European Countries in the Midst of the Global Economic Crisis*, Contributions to Economics,
DOI 10.1007/978-3-7908-2873-3_11,

knowledge are becoming a strategic resource of society comparable with natural, human and financial resources (Alexeeva 2009).

The creation of the Information Society was one of the strategic aims of many countries. Japan was the first to create it. The Japanese government submitted the following reports: "Japanese Information Society: issues and approaches" in 1969, and "Plan of the Information Society" in 1971. Since that time strategy has been regularly renewed.[1]

Following Japan, the US government adopted the "National Information Infrastructure: Agenda for Action" (1993) the number of important regulations.[2]

"Europe's Way to the Information Society" was adopted by the EU Commission in 1994. It has been followed by a number of national programs.[3]

The transition to the Information Society was regulated in the CIS later. "Assistance in widening of ICT use of in the Republic of Belarus" was adopted in 2003, "Strategy of Information Society development in Russia" – in 2007.

Since the late 1990s a number of the documents for regulation for the Information Society have been adopted in Ukraine: "National Information Program" (1998), "Electronic Documents Act" and "Electronic Digital Signature Act" (2003), "Basic Principles of the Information Society in Ukraine 2007–2015" (2007), "The concept of E-Government" (2010).

According to the recent research in developed countries the Information Society is considered a major priority for all governments; these countries have already spent significant effort and resources on widening ICT use and infrastructure development (Duff 2000; Feenberg 2001; Iosifidis and Leandros 2003; Kaplan 2005; Tapper 2001; Uotinen 2003). Currently, the focus is concentrated on competence and skills, quality of life, accessibility and modernization of public administration through ICT (Magda 2010; Mansell 2010).

---

[1] "Action plan of transition to digital administration process" (1991), "Access to information held by authorities Act" (1999), "Interception of Communications Act" (1999), "Electronic Signatures and Certification Services Act" (2000), "Formation of Advanced Information and Telecommunications Network Society Act" (2000), "Protection of Personal Information Act" (2003), and other laws and regulations.

[2] "The regulation for reducing paper work" (1995), "The Freedom of Information Act" (1996), "Government Paperwork Elimination Act" (1998), "Electronic Government" and "Use of Informational Technology to Improve Our Society" (1999).

[3] "Info-Society 2000" (Denmark, 1994), "Finland towards the Information Society – A National Strategy" (1994), "Action Programme for the Information Superhighways: From Metaphor to Action" (Netherlands, 1994), "A Government Agenda for Promoting the Development of the Information Society" (Italy, 1995), "Greek Strategy for the Information Society: A tool for employment, Development and Quality of Life" (1995), "Info-2000: Germany's Way to the Information Society" (1996), "National Information Society Initiative" (Portugal, 1996), "IT Government Bill defined the first IS strategy" (Sweden, 1996), "Information Society Initiative" (UK, 1996), "Austrian strategy and Action plan for Information Society" (1997), "Federal Action Plan for the Information Society" (Belgium, 1997), "Information Society Ireland: Strategy for Action" (1997), "Prepare the entry of France in the Information Society" (1998).

The analysis of the IS strategies of the CIS countries (UNDP Projects 2003; Strategy of Information Society development in Russia 2008; Basic Principles of the Information Society in Ukraine 2007–2015 2007) shows that they consider the same issues, but not enough attention is paid to the priorities of the tasks, there is no clear understanding of which problems should be solved first. In our humble opinion this is one of the main reasons for the gap between the CIS countries and leaders of the IS development.

So, the objective of the studies is to form the priorities of IS strategy according to the particular stage of IS development.

To identify the stages of the IS development we have set the following tasks:

1. To create a list of indicators for identifying the stage of IS development.
2. To analyze statistical data on IS development in the regional context, by the components, in the dynamics, etc.
3. To identify statistically the clusters of the countries which are in the different stages of IS development using the data mining methods.

The main IS development indicator is the composite ICT Development Index (IDI), proposed by "Partnership on Measuring ICT for Development". It contains 46 indicators, divided into three groups, which are related to ICT access, use and skills (Revisions and additions to the core list of ICT indicators; 2009). These indicators form the basis of the Information Society's statistical profiles. We analyzed IDI statistics for 152 countries included in the list of IDI for 9 years, from 2002 to 2010 (Measuring the Information Society 2011).

Additionally, because the value of the ICT and their part in income directly influence ICT access and use, we are including ICT Price Basket and GNI per capita in the list of indicators for the detection of IS stages.

Based on the data mining methods we collected the data from the several sources, cleaning them and transforming into the comparable intervals. Then we chose clustering as a mining task, and Kohonen maps as a mining method. Next, we evaluated and visualized the results. Based on the identified stages, we propose the priorities for the IS strategy according to the proper stage of IS development.

2 Statistical Profiles of Information Society

2.1 Indicators of the Information Society: ICT Development Index

With the awareness of changes related to Information Society formation, there is growing understanding that the tools used to estimate the growth of industrial economy become less relevant to new conditions. The indicators based on statistical data (ex., GDP) do not take into account the factors that ensure the growth of the modern economy.

Table 1 IDI

Countries	IDI, 2002	IDI, 2007	IDI, 2010
Western Europe			
Sweden	6.05	7.50	8.23
Denmark	5.78	7.22	7.97
Netherlands	5.43	7.14	7.61
America			
US	5.25	6.44	7.09
Canada	5.33	6.34	6.69
Asia			
Korea (Rep.)	5.83	7.26	8.40
Japan	4.82	6.64	7.42
Singapore	4.83	6.57	7.08
Eastern Europe			
Estonia	3.93	5.97	6.16
Lithuania	3.17	5.29	6.04
Hungary	3.49	5.19	6.04
CIS			
Russia	2.71	3.83	5.38
Ukraine	2.50	3.80	4.34
Belarus	2.53	3.76	5.04
Moldova	2.13	3.31	4.47
Africa			
Guinea	0.75	0.85	1.31
Nigeria	0.69	0.86	1.85
Chad	0.60	0.73	0.83

To collect and analyze internationally comparable and reliable statistics on ICT, "Partnership on Measuring ICT for Development" was created in 2004 during the World Summit on the Information Society (WSIS). Now its members are Eurostat, the International Telecommunication Union (ITU), the Organization for Economic Cooperation and Development (OECD), the United Nations Conference on Trade and Development (UNCTAD), the United Nations Department of Economic and Social Affairs (UNDESA), the United Nations Educational, Scientific and Cultural Organization (UNESCO) Institute for Statistics, the World Bank, and four regional commissions of the United Nations.

The first edition of "Key ICT Indicators" was released by "Partnership" at the end of 2005. To estimate ICT development, a composite index (up of 11 indicators covering ICT access, use and skills) has been proposed. These three sub-indexes were chosen to measure the ICT because they were evaluated almost everywhere, covering most countries and long periods of time. This set of indicators has become the basis of the Information Society statistical profiles (Revisions and additions to the core list of ICT indicators 2009).

IDI varies from 0 to 10. It reached its maximum value (8.4) in Korea, and minimum (0.83) in Chad in 2010 (Measuring the Information Society 2011) (Table 1).

The "Measuring the Information Society 2010" report states that in comparison with 2002 all 152 countries included in the list of IDI increased their levels of ICT

Table 2 Regional leaders in ICT development (Measuring the Information Society 2011)

Ranking in region	Countries	Worldwide ranking
	Europe	
1	Sweden	2
2	Iceland	3
3	Denmark	4
	Asia-Pacific	
1	Republic of Korea	1
2	Hong Kong	6
4	Japan	13
	North and South America	
1	United States	17
2	Canada	26
3	Barbados	41
	CIS	
1	Russian Federation	47
2	Belarus	52
4	Ukraine	62
	Africa	
1	Mauritius	69
2	Seychelles	71
3	Egypt	91

development, confirming the current process of transition to the Information Society. Korea is the first in the top ten countries (Table 2).

Generally, the countries that take the first places according to IDI are developed countries, while most countries in the end of the list – are from the group of the least developed countries with the low incomes. Nevertheless, for the last few years, some developing countries have also achieved significant IDI improvements – they are Saudi Arabia, Qatar, Bahrain and Vietnam. The most dynamic countries from the CIS are Armenia, Belarus, Azerbaijan, Georgia and Moldova.

In developing countries the IDI growth has accelerated significantly in recent years, but the "digital gap" is still huge (Fig. 1).

Taking into account the short time measurement of ICT indicators in comparison with the other indicators of development, the countries with low IDI could quickly catch up if their ICT sectors are given the necessary attention.

If we analyze the "digital gap" based on the number of years a country or region is lagging behind the leading country, we can say that it is relatively small, especially compared with the other indicators (for example life expectancy or infant mortality). Indeed, in 2008 penetration levels of mobile cellular and fixed broadband in developing countries reached the level of Sweden a decade earlier, and the number of internet users per 100 people was the same as it had been in Sweden 11 years ago.[4]

[4] Developing countries lag behind Sweden for 66 years by life expectancy and for 72 years by infant mortality.

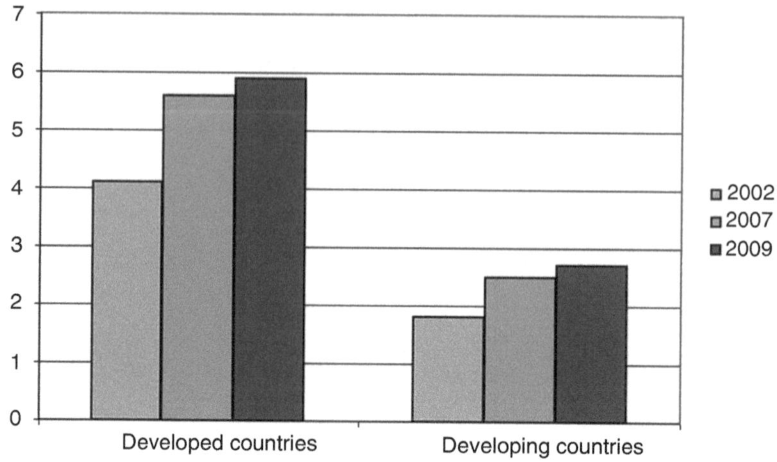

Fig. 1 IDI dynamics

2.2 *Information Society Development: The Analysis of IDI Dynamics*

The analysis of IDI dynamics shows that at the beginning its growth is mainly due to an increase in IDI-access, while progress in use and skills is relatively small (Fig. 2) (Measuring the Information Society 2010). This could be explained by the model of index construction: first ICT infrastructure is created, then the intensity of its use increases, and then the effect of ICT appears.

However, later, the IDI access and use sub-indexes are growing on average at the same rate. This indicates a shift towards a more intensive use of ICT. In spite of the economic recession, the use of the information and communication technologies has grown all over the world (Fig. 3) (Measuring the Information Society 2010).

Recently Armenia, Croatia and Estonia have achieved the greatest progress in IDI-access. The countries, that achieved the most significant improvements in IDI-use, are Bahrain, Georgia, Greece, Kazakhstan, Laos, Luxembourg, Nigeria, Sweden, Singapore and the UAE. The IDI-skills sub-index was growing slightly.

The data analysis shows that the leading IDI countries also take high positions in the classification by sub-indexes. As we see from Fig. 4, the CIS region[5] lags behind in IDI access and use sub-indexes, although IDI-skills is above the average here (Information Society Statistical Profiles 2009).

[5] Armenia, Azerbaijan, Belarus, Georgia, Kazakhstan, Kyrgyzstan, Moldova, Russia, Tajikistan, Turkmenistan, Ukraine, Uzbekistan (Georgia left the CIS in 2009 but it included to the report).

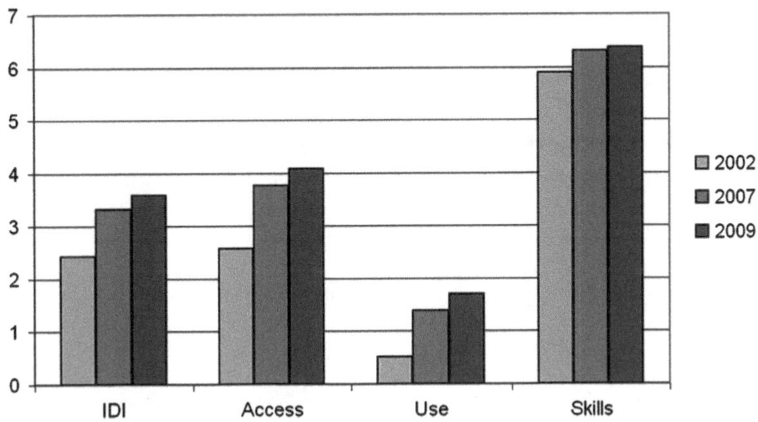

Fig. 2 IDI sub-indexes dynamics

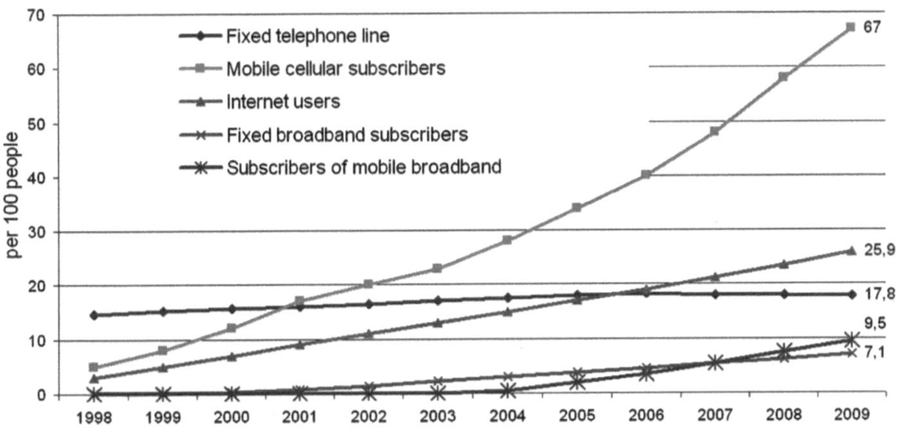

Fig. 3 Development of ICT-access in the world, 1998–2009

2.3 *Development of Information Society in the CIS*

Let us consider in detail the IDI sub-indexes dynamics in the CIS. Azerbaijan, Belarus, Moldova and Russia have achieved the greatest progress in the IDI-access. All four countries have increased household ICT access and internet bandwidth substantially. But primarily, progress in the IDI-access has been achieved due to the increase in the number of the mobile cellular subscribers per 100 people (9 % in 2002 up to 94 % in 2007) – Fig. 5.

Although the increase in mobile cellular penetration is a worldwide trend, it was stronger in the CIS than in the other regions – Fig. 6.

As for the IDI-use, one can observe a rather weak growth – only half of the overall rate of growth worldwide for the same period (Information Society

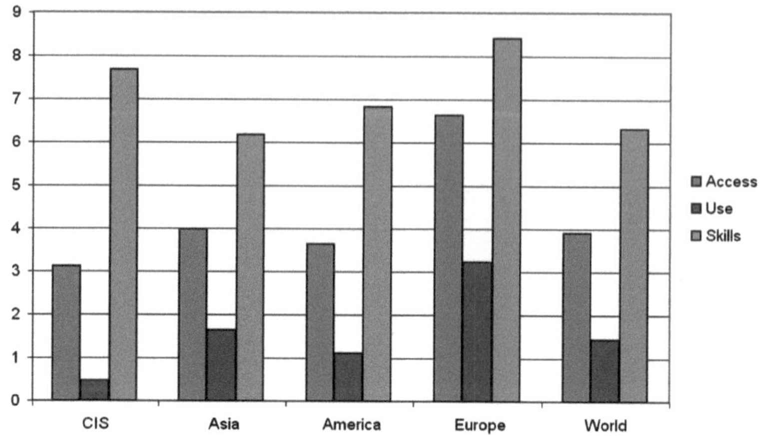

Fig. 4 IDI sub-indices by region

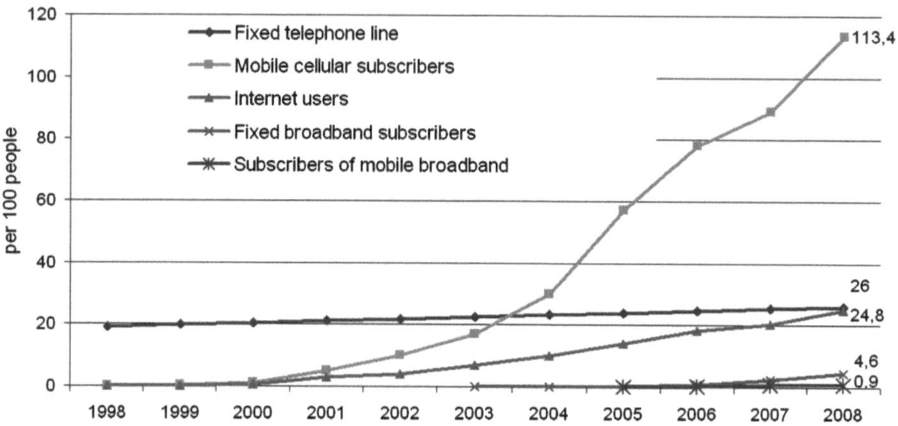

Fig. 5 Development of the ICT-access in the CIS, 1998–2009

Statistical Profiles 2009). The main source of the growth in IDI-use was the increase of the internet users (from 3 % in 2002 up to 28 % in 2010). Dynamics of the users' number shows the exponential growth in Ukraine (but mostly due to a very low initial level) (Fig. 7).

However, despite the rapid growth in the number of the users in Ukraine, coverage by these services is still behind the developed regions (Table 3).

The average increase in the IDI-skills is the lowest among all three sub-indices in the CIS; however, its value is higher than the world one.[6] The indicators of adult education

[6] It is important to keep in mind that changes in education have an impact over a longer time than the change of the ICT-access and use.

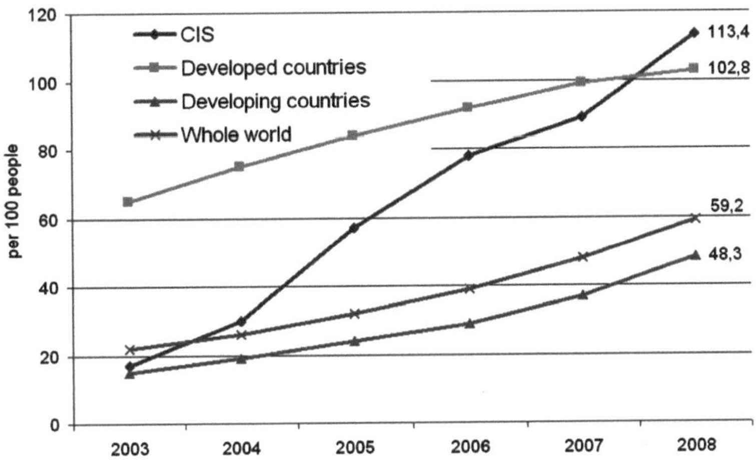

Fig. 6 Mobile cellular subscribers in the CIS and the world, 2003–2008

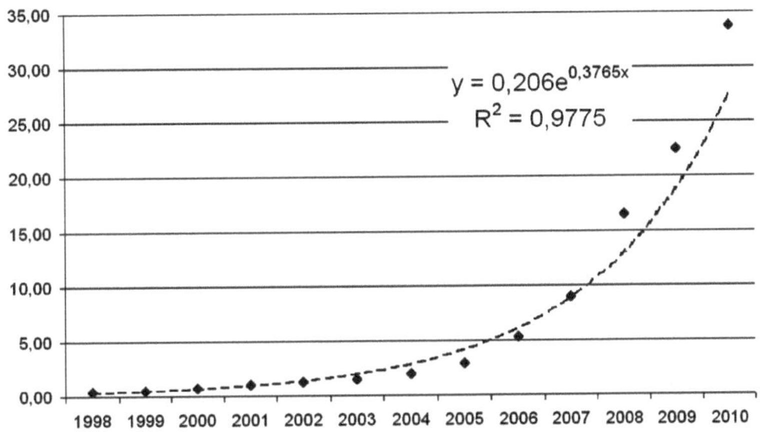

Fig. 7 Number of the internet users in Ukraine

did not change much from 2002 to 2010 in the CIS because they achieved 99 % in 2002. The level of secondary education has been improved slightly, being approximately the same as the global data for the same period. The rate of access to the higher education in Ukraine has shown impressive dynamics (growth from 57 % to 76 %), which allowed it to become the country with the highest level of the higher education accessibility in the CIS. But our country is the one which has lost 3 points in global ranking since 2008.

2.4 *The ICT Price Basket*

The cost of ICT services directly affect their implementation and use: lower prices lead to increased access and use, and higher levels of ICT lead to lower prices. In

Table 3 World internet usage statistics (World internet usage and population statistics 2011)

World regions	Internet users	Penetration (% population)	Growth (2000–2010) (%)
Africa	110,931,700	10.9	2,357.3
Asia	825,094,396	21.5	621.8
Europe	475,069,448	58.4	352.0
Ukraine	*15,300,000*	*33.7*	*7,550.0*
Middle East	63,240,946	29.8	1,825.3
North America	266,224,500	77.4	146.3
Latin America	204,689,836	34.5	1,032.8
Oceania/Australia	21,263,990	61.3	179.0
World total	1,966,514,816	28.7	444.8

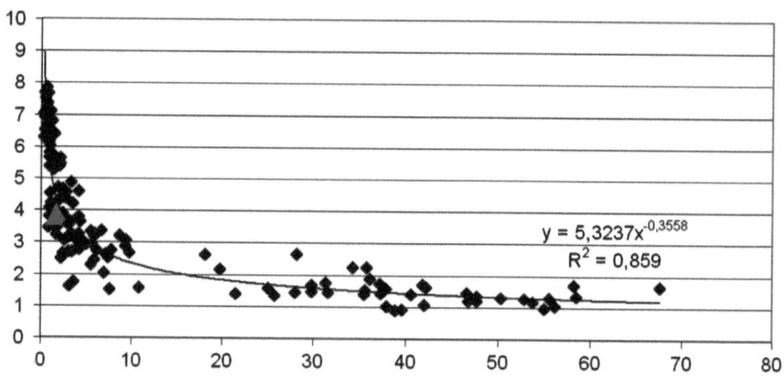

Fig. 8 Ratio between ICT Price Basket and IDI

general, the residents of developed countries spend relatively less of their income (1.5 %) on ICT services than people in developing countries (17.5 %) (Measuring the Information Society 2010). The analysis shows that in the countries where the IDI is more than 5, the ICT Price Basket is less than 2 % of monthly GNI per capita; in those countries where its share exceeds 10 %, the IDI is less than 3. This means that prices are a significant factor in ICT development only if they come down to a certain level, making ICT services affordable for the majority of the population.

The correlation between ICT Price Basket and IDI is described by an exponential function. It should be noted that in Ukraine (in the diagram it is marked with a triangle) ICT prices are lower than could be expected (Fig. 8).

However, the ratio between IDI and GNI per capita is quite weak ($R^2 = 0.74$) in the CIS compared with the global ($R^2 = 0.89$), European ($R^2 = 0.83$) or American one ($R^2 = 0.88$) – Fig. 9.

The levels of IDI in Belarus, Ukraine and Moldova are higher than they might be expected, taking into account the income per capita in these countries. This indicates that targeted strategies can successfully develop the adoption of ICT, even in the countries with relatively low income per capita, and promote them to the Information Society.

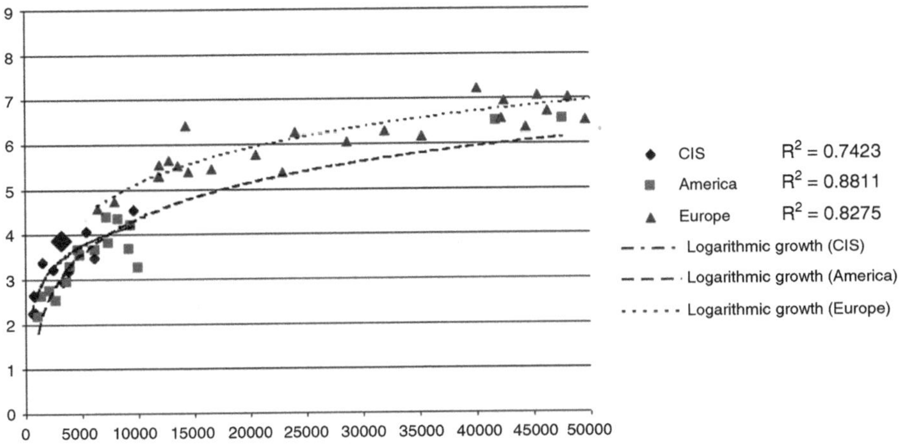

Fig. 9 Ratio between GNI per capita and IDI

3 Development Stages of Information Society

3.1 Grouping of the Countries According to Their Levels of ICT Implementation

One of the main advantages of the IDI is that countries can be grouped according to their levels of ICT implementation (Table 4) (Measuring the Information Society 2011).

The high group is composed of 33 countries, mainly from OECD members as well as Croatia, Hong Kong, Malta, Singapore and United Arab Emirates. Countries in this group have the highest ICT access, use and skills values.

The upper group is composed of 33 countries from Latin America, the Arab region and Eastern Europe. It also includes the Russian Federation. Countries in this group have achieved high levels of ICT access, use and skills.

The medium group is composed of 43 countries from Latin America, the CIS region and the Arab States. Countries in this group have an average level of ICT-access, but they are still relatively low in ICT-use.

The low group is composed of 43 countries, mainly from Africa and South Asia (including India). Countries included in this group have very low levels of ICT access, use and skills.

But the previous analysis shows the strong correlation between the IDI and the national income. So, we have decided to include ICT Price Basket and GNI per capita to the list of the indicators to detect the IS stages.

To implement the data mining methods for the identification of IS development stages we collected the IDI statistics (Measuring the Information Society 2011),

Table 4 Grouping of the countries according to their levels of ICT

Group	Number of countries	IDI, 2010	
		Minimum	Maximum
High	33	6.16	8.40
Upper	33	4.09	6.04
Medium	43	2.59	4.05
Low	43	0.83	2.55
Total	152	0.83	8.40

ICT Price Basket data (Measuring the Information Society 2010) and GNI per capita (Measuring the Information Society 2010), cleaned it and transformed into the comparable intervals. Then we chose clustering as a mining task and Kohonen maps as a mining method.

3.2 Data Mining Methods: Analysis with Kohonen's Self-Organizing Map

Self-organizing Kohonen maps are a data visualization technique, invented by Professor Teuvo Kohonen (Kohonen 2001), which reduces the dimensions of data through the use of self-organizing neural networks. Self-organizing neural networks have been created to solve clustering problems. Clustering is the division of the objects into clusters based on the parameters of the objects. The objects within a cluster are equal as for their attributes. Clusters themselves are often unknown in advance, they are formed dynamically.

The standard clustering algorithm can be easily presented as a Kohonen map. The problem of minimizing the distance from the objects to the cluster's core is the analog of neuron weighted sum $\sum w_{ij}x_i$, where x – the object parameters, w – the weights (analog of the cores). Each Kohonen neuron associates with one core, the greater the value of the neuron, the closer the object to the core cluster. The number of the clusters corresponds with the number of Kohonen neurons. The learning algorithm of Kohonen network is unsupervised. This concept does not require the target vector for the outputs.

The undoubted advantage of Kohonen maps is that they "learn" latent structures in data without any experts, thus allowing the data to structure itself automatically. Another advantage of self-organizing maps is the reduction of multi-factor information to two coordinates. Kohonen maps propose a comprehensive overview instead of numerous local cross-selections. Such holistic approach to data makes them a convenient tool for database analysis, based on associations between neighbouring parts of the map.

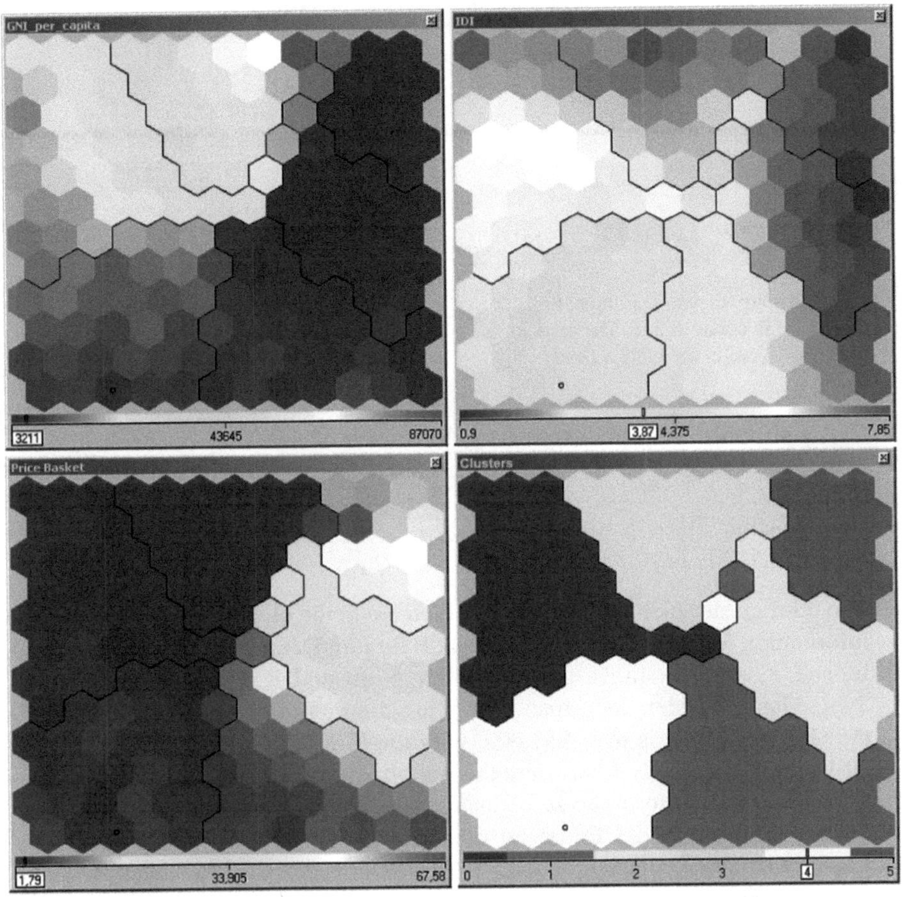

Fig. 10 Kohonen maps (Ukraine is marked with a dot, the values of indicators are given in the legends of the maps): map of GNI per capita, map of IDI, map of the ICT Price Basket, map of the clusters

3.3 *Identifying the Information Society Stages with Kohonen's Self-Organizing Map*

To identify the Information Society stages statistically we have constructed Kohonen's Self-Organizing Map [29] based on IDI, ICT Price Basket and GNI per capita of 144 countries. As a result, the homogeneous groups of countries have been identified.[7] It has allowed to allocate six clusters according to the stages of IS development (Fig. 10).

[7] The analysis was performed using Deductor Studio Academic 5.2.

		Clusters					
		1	4	0	2	3	5
Indices	Values	35 (24,5%)	29 (20,3%)	23 (16,1%)	21 (14,7%)	18 (12,6%)	17 (11,9%)
9.0 Price Basket	Relevance	100,0%	99,8%	99,8%	100,0%	99,6%	100,0%
	Average	5,8843	2,3031	1,13	32,245	0,65444	50,776
9.0 IDI	Relevance	100,0%	49,1%	100,0%	100,0%	100,0%	100,0%
	Average	2,7266	3,9734	6,0409	1,6143	7,0128	1,3412
9.0 GNI_per_capita	Relevance	100,0%	84,9%	98,8%	99,7%	100,0%	99,4%
	Average	2948	7782,4	21935	1006,2	51324	525,88

Fig. 11 Clusters' cores (The indicators are in the first column, the cores and the importance of indicators are in columns 3–8. The number of clusters (row 1) and the number of countries in each cluster (row 2) are in the table's head)

Clusters' cores are characterized by the values of the weights attached to the Kohonen layer (Fig. 11); they reflect the characteristics of the typical objects of each cluster.

The selected clusters are considered in order of increasing stages of IS development.

6. The third cluster includes countries, which are at the highest (sixth) stage of the Information Society: Australia, Austria, Belgium, Denmark, Germany, Iceland, Ireland, Korea, Luxembourg, Netherlands, Norway, UK, USA, Finland, France, Switzerland, Sweden and Japan. These are the richest countries in the world – the GNI per capita is over $50,000, with the lowest ICT Price Basket – $0.65 USD, the IDI exceeds 7 here, and the importance of all indicators is 100 %.
5. The countries that form the zero cluster are at the fifth stage of the Information Society. It includes 23 European countries – Hungary, Greece, Spain, Italy, Latvia, Lithuania, Poland, Portugal, Slovakia, Slovenia, Croatia, Czech Republic, Estonia; and Asian countries – Bahrain, Hong Kong, the UAE and Singapore. The ICT Price Basket is $1.13 here, IDI – 6.04, and the GNI per capita – $21,935.
4. The fourth stage of the Information Society corresponds to the fourth cluster. It includes 29 countries (20.3 %): the CIS countries – Belarus, Kazakhstan, Russia, Ukraine; Eastern Europe countries – Bulgaria, Bosnia and Herzegovina, Romania, Serbia; Latin America countries – Brazil, Chile, Colombia, Mexico. Its core is described by the next values of the indicators: the ICT Price Basket is $2.30; IDI – 3.97; the GNI per capita – $7,872. However, the indicators' importance of this cluster is the lowest in the calculation. It is 99.8 % for ICT Price Basket, 49.1 % for IDI, and 84.9 % for GNI per capita.
3. The next (third) stage of the Information Society corresponds to the first cluster formed out of 35 countries: the former Soviet Union – Armenia, Azerbaijan, Georgia, Moldova; Asia – Vietnam, China, India; Africa – Algeria, Egypt, Morocco; Latin America – Bolivia, Paraguay and Peru. The level of IDI in this cluster is 2.73, the ICT Price Basket – $5.88 (five and half times lower than in the previous stage), the GNI per capita – $2,948. The importance of all indicators is 100 %.

2. The second cluster corresponds to the second stage of the Information Society, with slightly higher level of IDI – 1.61, ICT Price Basket is cheaper here – $32.24, which is only 3.2 % of GNI per capita. Importance of all indicators is almost 100 %. This cluster includes 21 countries. Almost all of them are in Africa (Angola, Guinea, and Zambia) and South Asia (Bangladesh, Laos, and Nepal). Also there are three post-Soviet countries – Kyrgyzstan, Tajikistan and Uzbekistan.
1. Finally, 17 countries (Benin, Niger, Rwanda and the other poorest countries of Africa) are at the lowest (first) stage of IS development. They form the fifth cluster. They are characterized by the lowest value of IDI – 1.34; however, the ICT Price Basket is very expensive here – $50.78 with a minimum of GNI per capita – $525. The importance of all indicators exceeds 99 %.

3.4 The Main Priorities of Information Society Formation According to Development Stages

Let's consider clusters' cores in the attribute space (Fig. 12).

The cluster's core, formed from the countries which are at the highest (sixth) stage of the Information Society, is marked "6". We see that these countries are leading with a large margin on all the attributes. So here the focus is on the sustainable Information Society and people's needs. Social issues are becoming significant.

Then the "5" cluster follows, formed from the countries which are at the fifth stage of the Information Society. IDI is only one point less than at the previous stage; IDI-access, use and skills are relatively high; the majority of the ministries and public agencies are presented on the Internet. So the main issue on this stage is the E-Government concept.

The "4" cluster is formed from the countries which are at the fourth stage. IDI is more than two points less here (mainly due to lower level of IDI-use). So the main objective at this stage is the development of customer oriented electronic services (authentication, signature certifications, electronic forms, help-desks and call-centers, etc.).

The "3" cluster is formed from the countries which are at the third stage. IDI is two and a half times less than at the sixth stage. The levels of IDI-access and use are low here. So the key point here is ICT infrastructure creation.

The "2" and "1" clusters, formed from the countries which are at the initial stages. Average ICT Price Basket is 80 times more expensive then at the highest stage, but GNI per capita is just 1 % of it. IDI is around 1 here. So the main objectives at this stage are: the widening of access to ICT, improving of information literacy, and price reduction of ICT Basket.

As a result, based on the clusters' characteristics, we can define the main priorities of Information Society development.

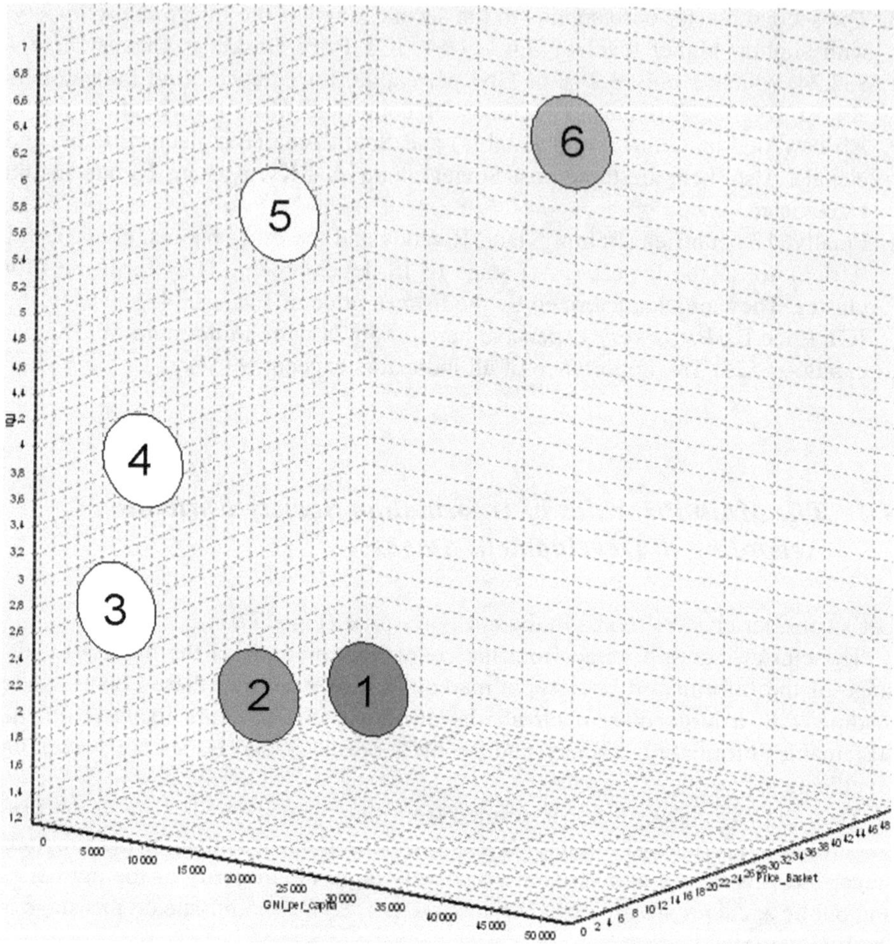

Fig. 12 Clusters' cores in the attribute space

Stage 6. The attention must be focused on Electronic Democracy and Good Governance, which includes the following key features: Participation, Rule of Law, Transparency, Responsiveness, Consensus, Orientation, Equity and Inclusiveness, Effectiveness and Efficiency, Accountability.

Stage 5. The priority is on the realization of the E-Government concept.

Stage 4. Key points are e-commerce Regulations, electronic payment systems development, and increasing transactions and services security.

Stage 3. Strategic directions of development are providing universal access to the network technologies and training of highly qualified staff.

Stage 2. The focus of the ICT implementation strategy has to be directed at creating information and communication infrastructure and price reduction of ICT Basket.

Stage 1. The IS Strategy has to be directed to expanding access to ICT and to improving information literacy.

4 Conclusions

According to the report "Measuring the Information Society 2011", Ukraine ranks the 62nd place (after Russia (47th), Belarus (52nd) and Moldova (57th)). Despite a slight lag behind other CIS countries, Ukraine shows a positive trend of the IDI – from 2.5 in 2002 to 3.8 in 2007 and 4.34 in 2010. But since 2008 our country has lost 3 points in global ranking.

If we consider IDI in detail, we can see that in Ukraine the progress in IDI-access has been achieved primarily through the increase in the number of the mobile cellular subscribers. The main source of the growth in IDI-use was the increase of internet users (from 3 % in 2002 up to 28 % in 2010). The average increase in the IDI-skills is the lowest of all three sub-indices in Ukraine, but the rate of the access to higher education in Ukraine has shown impressive dynamics (growth from 57 % to 76 %), which allowed it to become the country with the highest level of higher education accessibility in CIS.

It was shown that the level of IDI in Ukraine is higher than might be expected, taking into account the income per capita and the ICT prices in the country. This indicates that targeted strategies can successfully promote the adopting of the ICT here. These strategies should be based on the priority aims and objectives according to the IS development stages.

According to the computation, Ukraine is on the fourth stage among the six Information Society stages illustrating that the most urgent problems here are e-commerce regulations and security of transactions and services. Thus Information Policy in Ukraine should be directed primarily at solving these problems. The prospects of E-Government in our country can be discussed only after these mechanisms start working efficiently.

References

Alexeeva I (2009) What is knowledge society? Kognito-Center, Moscow

Barney D (2003) The network society. Polity Press, Cambridge

Basic Principles of the Information Society in Ukraine 2007–2015 (2007) http://search.ligazakon.ua/l_doc2.nsf/link1/JE0MN00I.html. Accessed 11 Dec 2010

Bell D (1973) The coming of post-industrial society. A venture in social forecasting. Basic Books, New York

Bell D (1980) The social framework of the information society. Blackwell, Oxford

Castells M (2000) The rise of the network society, the information age: economy, society and culture, vol 1. Blackwell, Cambridge, MA/Oxford, UK

Clark C (1957) The conditions of economic progress. Macmillan, London

Drucker P (1969) The age of discontinuity. Heinemann, London

Duff A (2000) Information society studies. Routledge, London/New York, Routledge Research in Information Technology and Society

Feenberg A (2001) Looking forward, looking backward: reflections on the 20th century. Hitotsub J Soc Stud 33(1):135–142

Information Society Statistical Profiles (2009) http://www.itu.int/dms_pub/itu-d/opb/ind/D-IND-RPM.CIS-2009-PDF-E.pdf. Accessed 5 May 2010

Iosifidis P, Leandros N (2003) Information society strategies in the European context: the case of Greece. J Southeast Eur Black Sea Stud, 3(2): 67–96(30), Routledge, part of the Taylor & Francis Group

Kaplan D (2005) eInclusion. New challenges and policy recommendations. http://ec.europa.eu/information_society/eeurope/2005/doc/all_about/kaplan_report_einclusion_final_version.pdf. Accessed 13 July 2007

Kohonen T (2001) Self-organizing maps. Springer, New York, Third Extended Edition

Lyotard JF (1984) The postmodern condition. Manchester University Press, Manchester

Machlup F (1962) The production and distribution of knowledge in the United States. Princeton University Press, Princeton

Magda D (2010) A study on how public policies affect legitimacy in virtual communities. J Inf Commun Ethics Soc 8(1):7–21

Mansell R (2010) The information society and ICT policy: a critique of the mainstream vision and an alternative research framework. J Inf Commun Ethics Soc 8(1):22–41

Masuda Y (1983) The information society as post-industrial society. World Future Society, Washington, DC

Measuring the Information Society (2010) http://www.itu.int/ITU-D/ict/publications/idi/2010/Material/MIS_2010_Summary_E.pdf. Accessed 23 Feb 2011

Measuring the Information Society (2011) http://www.itu.int/ITU-D/ict/publications/idi/2011/Material/MIS_2011_without_annex_5.pdf. Accessed 10 Dec 2011

Porat M (1977) The information economy. US Department of Commerce, Washington, DC

UNDP Projects (2003) http://un.by/ru/undp/db/00011749.html. Accessed 10 Nov 2010

Revisions and additions to the core list of ICT indicators (2009) http://unstats.un.org/unsd/statcom/doc09/BG-ICTIndicators.pdf. Accessed 10 Sept 2010

Strategy of Information Society development in Russia (2008) http://www.rg.ru/2008/02/16/informacia-strategia-dok.html. Accessed 7 Oct 2010

Tapper H (2001) Information society strategy. The case of Finland. http://www.nordicom.gu.se/common/publ_pdf/13_079-088.pdf. Accessed 20 Dec 2010

Uotinen J (2003) Involvement in the information society. New Media Soc Number 5:335–356

Webster F (2002) Theories of the information society. Routledge, Cambridge

World internet usage and population statistics (2011) http://www.internetworldstats.com/stats.htm. Accessed 12 Jan 2011

FSC
www.fsc.org
MIX
Papier | Fördert
gute Waldnutzung
FSC® C083411

Kolibri 360 GmbH
Ferdinand-Jühlke-Straße 7
99095 Erfurt, Deutschland
produktsicherheit@kolibri360.de